America Votes Obama to Biden Past Trump

A KALEIDOSCOPIC VIEW OF THE TRUMP PHENOMENON

Helen Fogarassy

Copyright © 2021 by Helen Fogarassy

Book design by Luna Faust

All rights reserved. No part of this publication may be reproduced, distributed, or transmitted in any form or by any means, including photocopying, recording, or other electronic or mechanical methods, without the prior written permission of the publisher, except in the case brief quotations embodied in critical reviews and other noncommercial uses permitted by copyright law.

ISBN: 978-1-63945-216-3 (Paperback)
    978-1-63945-217-0 (E-book)

The views expressed in this book are solely those of the author and do not necessarily reflect the views of the publisher, and the publisher hereby disclaims any responsibility for them.

Writers' Branding
1800-608-6550
www.writersbranding.com
orders@writersbranding.com

We often take for granted the very things that most deserve our gratitude. –Cynthia Ozick.

Dedicated to Robert Hamilton Johnston, the all-American love of my life who had the courage to marry this immigrant. **He was an Army vet from the Viet Nam Era and a cracker-jack defense attorney who had a heart. Honesty was our delight.**

Acknowledgments:

A book about America written by an immigrant has more acknowledgments due than can be listed in words. A mere thumbnail sketch needs to suffice.

The real authors of this book in terms of perspective are my departed parents, Janos and Ilona Skerl Fogarassy. They fought for liberation of their beloved Hungary from Soviet occupation behind the Iron Curtain until the cost of staying was death.

Two young children were the impetus for survival. The family fled at night. They were received as refugees in Austria and were placed with the Skerl elders who had found asylum there after the Second World War. Their relocation to a permanent new home in America involved numerous Austrian, American, international and religious organizations, in addition to the countless strangers willing and even happy to help newcomers who were grateful for help while lost in unfamiliar lands.

One of those grateful newbies to America was the Reverand Alphonse Skerl, a Catholic priest affiliated with the St. Meinrad Seminary near Indianapolis through an Austrian Seminary. He sponsored the Fogarassy family, which included the author and her big brother Steve.

Under the wing of Father Skerl, the Fogarassy family was welcomed by successive parish neighborhoods in Northwest Indiana affectionately known as "da region." It was an industrial center on the Illinois border near Chicago.

The Fogarassy parents struggled with homesickness but the kids helped them adjust as they thrived among peers at schools in the Holy Rosary and Holy Angels parishes and then at Andrean High.

Those schoolmates were quick to help with both English language and American ways. In adulthood, some were still in their home state. Others had spread across the country. Today's social media reunited many and they remember fondly those early fun days of learning with each other.

Likewise, such early warm ties were anchored for life in St. Louis when Father Skerl was assigned to St. Mary of Victories Church near the Gateway Arch. The Schuler family from that period has remained a lifelong Fogarassy friend. They're scattered across the country but shared memory brings them back together however distant the memories first laid.

Formative memories have remained dear from Indiana University days during the Vietnam protest era when the institution adapted and still maintained its standards. Outdoor classes among rolling hills were allowed but thoughtful term papers still required. The author owes much gratitude to the Comparative Literature Department, the Uralic Altaic Department and the freedom of thought initiatives that led her to cell biologist Karl Matlin in a marriage that took them to New York where they parted.

From that period of the author's life came a lifelong friendship with the Finnish Helenius family, now of Zurich Switzerland. During their tenure at Yale, the Helenius science lab was home to international students from the world over. The family lived in nearby Guilford and their spacious, historic home was a center for social events. The author was privileged to be a close friend included with other warmly welcomed guests.

An equally warm welcome was extended by Father Skerl to parishioners upon his return to Northwest Indiana. As pastor of the Holy Trinity Hungarian Church in East Chicago, he created a cultural center for changes in "da region" during the Church's 100-year history. Old timers talked of turf wars between East European newcomers for work in the steel mills. Displaced persons from the WWII era debated with 1956 refugees, all groups that became dated as new arrivals found their way after escape from Hungary still behind the Iron Curtain. The influx eased once the Curtain fell along with the Soviet Union. By then, American Blacks were emerging in "da region." Some joined Holy Trinity,

Racial harmony was nowhere near the radar at Holy Trinity Hungarian, but the Church was a safe harbor for bridging differences. Old timers reminded others of turf wars between Hungarians and Poles. Black parishioners took part in Church and social activities. Occasional friendships sprang up and translated to work situations.

This author in New York kept up with Indiana events through her big brother Steve, who worked in the steel mills, raised a family and never lost interest in the life of his little sister. Between the two, news about half the country was covered. Additional input came from friends and relatives across the country and overseas.

With that long lead-in, the author expresses thanks to friends and colleagues who have contributed to the formulation of the ideas in this book. The United Nations and UN colleagues top the list. While America struggles with racial reckoning, the UN just up the street offers a template for global racial equity. Racial, cultural and national traits are marked at the UN, but they intersect on a level playing field for universal human nature to express itself. The UN is a personal free-for-all played by strict rules that are badly in need of upgrade.

Among UN Associates who were most influential in the development of the ideas in this book were George Parker of the Public Information Department, Maria Carlino of the UN Press Office and Andrzej Abraszewski of Poland's Mission to the UN.

The author was privileged to take part in the 1993 joint US/UN intervention in Somalia and the experience left an indelible mark on her perception of how the world worked. In her view, the UNOSOM mission was a badly misperceived trapdoor in global relations. American media urged the intervention with images of famine-starved children. Internationals barged in with best intentions and poor coordination only to find the Somalis eager to provide the outrage that the US media craved. In 2021, that contradiction between promotion of good and reward for outrage is in greater need of resolution than ever.

Following publication of the author's book about the UNOSOM experience, expressions of support for her views were sent by Jimmy and Rosalynn Carter, diplomats Anthony Lake and Richard Holbrooke, Colonel Joseph Celeski of the US Army and Admiral Jonathan Howe of the US Navy. Based on his own experience in Somalia, Admiral Howe also called for the recruitment of capable people for missions at faster than bureaucratic speed. Information efforts were critical to success, he added.

Based on subsequent experience with the US Veterans Administration, the author believes that the viewpoint of US veterans is a great untapped resource in America's full entry into a global world. The cultural shocks involved in transiting between countries at varied levels of development would be better understood with the input of service members who had undergone the changes at first hand. Likewise, the work of the United Nations would be facilitated by such input from service members of member nations.

While the cultural shock of Somalia along with its neighbors of Kenya and Ethiopia were a shock even to an immigrant who began life in war-ravaged Hungary, her subsequent sojourn in the Bronx proved baffling to one accustomed to the easy UN cultural flow.

Perhaps because of population density, racial and ethnic groups in the Bronx were slow to integrate. Inroads were made at neighborhood watering holes through the convergence of location and the growth of surrounding industry. Thus, the homey intelligence of a local bar or club drew in minority stragglers from expanding hospitals and AT&T stores. Word of mouth about a satisfying welcome brought in friends of repeat customers.

Of particular help to the author in negotiating the Bronx experience were Charles Whalen and his wife Carol, now of North Carolina. Suzanne Sheppard introduced the author to the Brons. Others adding to the evolving American fabric as reflected in the Bronx were the local business owners who shattered mystery about previously unknown cultures. Bangladeshis, Yemenis and Pakistanis welcomed all. Few customers complained when check-out slowed while clerks paused to pray.

In that vein, the Small Business Administration deserves gratitude for providing a sympathetic resource during the Covid pandemic. Unfortunately, bureaucratic constraints prevented them from being helpful. The staff, however, was at least sympathetic in contrast to government and commercial entities where hour-long waits were liable to end in a broken line.

For a writer who made her bones in the tedious, time-consuming and debilitating process of SASE submissions and rejects, the ease of web publication has been a daily treat with Twitter. Other avenues for easy posting of articles have been less reliable over the years in the fast-evolving field. Writers' organizations such as the International Women's Writing Guild, Poets & Writers and most especially the Authors Guild have helped sustain the author's tenacity in getting across her cross-cultural message.

This author aims to put complex ideas into plainly understood words, a task that can involve hours and even years of agonized concentration. For an independent writer with plenty of experience under her belt, the final step of communicating the words to the public makes a Web presence essential. Thanks for development of the helenfogarassy.com website go out to Jeanne Roitman, Wordpress, GoDaddy and now the Angela Collins team at Calcoastwebdesign.com. The Webcoast team has been patiently accommodating with untutored requests.

With English as the third language learned as a child, the author is grateful for help in detangling her text. That invaluable help for this book came from James Bradley, a solid friend and UN colleague until he joined the UN-affiliated Association of Southeast Asian Nations (ASEAN). His all-American cautious approach to expressing views helped tame those of a Hungarian immigrant to America who was witnessing a replay of the disaster that had befallen her birth country 70 years earlier. The mediator between the two views was mutual friend Myat Thi Ha of Burma/Myanmar.

For publication of the book itself, thanks go to the team at Writers' Branding, an independent self publisher. Their team has proven to be a reliable, responsive and capable publishing partner. Their support on a personal level has served as a nurturing source of inspiration in the confusing and often lonely world of the writer.

On the purely personal level that makes all the difference in any culture at every level, thanks go out to Sally Nemeth, Peggy Hammond, Igor Koulichkov, the Spahi family and the Leo Gonzago family. Though departed, lifelong thanks go out to Dr. Margaret Mahler, Juliane Koennecke and Frank Wetzel, for whom justice is still to be achieved.

Finally, thanks go out to the people of Hungary, who continue to battle their way to freedom beyond the continuing fallout from the Soviet era in their country. Barbed wire has now been replaced with welcoming tourist guides. The Hungarian gusto for life has never been lost. It is carried on by the expatriot Hungarian communist in the US, Canada and beyond. At the age of 92, Father Skerl has retired from Holy Trinity Hungarian Church in East Chicago. He continues to bring the soothing presence of vocational wisdom to Covid patients as chaplain to Northwest Indiana hospitals.

Table of Contents

Overview	1
Part I. America 2008	27
The Racial Red Herring in the 2008 American Election	29
The UN as a Friendly Window on the World	32
A Bird's Eye View of the Pope at the UN	34
A New American President for a Modern World	37
Olympic Messages to America in its 2008 Election Year	39
Two Weeks to an Olympic-Sized World	42
Winning and Losing with Olympic Aplomb	44
The Olympic Flame Beyond the Two-Week Strobes	46
From Global Olympics to National Convention – America at World Center Stage	48
What America Wants in a Woman – as Judged by the 2008 Presidential Line-Up	50
What Drives Palin – Firing a Chef When She Has a Big Job and Five Kids to Feed?	52
No Nation is an Island in the 2008 American Election Year	54
Better a Black Man in the White House than a Right-Wing Zealot a Heartbeat Away	56
Candidate Families Do Matter in the 2008 US Presidential Election	58
A Black Family in the White House with the 2008 US Election?	60
The Meaning of "White House" in the 2008 US Presidential Campaign	62

Where Does a Palin Family Wedding Fit
    with the 2008 American Election?   64
America Cracks a Global Glass Ceiling with
    the 2008 Elections   66
The New American Revolution with the
    2008 Presidential Election   69
It Serves to Remember Rove is Palin's Tutor in the
    2008 US Election   71
Flirty Sarah Palin as America's WMD in the
    2008 US Presidential Election   74
A Frankenstein's Monster in the 2008 US Transition   76
Breaking the Bank Before Leaving in the 2008 US Transition   79
A New Form of "White Flight" in the 2008 US Transition?   82
Can an Invader be a Liberator in the 2008 Transition?   86
A Ticking Time Bomb in the Oval Office as the
    2008 Transition Clears?   89
"We Had Fun," the President Tells a Tanking America
    in the 2008 Transition   92

Part II. America with Obama   95
Privilege Dies Hard, Even After the 2008 US Transition   96
The Emancipation of America with the 2008 Transition   99
Sport and the Olympic Perspective on 2010 America   102
A Spotlight on American Goodwill in the Obama Era   105
Is Obama's Approval Rating Slipping because
    2009 America is Myopic?   108
The Cure for America's Economy is to Mainstream a Global
    Mentality   111
The Last Shall be First with the 2012 Election   114
America Belongs to The World   119

Part III. America 2016   123
Master Con Don   124
Champ Turns Chump with Trump   128
Tempest Trump Riled by Woman Hillary   131
The People vs. Ultra-White Trump   136

Part IV. America with Trump — 141

- The Trumps Invade the Capitol — 142
- White Hot in the Melting Pot — 149
- Puny Trump in Grand UN — 152
- Moscow Towers Over Trump — 156
- Trump Chutzpah and Russian Gelt — 159
- Trump/Russia, Hungarian-American Eyes — 162
- Trump Tower Apprentice — 169
- Toxic Trump — 172
- No Dangerfield, this Don — 174
- The Pathetic Prez — 177
- Twitter Trump — 180
- Blow Them Whistles — 183
- The White House Born Loser — 186
- Trump, the American Absurd — 190
- The Runaway Trump Train — 193
- Chill Out America, Kick Trump & Opioids — 196
- 10 Things to Love About America on Trump Days — 200

Part V. America 2020 and Beyond — 203

- Stranger than Fiction Trump — 204
- The Snookered Trump Base — 208
- The Deadly American — 212
- Dead Duck Dino Don — 215
- Uncle Sam on Life Support — 218
- Please Mr. Postman, Count Me Into the Vote — 221
- Speak Up, Dems, the Ruskies R Here — 225
- Dems and the Status Quo — 228
- Kamala's Busing Scars — 231
- In Praise of Age and Biden — 234
- Do Your Homework, Dems — 237
- 2020 Belongs to Biden — 240
- America to Trump, You're FIRED — 244
- The Chucky Trump Horror Show — 247
- Debunking the Trump Mystique — 252
- Uncle Scam Undone — 255

America Comes of Age in 2020	259
States United by US Election 2020	262
Trump the Dumped	269
Biden Buries Trump	275
Where's the Beef in Trump America?	284
Defusing the MAGA Mob-sters	290
Devil in Disguise Qanon Don Does CPAC	298
Bonkers America in a Tech-Addled Covid World	304
Nations United by the US 2020 Election Debacle	314

Overview

The beacon of democracy had little in common with the greater world until the world attacked it on 9/11. Over the next 20 years, America bumbled its way in an alien world until an American opportunist grabbed the country's democratic liberties to exploit them for personal gain. His response to losing the next election woke America to global reality. Its challenges were the same as those of emerging democracies across the world and those boiled down to power struggles at all levels everywhere.

While technically the US was a constitutional federal republic, it became the paragon of democracy because of the ideals set out in its founding Constitution. Namely, those included the proposition that all people were created equal and that all were to be treated as equal under the law. That rule of law protected democracy and it was the very point on which Donald Trump challenged democratic norms to level the playing field between America and the world's near-200 other countries.

In the 21st century, governments were enormously complex, ranging from monarchies and democracies to autocracies and totalitarianisms. Most were hybrids, as in many Islamic and Asian States. Further, most countries had anarchic elements within them, as well as extremist groups with various agendas generally at odds with the existing government. Some local anti-government groups were associated with pan-national organizations such as the al-Qaeda that carried out the 9/11 terrorist attack on the US. That group morphed into the broader Islamic State or ISIS during America's misguided 20-year War on Terror, which was focused on the Middle East but in actuality had global tentacles often affiliated with local anti-government groups. In short, terrorist attacks occurred worldwide and it took global cooperation to curtail them.

Into that global mayhem spread largely through the internet stepped American real estate magnate Donald Trump with the message that he would Make America Great Again by building a great Wall to keep out immigrants and would keep America safe by banning travelers from suspected terrorist countries. While that message ignored the fact that home-grown terrorist organizations were on the rise in the country, the message delivered with ample manipulation of both the political system and the media network won the election for Trump. That Trump miasma became the law of the country for four years until Trump lost the next election and the result was an attempted coup on the world's paragon of democracy...

By the time Trump supporters stormed the US Capitol to overturn the election he lost, a month of legal wrangling had failed to produce any evidence of voter irregularities. The coup had formed organically with no basis for need except that the leader had called on them to fight and change a vote he lost because he said it was stolen. If that kind of deception could be pulled off in a stable democracy like the US, it was no wonder that emerging democracies and hybrid governments needed help to stabilize in an interconnected global world. The dynamic between America and Afghanistan was a case in point.

Joe Biden was the seasoned American politician with the integrity to defeat Trump and withstand his assaults on basic decency. He had been vice president to Barack Obama and it fell to his new administration to clean up the mess in Afghanistan that began 20 years before with the ill-advised Bush War on Terror, and which was set to incendiary momentum by the White House showman Trump in his final year as president when he plotted a surprise Camp David meet with the ousted Afghan extremist Taliban movement still waiting to regain power once Americans left. Thus, as Biden grappled with fall-out from an insurrection denied by the conservative Republican party of his own country, he followed through on the Trump plan to withdraw American forces from Afghanistan. That produced a huge backlash when the hurried drawdown disclosed the strong bond democracy had forged between Americans and Afghans newly threatened by the return of a medieval Taliban regime.

Democracy was far from perfect but it was more productive than anarchy and certainly more compatible with a benevolent human spirit than autocracy or totalitarianism. In that vein, while the world awaited the outcome of the Taliban return touted as more tolerant than before, America's own experience after its brush with autocrat Trump could serve as a model for how democracy could save itself and others from a hostile take-over.

In 2008, America was embroiled in a misguided War on Terror overseas while its tanking economy at home threatened to bring down global economies. A brilliant young Barack Obama offered the hope of radical change to spark enthusiasm into a dismal world. The only drawback was that Obama was racially mixed and few outside his circle believed America was ready to elect a non-all-white president. Still, the prospect was invigorating as America held its two national Political Conventions prior to the world-affirming summer Olympics held that year in Beijing,

At their Convention, Republicans introduced war hero John McCain as their presidential candidate and the self-proclaimed "mama grizzly bear" Sarah Palin as their Vice-Presidential candidate. Democrats introduced the idea that the pale male monopoly on power was over. When Obama won the election, the world rejoiced. Domestically, the conservative backlash was fierce.

In the 2008 election, Democrat Barack Obama won handily over Republican John McCain in part because the incumbent Republican George W. Bush had lost favor with America. The infamous 9/11 terrorist attack on the US occurred during the first year of his presidency. After the attack, Bush came out a hero at first by rallying and uniting the country to draw empathy from the world at large. He launched a war on terror starting with suspected terrorist targets in Afghanistan. Then he engineered a war on Iraq with manufactured facts presented to the world at the United Nations. That war produced fallout in neighboring Middle East countries, including Pakistan, Iran and Lebanon. It also complicated the ongoing war in Afghanistan.

At home in America, scant attention was paid to those distant involvements except through a direct connection with a military service member. That may have been due in part to the brewing great recession precipitated by the deregulation in this country's financial sectors under the Republican Bush administration.

When Obama took Office in January 2009, he fixed problems by bailing out the distressed entities, including the banking and auto industries. In short, Obama's policies averted collapse of the global economy and yet he received little credit for the yeoman's work. His White Vice President Joe Biden urged him repeatedly to devote more time to playing the political game, as was later revealed through interviews and memoirs. Obama declined. In the first place, that was not Obama's style. Secondly, he was focused on more pressing issues related to his unique role in history.

Half-Black Obama was a self-contained, confident man. He wanted achievements to stand on their own, not seen as a concession to a political newcomer. In hindsight, that position may have been a miscalculation. He may have underestimated just how far he was from winning concessions of any sort.

Within a month of Obama's inauguration, the conservative Republican Party gave rise to the even more fundamentalist Tea Party movement. Dedicated to core Republican principles such as fiscal responsibility and small government, the group's primary focus was to defeat the progressive Obama agenda.

The conservative rally cry resounded throughout the country as Republicans at state and local levels primed for the 2010 midterms. The result was a Republican wave. They gained 7 seats in the Senate and still failed to reach majority. They gained 63 seats in the House of Representatives, won governor seats in 6 states and flipped control of 20 state legislatures, which put those states in good position to redistrict based on the 2010 Census. The consequence was predictable.

Obama was blocked by Republicans throughout his eight-year term. His big victory was the Affordable Care Act, a national health care plan that met with much opposition until realization of its benefits overrode resistance and it became known as Obamacare. More ominously during Obama's eight years in Office, openly racist groups were flourishing on the Internet and infiltrating into the general web population.

No doubt the information superhighway has been a blessing for global humanity, but the downside has been the unsettling effect of erasing the line between personal and social norms of communication. In fact, the very barriers between thought and expression have broken down, with thoughts no longer confined to the guarded privacy of diaries or even filtered naturally in polite social conversation. Instead, private thoughts were blasted unedited into the world. Instant feedback fed the ideas or else they smoldered until finding a more responsive forum.

In that whole new social arena, personal thoughts became impersonal messages making lightning rounds across the personal grapevines of followers, bff's retweets, classmates from 40 years back and bff's of old school chums hardly remembered. In the scramble for numbers of "likes," "follows" and responses to posts, correlation was lost between posts and their sources.

HELEN FOGARASSY

Basically, the social media world was little more than ordinary gossip pumped up on steroids. The freedom of casual exchange, however, made it a fertile hunting ground for the white supremacist and racial hatred groups that had been proliferating on the Web since the 1990s. Obama's 2008 election was welcomed by these groups as a focal point for their message that Whites were losing out to inferior races. While ultimate subscribers to those sites were no doubt true racists, others were probably lured by that sheer sensationalism that dominated interest in any form of gossip.

By 2016, Donald Trump had long groomed himself to be a social and media sensation of the renegade variety. He was known in his native New York as a high stakes hustler who had lost all credibility with legitimate financial backers. The country knew him as the harsh CEO of the Apprentice reality show. Politically, he had been a vocal champion of the "birther movement" questioning Obama's legitimacy as a native born American eligible to be President.

Trump fused all those aspects of his persona to suddenly announce that he was running for President as a candidate of the Republican Party. The announcement was made in a flash of drama in a dictatorial style that emphasized an openly racist flourish.

That entrance of Trump into the political arena was the opening salvo for all-out war between America's dueling factions rising up in the American pool since way before Obama's election. Roots of the divisions went back beyond the KKK and the US Civil War over slavery. They encompassed waves of immigrants in which newcomers from distressed parts of the world made their bones by fitting in with those already here.

Like any skilled hustler, Trump probably took measure of the playing field he finally entered. Then as field marshal, stage director, puppet master and ace card shark, he took America for the ride of its life.

No one of any political stature took Trump seriously at first. He was considered wholly unfit for Office and his candidacy was seen as a joke. But much of America under the radar was hooked by the televised image of Trump descending a golden escalator into a cheering crowd of fans. Whether or not the scene was staged, a large swathe of America sat up and took notice. Conservative Republicans started to pay attention.

Trump won the Republican party's nomination for president by mowing down his opponents with insults and attacks during primary debates. The tactic became more pronounced during the presidential campaign itself, when his Democratic opponent was the widely recognized and highly respected Hillary Clinton, a woman who ran her campaign against Trump by taking the political high road. The approach proved to be catnip for Trump.

Refined America was aghast at Trump's crude antics, but rugged individualist fans saw him as the salvation for an America growing soft under book culture. Massive rallies served to feed the fan base ardor as Trump "ad libbed" random promises tailored to the location. Applause heightened his mockery of opponents, especially his opponent and the mainstream media reporting on her favorable ratings. In fact, he branded the media as the fascist "enemy of the people," which led to physical threats to press members covering an event. Despite the hostility, the American media was hooked into Trump.

First, Trump outrages were fishing chum for viewers. Secondly, the media was obliged to give equal coverage to candidates in a presidential election. Thus, Trump became a media magnet on all fronts. He pumped the right-wing media, toyed with the mainstream and liberal, dissed the media as a whole during rallies and trolled the social media that carried the exhilaration of a rally far beyond those in attendance. The combined media impact was to inflate the image of Trump as the outsider hero. The more he was legitimately faulted for misrepresentations and outright lies, the more he came to be seen by fans as the little "David" who would take on the establishment "Goliath" and drain "the swamp" as proclaimed.

Clinton with her establishment background won the popular vote by 2.8 million votes. Careful targeting of relevant Electoral College states, however, gave the victory to Trump in the election. America as a whole was in shock along with the world. Trump in turn began his tenure-long claim that he won the election by a landslide.

Throughout the campaign, Trump boasted that he would bring in only the best people to "drain the swamp." Numerous sources as distinguished as the Brookings Institute have tracked strands of the chaotic Trump administration. The turnover rate in his administration was well over a record 92% of senior advisors. Eight White House-related Trump allies were arrested, indicted or even convicted. Most were granted pardons shortly before Trump left Office. And while it was a truism that all politicians lie, Trump's whoppers throughout his White House career topped daily records. Accredited fact-checkers and venerable news outlets like the Washington Post and New York Times barely kept up as the great US Presidential powers in Trump's hands were used not to "drain the swamp" but to trash the Constitution and sack the Treasury.

To accomplish the incredible feat of fleecing the great "land of opportunity," Trump had only to bring into the Oval Office the basic business model he perfected throughout his career. He skirted the Constitutional constraint against nepotism by appointing family members to key advisory positions. He ousted experienced institutional staff and replaced them with team players willing to do his bidding. He carried out actions with such reckless abandon that for the first time in history, an American President was impeached not just once but twice.

A key strategy of the Trump administration was to blur the mandates of the three branches of government. A cornerstone of the American Constitution was its provision for three separate branches of government to act as a check on the others. The Legislative branch made laws, the Executive put those laws into practice and the Judicial arbitrated differences between the other two. Trump compromised and confounded all three to maximize gains available to him from the Oval Office.

Abuse of power was a poorly defined area of US law since the issue had seldom come into question at the Presidential level. Yet since that was the Trump specialty, he honed the skill well enough in the Oval Office to escape impeachment twice, simply by erecting the legal scaffolding for transgressions without borders. As head of the Executive Branch, Trump was able to invoke Justice Department norms to protect him by virtue of his position. When the going got tough, he appointed a new and more amenable Attorney General. In the Legislative branch known as Congress, politics overrode the legal process. With those politics centered on the miasma of the Trump identity.

Mystery was a big part of the Trump charisma. He fascinated fans with his seamless flip between actual and manufactured bits of information. He claimed great wealth but would not show tax returns, nor did he use personal money for political goals as he had at first bragged he would. Fans enamored of his ability to shape-shift did not care to parse details, especially after the Trump team labeled obvious falsifications as "alternate facts."

Since the Trump base was loud and fervid, Republicans who may have been skeptical of alternate facts stayed mum. From Washington, there was no telling how large was the Trump throng among the more moderate constituents back home. Further, had Republicans dared to speak out, their political careers would be shattered by a vicious Trump Tweet and his endorsement of a rival in the next Republican primary election.

HELEN FOGARASSY

Congressional Republicans were over a barrel when it came to crossing Trump. Few dared and they paid consequences. Between Trump, media coverage and peer pressure, Republicans with integrity lost stature while those amplifying the sensational Trump discord were elevated to stardom.

Overall, Trump was an endless stress-filled adrenalin rush for America and the world. He and the base obviously thrived on the "All Drama Trump" that followed "No Drama Obama," but others grappled with the Trump rhetorical abuse that defied logic and sent decoys down rabbit holes with the dramatic device called suspense.

"A health care plan much better than Obamacare," was dangled for four years, by the end of which the plan was to be unveiled after the election. "Another meeting soon," he told the press after his ill-fated Summit with the North Korean dictator that went nowhere. Talk of another summit faded in the suspense of whether Trump would withdraw the US from its long-standing European alliance with NATO. "Good people on both sides," he declared after a white supremacist rally in Charlotte NC killed a peace activist. The equivocation invited speculation about just where he stood on fascism and race.

According to grassroots journalist David Keegan, ambiguity was the main Trump tool for hooking both moderate and far-right Republicans. He excelled in vague generalities that could be interpreted according to prior beliefs. Then he threw in a loaded specific word like "Antifa" to divert attention onto a common enemy he had elaborated. "Antifa was a loosed political movement of anti-fascists until Trump branded it as a powerful force intent on destroying the country. That tactic of pivoting onto an explosive subject served a dual purpose. It appeased moderates by identifying a culprit and it riled extremists into a frenzy. The truth of a matter was wholly beside the point.

The entire MAGA campaign was based on a mix of concrete images and whitewashed evasions. The Trump plan to Make America Great Again was to insulate America from a globalizing world. Representing that goal were a border Wall, the hounding of immigrants and a severance of global alliances that he claimed were "ripping off" America. "Getting along is a good thing," he said as he cozied up to the world's most notorious dictators. At rallies, the MAGA crowd in red MAGA hats exploded into cheers at every mention of the Wall. At rallies, Trump rarely mentioned his affinity for despots.

Based on subsequent developments with those like North Korea's Kim Jong-un, the perception of friendship was one-sided and easily sold to a man readily won with mere flattery. But that foreign perception of Trump made no appearance at MAGA rallies or on Trump-friendly media and social media circuits. That kept Republican legislators chained to home constituents while in Washington they implemented the conservative agenda of stacking the country's courts with Republican judges whether qualified or not.

In a way, MAGA fever was an optical illusion, a reverse eye-on-the-ball game where the objective was to deflect attention away from events in reality. It was a baseball game where Trump stole to home plate while all eyes were on the fast ball pitch. Magicians and three-card-monte dealers worked with similar sleights of hand. At the highest, most consequential political level, the MAGA constellation of Trump, his base and conservative Republicans anesthetized America to the frustrations produced.

Unable to break the Trump cycles of marauding the Constitution, Democrats drooped after every defeated bout and MAGA glee billowed. The dynamic shot to nuclear speed when the Covid pandemic hit early in the 2020 election year.

Once started, the pandemic spread like wildfire and the economy hiccupped under stab-in-the-dark approaches. At first Trump downplayed the health hazard, but as deaths mounted he agreed to a national stimulus plan to save the economy expected to breeze into re-election. As deaths still mounted, he instituted daily press briefings and mandated states to institute their own plans. In the frenzy of equipment shortages, health care burn-out and mounting contagion, Trump seized the opportunity to make hay for the coming election by politicizing the Covid pandemic.

Like the red MAGA hats, face masks became the Trump branding tool for instant display of political stance. Those wearing masks were timid establishment drones. Those without masks were hardy, salt-of-the-earth Americans. From that start and in line with the political affiliation of their Governor, states came to the fore as Republican red or Democrat blue. Then under Trump and his social media bullhorn, the defiance of face masks morphed into a call for asserting patriotic liberty. Finally, as the majority of America hunkered in quarantined isolation, a Black man was murdered by a White police officer in plain sight and a long-overdue racial reckoning exploded.

George Floyd's alleged misdemeanor offense was to pass a bogus twenty-dollar bill. In the course of seizing him for that minor infraction, police officers allowed one of their own to torture Floyd to death by deliberate asphyxiation. The excruciating encounter was caught on camera, broadcast to the world and racial realities struck a global nerve.

Particularly striking on the global stage was the American link to the slave trade that flourished across Europe and in its colonies some 300 years back. The colonies were spread across the world from Asia to Africa and the Americas. In time, slaves from African colonies were sold into colonies located in the Caribbean and the Americas for work on developing plantations. By the time the trans-Atlantic slave trade was gradually abolished starting in the early 1800's, the North American South was a major market for cotton and tobacco plantation labor.

For Europe, the George Floyd murder was a grim reminder of a colonialist heritage that has led to a modern influx of immigrants from former colonial countries. Europe as a whole was coming to terms with its own racial past, and George Floyd's murder had globalized racial reckoning. America could not contribute to the global effort until its own more urgent situation was addressed. Under Trump, the drive for racial reckoning accelerated to warp speed.

Much of America was moved to the racial justice position by the concrete image of the George Floyd murder video. The instant urgency for racial reckoning, however, created broad generalizations in the narrow American lens of history that stretched only 400 years back. As Blacks rallied and brought attention to routine instances of fatal encounters between White police and Black persons, all Whites in America became lumped into the privileged group that continued to block Blacks from equality. Trump's response was a square-out challenge to the validity of the Constitution itself.

All men were created equal according to the Constitution, with the concept amended over years to include all people as society evolved. Trump's reaction to the Black protests against injustice brought into question that proposition because he called the events riots right off the bat, then praised law enforcement while ignoring victims even when obvious violations of civil rights were caught on videotape. His overall rhetoric evoked the ugly historical fossil of colonialism when he recast actual events to convey a racially-charged image of yet another incident in which White police officers were called upon to subdue an unruly Black mob that was "uprising."

With the authority of the US Oval Office, Trump may have continued his colonialist divisiveness had Joe Biden not become his rival as the official Democratic candidate for the presidency in the 2020 US election. The contrast could not have been more stark.

In a nutshell, Trump advocated for forceful crackdowns on mostly peaceful protests against racial injustice, calling them riots. Biden visited both the families of victims and police precincts to offer empathy and to reassure that change would come once he was in Office. His tone was confident and it carried the weight of authority.

Biden had nearly lost the 2020 Democratic primary when he landed the support of South Carolina Representative James Clyburn, a Black man well familiar with Biden from Congressional days. His assurance of Biden's integrity was so unequivocal that other Democratic candidates in a crowded field withdrew from the race and threw their support behind Biden. The Democratic alliance overrode progressive and centrist differences in the party, which proved fortuitous for America in a globalizing world.

Throughout the Covid-laced campaign season, Trump mocked his rival for following Covid precautions. Steady Joe Biden remained unflustered. He also refused to engage in the Trump attempts to bait him even as tough guy Whites and Republican leaders pumped the Trump trail. They underplayed the Covid threat, made defiance a badge of independence. Some even took up arms to defend their liberty and attack the state leaders restricting their freedoms. By October of election year 2020 n Michigan, the national FBI announced that 13 men had been arrested for a plot to kidnap the Governor and overturn the state government.

Biden, meanwhile, called for a level-headed plan to defeat Covid, restart the economy and heal the country's divisions. As Biden's approval ratings soared, Trump doubled down on his pathway to staying in Office.

Covid statistics ignored, Trump insisted that rallies be arranged. There he dangled the notion to cheering fans that "sleepy Joe

Biden" could only win if the election was rigged. At rallies and on social media, he hammered home the idea that the election would be lost only if stolen. In increments, he alerted fans to be ready and defend the Constitution if the election was stolen from him. And stolen from them, he added, reinforcing the notion that he was acting on behalf of fellow outsiders.

Those outsiders on the Trump train by then were a motley crew of web denizens gone haywire with White supremacy, racial hatred and conspiracy theorists whose main focus was fear and loathing of Democrats. A similar composition would show itself later during the 6 January assault on the US Capitol. Also on the Trump train were Republicans who had not yet left the party, many reliant on donor funds the Trump machine seemed to abundantly tap from both major and grass roots sources.

By the time Trump lost the 2020 election, the social media circuits were on fire about the fraudulent vote. The emotional fervor that Trump had stirred and fanned throughout his Presidency had permeated the American central nervous system. A good portion of the country had grown irrational enough to dismiss any relevance of facts. "I just feel" was the common phrase of Trump supporters who refused to accept the vote results. The reasons for the feelings varied. Some were sure the election was rigged with no basis for the certainty. Others just felt Biden didn't win. Still others felt that Trump had won because Biden couldn't have won. He didn't even campaign, they said. Look how hard Trump worked to get reelected. Brainwashing, wishful thinking and faulty logic had fused. That was the cue for Trump to continue his presidency regardless of facts.

Reliable electoral analysts have concluded that the Trump base so fervently devoted to him had simply failed to vote for his re-election in sufficient numbers to beat Biden. As indicated by Republican votes for other candidates on the ticket, Trump had drawn voters to the polls, but they had declined to vote for him a second time.

Such facts had no meaning and they held no interest for Trump allies. To them, he had won because he said so and was proving it by refusing to concede.

Concession was an American electoral norm for a peaceful transfer of power from one administration to the next. The precedent was set in 1800 when a three-way Electoral College tie between incumbent John Adams and candidates Aaron Burr and Thomas Jefferson was settled by a vote in the House of Representatives. The vote handed the victory to Jefferson. Adams conceded but skipped the inauguration.

The tradition at the Presidential level had continued unbroken ever since. At the gubernatorial level, the first modern refusal to concede occurred at the primary level in the 2010 Republican midterm wave after Obama's 2008 election. Trump not only broke the Constitutional norm of concession but he kept up his campaign to vigorously push the baseless claim of election fraud.

In the American form of democracy, Federal standards regulated overall voting rules but individual states had the right to conduct elections in line with state preferences and needs. Thus, states varied in their use of canvassing methods such as early, mail-in, and absentee voting. The Covid pandemic in an election year had required states to quickly make adjustments for making the voting process both safe and accessible. States had responded resourcefully to an unprecedented global health crisis. Trump turned that asset of states into an all-out drive for keeping himself in Office.

Trump's antics over vote tallies stretched the nail-biter 2020 US election to more than a week before the Biden win was called by mainstream media based on recounts and audits confirming the original outcome. Trump still refused to concede, instead tying up the issue in legal cobwebs.

Depending on the count amongst local, state and federal procedural rules, Trump and his Republican allies instituted somewhere between 40 and 80 lawsuits challenging the validity of an election based on such parameters as mail-in, early and drive-in voting methods. Nearly all lawsuits were summarily dismissed or dropped in successive court proceedings all the way up to the Supreme Court in which three of eight justices were Trump appointees. Undeterred, Trump called for recounts in swing states where he had lost and when audits, recounts and court challenges failed to yield him a win, Trump turned to his social media base hazily tied to conservative Congressional Republicans.

That base had been primed during the Covid-laced presidential campaign. The QAnon conspiracy group had made its debut at a Trump event. The White group of Proud Boys had been told to stand by. As the January 6 date neared when Biden's Electoral College win would be confirmed by Congress, Trump invited fans on Twitter to "Stop the Steal" and meet in Washington that day for an exciting and "very special time." It will be wild, he teased as the day neared.

The back story of the Trump-branded "Stop the Steal" campaign has yet to be unearthed. Republicans have blocked full investigation, claiming there was nothing more to learn about the attack on the US Capitol that began with a Trump rally and ended in an assault that in any other country would be identified as an attempted coup. What had made the American version of a coup so unbelievable was the same convolution that marked the entire Trump tenure.

Trump won the US Presidency in 2016 with no basis for being qualified to even run. When he lost that same position in 2020, he refused to concede even though there was basis for the contention that the election was flawed. He lost both the popular and Electoral College votes in an election that was pronounced by his own Homeland Security cyber chief as the most secure ever. Reinforcements had been put in place after the 2016 election were found to be tainted by foreign interference. And still, as a result of his once having attained the Oval Office, Trump was able to imperil the entire American democratic voting structure just be refusing to leave.

The incredible feat of nearly toppling the world's foremost democracy was a product of a toxic combination in a land of opportunity. An opportunistic hustler hooked a base. A conservative Republican party striving for a plutocracy seized the opening.

The mystery and suspense of the Trump years stretched into 2021 America as Trump refused to concede. In retirement, he continued to hold court in his Mar-a-Lago retreat with aspiring Republicans who believed he could help them carry his mantle into the future. Republican governors and legislators in swing states where Trump lost rewrote voting laws to make voting harder in future elections. Republican legislatures authorized illegal "fraudits" that served no purpose but to erode voter confidence in the system. Electoral officials were threatened and replaced. Republicans even restructured state electoral systems to allow for the option of overturning elections.

Allegedly, all those measures put forward by state Republicans were instituted to ensure the security of the vote and to restore voter confidence in the system. Democrats identified elements that were obviously meant to suppress the vote, Those ranged from prohibiting the distribution of water to those standing in line for upwards of five hours to restricting voting hours to preclude initiative like "Pray and Vote," which provided for transportation of Blacks to the polls after Sunday Church services. The institution of such classic "voter suppression" tactics suggested that Republicans knew Trump was a fluke who could return to the White House only if the electoral bedrock of democracy was destroyed. The speculation gained credence when steps at the federal level to override those state mandates were stalled by Republicans refusing to cooperate with Democrats.

The Trump phenomenon occurred at a watershed time in both American and world history. The racial glass ceiling was broken by the 2008 election of Obama with Joe Biden as his Vice President. Trump was the backlash between the two. With the solid election of Biden who won both the popular and Electoral College votes, America was set to resume its role in a globalizing world except for the status quo in which conservative Republicans had been hijacked by Trump. In 2020, America chose Biden to liberate it from the Trump sand trap.

Young, half-Black Obama had chosen seasoned White Biden as his 2008 running mate because of the elder's experience with both the US Congress and the Foreign Relations Committee of its Senate. Both those qualifiers served America well beyond 2020.

Renegade showman Trump caused great damage to America both at home and abroad. At home, his trade policies, mixed messaging and rampant misuse of misinformation created a chaos that was exacerbated by his mismanagement of the Covid pandemic. Overseas, confidence in America declined sharply under Trump. An early 2021 Pew Research Institute survey indicated that America's favorability around the world jumped from 32% in 2020 under Trump to 74% in 2021 under Biden in Office for mere months even with no transition help from Trump. However, the Pew poll of 16 countries also found that confidence in America was undercut by concerns over the stability of its government after the 1/6 attempted coup and the continuing domestic turmoil.

Those outside views of America may have influenced the Biden approach to both the domestic and global challenges facing America after Trump. Promptly he nominated and got confirmation of veteran advisors and Cabinet members across the diversity spectrum. With an emphasis on getting things done, he unveiled a Covid vaccination plan with targets and strategies that met expectations ahead of time. Unable to achieve bipartisan support, he tapped a reconciliation function to launch the America Rescue

Plan that covered both relief and economic stimulus programs. Then when America was at least stabilized under the continuing Trump barrage, Biden stepped away to give America an outside view of itself.

In eight short days, Biden went abroad to convince the world that "America is back." He went first to Great Britain beset with its own domestic ills since the country withdrew from the European Union in a move known as Brexit during the same 2016 year in which Trump took the helm in America, while in Britain, Biden took part in a meeting of the G-7 group of countries representing the world's most economically advanced and politically liberal systems. From there, Biden met with the European Union countries to reaffirm alliances and set a common course for advancing democracy around the world. As a punctuation mark to that message, he held a face-to-face meeting with Vladimir Putin of Russia, one of the world's leading autocrats.

The purpose of the meeting, Biden matter-of-factly told the press, was to set down markers on behavior in a global world. Contradicting US Intelligence reports, Putin denied meddling in American elections or engaging in the cyber warfare bedeviling the US. Biden responded by simply reminding Putin that the US had vast cyber resources that could be unleashed if attacks on its critical infrastructural components did not cease.

Further on his campaign to let the world know "America is Back," Biden reaffirmed his country's commitment to its democratic values. America would again speak out on issues like human rights in a global world by a clear statement of position.

The Biden message was enthusiastically received overseas. Back home, the news was slow to penetrate into the continuing stalemate between human-centered Democrats and the status quo of conservative Republican enthusiastically bound to the Trump web

As a land of immigrants, America could be seen as a hybrid microcosm of the wider world. People of all colors, races and ethnicities became American once settled. The diversity and freedom offered by American democracy raised immigrants above the performance levels achievable in their countries of origin. Those early ties, however, did endure, which preordained America to lead in guiding others through a period in human history that could otherwise overwhelm and make tyranny enticing.

That message of the difference between democracy and despotism was the main point that Biden delivered to the world on his overseas tour. At home, the ideal of democracy still hung in the balance as a would-be rogue demagogue remained on the loose, along with a posse of apprentices vying for the same position.

"I know the system and I alone can fix it," Trump bragged in his 2016 campaign. In the reality of hindsight, he knew part of the system and his intent was not to fix but to milk it. But in 2021 after five years of such wrenching verbal fraud at the highest presidential level, America was reminded by Biden that leadership was not a matter of "going it alone" but a practical skill for cooperating with allies. Unbeknownst to the American public, America had already developed tools for such relations with allies. Like many family treasures stored in attic mothballs, they were ready for use with Biden.

By the time of Trump, much of America had grown complacent about freedom. The Trump phenomenon was a wake-up call for America to pay attention and protect its best aspects from its worst. Once the choppy waters in the wake of Trump died down and Republicans had less to fear from him and his base, legislative action would close loopholes that had let an unfit candidate seize America's Presidential powers. After Trump, "norms" no longer sufficed for the challenges of cross-border activities like foreign election interference and presidential exemption from prosecution. Norms formalized into law would strengthen the democratic framework, as was done in the earlier great abuse of Presidential power under Richard Nixon some 50 years before.

Further, as Biden showed with his presidential campaign, America's media could promote the cause of democracy by focusing on substance instead of staying stuck in the dated journalistic doctrine of leading with sensationalism. The Trump flair for outrage had nearly toppled democracy. The Biden briefings on cleaning up the Trump mess provided comfort and a sense of stability to a country still rocked by remnants of the Trump influence. In a Covid ravaged America upended by a basic disagreement over the nature of facts, reality was more compelling than manufactured sensation.

Likewise, the media could broaden America's horizons onto the wider world. A more far-reaching view could help America solve intrinsic problems such as racism. It would also help America appreciate its strengths and build on resources already established. For example, America led the Allies to victory over tyranny in the Second World War. Afterwards, it led the drive to establish the United Nations to avert such wars in the future. UN offshoots like the World Health Organization and the International Monetary Fund have been powerhouses behind global betterment in areas ranging from peace-building to refugee resettlement to fighting worldwide corruption, human trafficking and climate change. Those agencies would be immensely effective if the American public got behind them. Those global bodies would also provide great career opportunities for civic-minded young while improving the global social climate for commerce.

The world offered enormous opportunity to advance freedom to both America and its allies, but like America, the UN and its bodies were in dire need of upgrade. American roads, bridges, railways and dams built 50 years ago were in disrepair, in part because pioneering America liked to build and it balked at the boring work of repair. In a global world of environmental crises due to industrialization over the last 160 years in an overall human history of some 5,000 years, abandoning time-worn projects in need of repair was no longer sustainable.

For America and the world, the Second World War was the global Rubicon. From that point forward, humanity had the option to either survive or wipe itself out with the nuclear bomb. The wise choice of survival led to the establishment of institutions such as the United Nations, but after 70 years it too needed an upgrade to be useful. But like America in its transitional period, the UN was stalemated by "old think" vs. "new think."

Founded in 1945 San Francisco, the UN was structured on the basis of the five major powers that defeated tyranny and imperialism across the world. Those five powers with permanent seats on the UN Security Council had a veto power that killed an initiative of the other four. Like current conservative Republicans in the post-Trump Biden age, "old think" prevailed. Those in power would not cede until maybe total annihilation of humanity was at stake. By its 2020 vote, America gave Joe Biden the mandate to guide America into "new think." He was to fix the US and global logjams by picking up where the Obama mandate left off when Trump elbowed his agenda out of the way.

In 2021, America reckoned with its racial past as the rest of the world's near-200 countries waited to see how America fared with its social upheaval. Under Biden, the Juneteenth national holiday was signed into law to celebrate the date on which slavery in America came to an official in Texas. The proclamation was made the day after Biden returned from his overseas trip. It was a good example to the world of why western democracy offered the best pathway to an equitably evolving global future. The declaration had been passed by Congress in an overwhelmingly bipartisan consensus even as Trump still rode rough-shod over Washington Republicans. Beneath its great superficial differences, America came together to uphold a core value.

Such flexible recourse to basic national integrity was impossible in the communism of China, which imposed rules and restrictions insufferable to those accustomed to the freedom of personal pursuits. Autocracies like that in Russia squelched healthy discourse, with the penalty for speaking out ranging from imprisonment to death. History has shown that people do not take well to being subjugated or suppressed. America's experience in the Middle East during the first two decades of the 20th century also showed that people could not be rushed, nor could they be used as mere political tools.

America invaded Afghanistan in its war on terror after the 9/11 attack. While there, it saw opportunities to ensure that world-threatening terrorists could be contained. Progress was made but under the global political and media radar. It was only after Biden pulled the plug on the hapless mission that reality sank in around the world. Progress had been made, relationships had been forged and uprooted refugees needed homes. Organizations around the world were willing to help. What they needed to be effective was coordination under the already established United Nations streamlined just the way America was doing with its own infrastructure.

Bureaucracy was unavoidable in a complex world but stagnation was as curable as a clogged drain. It called for an assessment of blockage points and a direction of resources to clear the pathways for smoother flow. In that endeavor as well as in politics, the fresh perspective of immigrants was a major American advantage. They reminded America of how badly the human spirit was crushed behind barbed wire and military tanks on streets. Those ongoing global realities made immigrants the lifeline of America, the blood transfusion that saved it from indolence or arrogance. Together with the racial reckoning going on now for over 300 years, America was destined for global greatness under Joe "from Scranton" Biden with his Irish-American background giving him the gumption to defeat a tyrant and withstand the turmoil left in his wake.

The commentaries in this book present multiple perspectives of the one phenomenon that will go down in history as America under Trump. From any angle, the occurrence was hard to grasp. From the viewpoint of an American immigrant born into a totalitarian state, the American flirtation with a would-be dictator was a marvel of human valor. Having survived the ordeal, America was in a better position than ever to lead the world into a prosperous, cooperative future.

Part I.
America 2008

The Racial Red Herring in the 2008 American Election

The year 2008 was a critical one for the world as seen from inside the UN Secretariat, There is was possible to see ountries jostling toward development while a key player sat on the sidelines of the international scene.

From inside that lofty edifice, the 2008 American elections were seen less in terms of race and more in terms of generational warfare. Could a young American upstart unseat the long-in-tooth old order to jump start the country into the new century?

The world was patient with America as it went from an out-of-touch elder Bush to a rock 'n' roll President Clinto and then back to a younger Bush who made his father seem like a liberal icon in comparison. When the younger Bush was elected, the world was aghast and then bemused by America's acceptance of a leader proud to be illiterate.

In 2008, the world wondered if America would continue to indulge its fetish for the quaint by electing an elderly war her growler lwho admittedly didn't use a computer. Alternatively, America would go for a vibrant young man at ease in the modern world.

News about the campaign buzzed inside the UN and delegates heard the objections to Barack Obama. He was too young to be President of the United States. He didn't have enough experience. But to the world looking on, nobody could do worse than had been done during the eight years under outgoing President Bush.

The world's near-200 countries represented at the UN watched eagerly to see which side of America would emerge with the 2008 election. The undisputed world leader still maintained its reputation as benevolent, but the country had grown stubborn, bellicose and uncooperative since its heyday as the post-WWII hero. In 2008, it was still only one of two countries that refused to sign an international convention on the rights of the child, for example. Some of its provisions could impact on the interests of its corporations operating overseas.

In the possible election of Obama to the US presidency, the world saw a possibility that America would reverse that trend toward self-interest. Troubles and conflicts would continue throughout the world, but the march of overall prosperity and good will would outmatch them if America became part of solution instead of compounding problems.

The consensus was that young Obama with his savvy world view could bring about that change. The only question was whether America was ready to elect a Black man as President of the United States with its history of racial conflict.

Sadly enough, the common view was that America was not ready to take that step, that America would rather elect an out of touch white dinosaur instead of joining the global mainstream. America had a blind spot about race. That's why it remained obsessed with illegal Mexican aliens taking jobs Americans didn't want and failed to notice that Mexico had grown so agile in forging partnerships that it was building attractive, fuel-efficient cars that the whole world was eager to snap up.

To the world at large, the 2008 US election was not about race but about America's willingness to adapt for the needs of a globalizing world. Republican candidate John McCain might manage, but Obama was the modern marvel who appeared out of nowhere after a single speech and was solid enough to withstand the slippery slopes of sudden fame. He was a man at ease with thinking on his feet. He was the best match for a galloping world.

In the view of most at the UN, the US was not ready to elect a Black man as its president because of its racial history. But if Obama did win the election by some miracle of America adapting to modern geopolics, he would become a red flag signaling outrage to those who couldn't adapt. They would oppose Obama in a fight to the death.

The UN as a Friendly Window on the World

The world was a much friendlier place from a window of the United Nations Secretariat than from even a step beyond its guardhouses. At the UN, the only obstacle to a Black man as US president was the doubt that America was ready for that step. At the UN the majority of 200 world leaders were nonwhite. All were commanding figures. Some were even women, as was Liberia's Head of State, leading a troubled African country onto the global highway of progress that Americans didn't see on its mainstream GPS.

From the Secretariat window, countries were building a world beyond the cataclysms shown on American TV screens. In their daily lives people worked, prayed, worried and celebrated just as Americans did. Certainly, many were far poorer than poor Americans, but they knew about America through cell phones, the internet and aid agencies and the image alienated them.

From the Secretariat view and that of the world, America was a provincial giant separated from the wisdom of the enlightened among its own people. They included philanthropists like the Gates couple and the entrepreneur Ted Turner who became a quirky breath of fresh air in a UN adapting to global changes while America stagnated.

Americans in finance, trade, advertising and marketing knew about the world beyond American borders, But information about that world came to those specialists in the form of demographic and financial data. American mainstream media looked beyond its narrow parameters onto when a foreign disaster struck with enough force to merit American attention. Cable networks with news about the outside world were mostly gloomy, preachy and ultimately boring. For some reason, the American info machine did not apply the full force of marketing ability to making the world more user-friendly to Americans. America was the loser.

The UN Secretariat staff didn't need a Hurricane Katrina or Tsunami to see Asians, Africans, Arabs, Europeans and Americans interacting. Those from far-flung regions of the world adapted quickly among their peers and were soon well-heeled and savvy about the world's ways. When at ease, human commonalities emerged.

People from all over the world made mistakes. Some owned up, others denied, deflect and cast blame. Many UN postings came through national cronyism. Those ties tightened at UN HQ. And while hostilities, resentments and envy flared, the ideal of good will prevailed over the universal human weakness that the UN was designed to tame at a global level.

The world of 200 countries was full of people with a slew of frailties and strengths at all levels of development toward the ideals of justice and equality. That world was not about to turn into a Coco Cola ad overnight, particularly with a UN that had not been upgraded in 70 years and a US that had grown eve more disinterested in its work. But through the UN Secretariat window, progress toward the ideal was clearly visible.

Countries had emerged out of obscurity by forming regional alliances that secured funding for members through UN-affiliated agencies such as the IMF and World Bank. Rich countries partnered with poor to build highways, wells, clinics and markets to make the world safer, healthier and more prosperous for markets rich and poor.

In short, the world was a compassionate place from the UN Secretariat vantage. America would benefit from seeing that view. It would appreciate the good work being done by an organization it had founded. It would also lose its defensiveness about being asked for another hand-out.

A Bird's Eye View of the Pope at the UN

Press Officers in the Department of Public Information at the United Nations wrote on-the-spot press releases available to the world on the web. Few outside the United read those releases but when Pope Benedict XVI came to address the General Assembly April 2008, the Holy Trinity Hungarian Church in East Chicago, Indiana asked one Press Officer to describe the experience of seeing the world's spiritual leader interact with the world's leaders.

The Pope's visit was very exciting, she said. The vast Assembly Hall was filled to capacity. A few thousand people, waited for him to arrive, all buzzing with anticipation above and beyond the usual rustle of an important world leader appearing. When the announcement was made that the Pope was near, people got very quiet and turned to watch him walk up from the back in his red Prada shoes, accompanied by two bishops and UN security staff. The air was much more solemn than usual as the Pope reached the dais and was greeted by the UN Secretary-General and the Assembly President. After they all shook hands, the Pope gestured out to the Assembly and a protocol officer led the Pope to the white VIP chair at the side of the speaker's podium.

Since the press officer was not Catholic, she didn't know what the Pope gestures meant, but he seemed to be blessing the Assembly as he held out his hands and swept those assembled with his eyes. With all his greatness, he seemed very humble. He seemed to understate his position, which reinforced the sense of being in the presence of greatness. He was more gentle than charismatic and the crowd was obviously awed, as if sending his presence. When he finally spoke, his words were powerful and thought provoking.

The Pope's message was much the same as the ideas expressed daily at the UN, the press officer said. But the way the Pope expressed those ideas had a solemn rhythm that suggested there was deeper meaning beyond the words. He spoke about the need to protect people whose human rights were violated and that governments must not use state sovereignty as an excuse bad behavior in their countries. He talked about the need to help the very poor of the world, many of whom lived in Africa. So the message wasn't that different but the way he talked about the issues in a religious context gave them impact. He was talking about a concept that at the UN was known as the responsibility to protect. It was a shared responsibility to help those in need wherever they were, like those in Sudan who were being massacred, The responsibility also meant that governments must not be allowed to get away with mistreat-ing their people. In the religious context and expressed at an elevated intellectual level, the message was striking caught your interest.

The Pope ended by blessing everyone in all six official UN languages, The Secretary-General and the Assembly President then wished him a happy birthday. That was a nice light touch to the powerful presentation.

Overall, the narrator summed up, the Pope at the UN seemed to command total and obvious respect. World leaders were open to his message. They were open to his message and responded with smiles and nods. Some people got very emotional. Most diplomats maintained their air of formality and decorum, but a few cried as the Pope spoke, along with many of the UN staff. The feeling inside that grand hall seemed to go even beyond deep respect and closer to reverence. The UN is used to Presidents and Prime Ministers. In person, they are very impressive. But a religious leader of the Pope's stature was striking beyond mere secular power.

Catholics must have felt they'd seen light, the non-Catholic press officer went on. But even as a non-Catholic, she said she felt she was in the presence of greatness, that the Pope was a very powerful person, one of the most learned people in the world. In that sense, the experience was awesome. The pomp of his garments and entourage certainly add-ed to that sense. It's only fitting that world-level leaders reinforce the message of their countries with the most splendid garb of their nations. Overall, the Pope made a terrific impression on the UN and on New York City in general. He brought a spiritual depth to the city and it was very well received. That greater spiritual depth as a result of his visit was re-flected right back to the Pople as he made his way around the city in his popemobile. Throngs cheered. He smiled and gestured back, probably with a blessing.

For a Catholic perspective on the Pope's historic visit to the UN, a staff member snagged a seat at the press office desk. On first seeing the Pope walk up the aisle, she said she was struck by the sense that he was the person holding a position that was directly descended from the first Pope, St. Peter, who founded the Catholic Church. The context of that long timeline lent new emphasis to the UN message. The philosoph-ical edge common themes made them profound and closely aligned. Both Catholicism and the UN had the common goals of helping people and doing good in the world.

Further, she said she was happy to see the Pope as warm within the formality of his role. When he extended hands to bless, his fingers flut-tered with earnest feeling. In an address to a rally of young people the previous day, the Pope had shown real rapport with the kids who were obviously thrilled to be in his presence. He kept looking out at them as with admiration, as if to let them know they were important to him be-cause they were the future.

A New American President for a Modern World

America was a big hero to the world after the Second World War, when a spirit of kinship prompted the country to push for the United Nations. A series of misadventures on the global stage since then had sent the mighty United State into what seemed like an ever-deeper sulk.

After 9/11, the greatest military power in the world was seen by outsiders as holed up in a deteriorating once-glorious bunker. It seemed the wounded former giant only ventured out to lob water balloons at perceived bullies in a frenzy of preemptions that to outsiders was a confusion of "vigilance" and "paranoia. "

In the eyes of the global UN, America was the former hero that deteriorated drastically under a conservative administration. America had found global support after 9/11 but responded with increasingly unilateral actions while the world grew multilateral with cooperation. While the world agreed on the need to control nuclear arms, the US withdrew from the major arms control treaty. It refused to join the world on the Kyoto protocol to address global climate change, refused to sign a Convention to regulate worldwide child labor and obstructed global agreement on fighting racism. Finally, it dug in its heels against a world criminal court to limit the impunity of genocidal tyrants on the grounds that America would be open to frivolous lawsuits brought by enemies.

Taking such consistently obstinate stances on key issues to advance the global good could be interpreted in many ways. To some, America was the loner maverick with enough power to do as it wanted. To others, it was the defensive giant that saw enemies in every shadow. In 2008, the sagging economy provided a clue. Whatever the reason, America was growing irrelevant on the global stage.

While China was rebuked for its human rights and trade policies, China controlled America's purse strings by purchasing securities America needed to sell in order to bail out its flailing financial institutions. With all its problems and handicaps, China was growing in importance while the US stagnated.

The world rejoiced at the possibility that Barack Obama could be America's next president. The enthusiasm was proof that the world still believed in America despite its recent role as spoiler in world progress. The world wanted an American president who was aware that 200 other countries existed and mattered, one who spoke learnedly with a clarity that left no doubt about veracity.

America lost credibility with the world when it very publicly lied at the United Nations about weapons of mass destruction in Iraq. Even worse, America seemed unaware of just how severe the consequences had proven to be. Elected officials had backed the decision to invade Iraq. Subsequent claims of faulty intelligence had fallen flat. America's legendary competence had taken a hit.

The reputation of the fallen world hero continued to suffer through the conduct of the baseless war it had waged on Iraq. Reports disclosed a series of scandals. Contractors had scored windfalls. Illegal torture was employed at Abu Graib, third country detentions centers where extreme torture was legal and finally at Guantanamo Bay, where prisoners were held indefinitely and without due process. Executive privilege was invoked to cover up violations of rights.

In 2008, the pinnacle of democracy had much to set right with the world and with its own ideals. Above all, it needed a leader who commanded respect in the world to erase the incumbent image of an arrogant president who cavalierly waged war on countries he didn't like.

Olympic Messages to America in its 2008 Election Year

The quadrennial Olympics were a snapshot of the world at its best They were a portrait of a future in which nations competed as equals in the global arena and where individuals medaled in their fields of proficiency.

While governance was vastly more complex than sports, a number of principles applied to both when viewed from the Olympic perspective. Those were particularly significant for America as it prepared to elect a new president for the next four years.

*First, the Olympics showed that youth was good and that elders had nothing to regret about aging out of youthful vigor. The energetic endurance of youth created the opportunities for elders to remain relevant. There was no Olympic medalist without a coach and there were few without supportive parents.

*The Olympics also showed the world as a delightful mix of racially, ethnically, nationally and regionally interconnected people. Value judgments about other cultures were subsumed in the visceral reaction to seeing the exquisite beauty of the human mind and body working together.

*Experience was not necessarily an indicator of fitness for performance in Olympic competition. The most seasoned athletes made crushing mistakes. Novices benefitted from those errors. Graciousness in accepting the result was the measure of respect accorded the performing athlete. Gloating or mudslinging brought the greatest disgrace to an athlete or team.

*The Olympics were globally significant enough that in 2007, the 200 United Nations member countries adopted an Olympic Truce by an overwhelming majority. That agreement to stop hostilities for the two-week period of the Olympic Games did not deter the Georgians and Russians from armed engagement and it did not stop suicide bombers in Pakistan. The global compact needed enforcement mechanisms at local and national levels.

*The Olympics were a showcase for the world's most physically fit. Whatever their color or gender, Olympic athletes were attractive because they had integrity between all physical functions. Mind, body and emotions were brought into alignment for peak performance.

*Americans came across in the Olympic global mix as exuberant, vital and good natured. They dominated with their numbers and reflected the racial reality of their country. Most athletes were white, particularly predominating in equipment heavy sports. As with other areas of American life, the ratio was expected to come into alignment as equality was advanced.

*The Olympics presented the world in all its vast, diverse splendour. Media coverage focused on backstories of both athletes, communities and countries they represented, along with cooperation for the training of athletes. That wholesome view of the world found acceptance in America. According the NBC network, the 2008 Olympics had a 16.3 rating with an average of 26.6 million primetime viewers on a typical weeknight. That figure was up from a 15.7 rating with 25 million viewers when the Games were held in Athens four years earlier.

*NBC TV coverage of the 2008 Olympic Games brought to light the hidden sides of America's cities and small towns where Olympic-level athletes were nurtured and trained. In Des Moines, Iowa, for example, American immigrant and Beijing-born Liang Chow coached gymnast Shawn Johnson for ten years before she won gold in 2008.

*Finally, the Olympics showed that nationalism was a universal trait as natural as family ties or preferences. When national identities were allowed to compete on a level playing field, they enhanced individual traits that in turn were reflected by team performance and national pride.

Two Weeks to an Olympic-Sized World

The quadrennial 2008 summer Olympic Games in Beijing opened with digitally-enhanced fireworks that captured the world's interest and kept it throughout the Games. According to Nielson, 4.7 billion people watched the games during the two-week airing, which was 70% of the world population. In comparison, 3.9 billion watched the Games in Athos four years earlier and 3.6 billion watched them from Sidney. In the US, the Games were the most watched TV event ever with 214 million viewers.

That level of global attention on the same event was bound to make an impact on shared awareness. Because of stars like record-smashing Usain Bolt, the world knew more than ever about Jamaica and Bahrain. Sports themselves gained new recognition. Softball was revived as an Olympic event after its expected demise as an American sport that only Americans could win.

The success of the Games depended in large part on the cooperation of key players in the event. The Olympic schedule was rearranged to provide morning live coverage of swimming events for Americans. Digi-tal services provided live internet and broadband coverage, as well as mobile phone clip downloads that were available worldwide. According to the Australia news source, 12 million video views enabled 12 million viewers to witness India's first individual gold win in the sport of air rifle.

The ability to achieve such a global impact was due in large part to the corporate Olympic sponsors who held global marketing rights to the Olympic logo, which was one of the most recognized symbols in the world. Those sponsors adhered to healthy Olympic standard in their advertising. They also provided special services for events. The twelve-time sponsor Panasonic, for example, designed state-of-the-art audiovisual equipment for Beijing, including the large-screen ASTRO-VISION display systems used at the opening and closing ceremonies.

Other sponsors included General Electric based in Fairfield, Connecti-cut, which expected to double its business with China by 2010 as a re-sult of its work with the Olympics. According to the International Herald Tribune, the news was a boost to the company that had lowered its yearly earnings forecast due to the US credit crisis. The increased rev-enues were expected to come in the areas of clean-energy technology and infrastructure development for fast-growing Chinese cities.

Other corporate sponsors of the Olympics included Coca Cola, Kodak, Johnson and Johnson, McDonald's, Visa, Samsung and Omega, among others. As a testament to the value of supporting the Olympic Games in exchange for concessions in accessing to the global marketing platform provided by the Olympics, the International Olympic Committee said it had the highest sponsorship renewal rate of any sports property.

HELEN FOGARASSY

Winning and Losing with Olympic Aplomb

Nearly five billion people worldwide saw the 2008 Olympics broadcast from Beijing. Few viewers outside an athlete's country paid attention to losers or even to winners who medaled at lower than the top gold level. While some athletes never expected to win and others were sorely disappointed, the sting of defeat was softened by the course of an Olympic athlete's lifestyle,

Athletes reached the Olympic level in their sport by competing in local, national, regional and interna-tional events. In those trial runs on their way to "going for the gold," they learned to lose well and re-cover so as to keep going until they finally won.

Gold medal Olympians were a rare breed indeed. In Beijing, for example, there were approximately 300 events with 600 athletes competing. Since three medals were awarded for each event, the total number of medals to be awarded was 900. Theoretically, every athlete could have won a medal and half could have won two. That potential was a strong incentive for competing and yet the reality was that Olympic stars won multiple medals.

The star status achieved by an Olympic athlete depended on numerous factors. Individual ability was key, of course, but team rapport was a factor, as was the support given to the sport by national sports organizations. Large countries with big budgets were usually topped the winners lists while 120 of the world's 200 countries won no medals before the closing ceremony.

Not surprising, host country China won a total of 100 medals that year. It was the largest national medal tally in Olympic history.

Nevertheless, the athletes of the 120 countries that won no medals took part in the closing ceremony with as much vigor and good will as they had brought with them to the opening. Their record proven performance took the sting out of defeat.

Each athlete competing in the Olympics was nominated by the national Olympic committee. By the Olympic charter, no more than three athletes for any event were entered per country.

To be one of three top athletes in any country was no small feat and no shabby honor regardless of how small the country. That's why national flags were carried so proudly by athletes under the Olympic banner.

The Olympic Flame Beyond the Two-Week Strobes

As the 2008 Olympic summer games wound down, the expected big winners from globally prominent countries got the lion's share of the attention. But the added value of the quadrennial events was the inexorable emergence of the world's little people into global consciousness in a favorable light.

The Olympic Games demonstrated that the people of troubled countries like Georgia and Somalia were more than mere victims of historic vagaries. They were in fact worthy participants in shaping the world through established channels.

The Olympics spoke forcefully for the justice of bettering the world. Sport was a universal language understood by all. It levelled some differences and brought others into relief. Sport was objective, complete with humanly subjectivity. It was an age-old device for constructive competition that could mitigate hostilities.

Somalia, for example, had been without a government for nearly 20 years and yet it sent athletes to Olympic events. While disrupted by national strife, Somalia's standing with the International Olympic Committee was reestablished in 1994 through the United Nations Operation in Somalia during the intervention. UN experience had shown that sport could put a pause on civil strife and improve conditions for negotiation. Indeed, the World Cup was televised that year on communal televisions donated by Cisco and powered by generators. As expected, fighting died down during broadcast hours.

The International Olympic Committee had a membership of 205 national committees. In 2005, the parent Committee teamed up with the 192-member United Nations to advance the global good by promoting the fundamental principles of sport and sportsmanship.

An Office for Development and Peace was established based on the premise that the principles of sport were the same as those for promoting global good. Those principles included respect for opponents and rules. They emphasized the importance of teamwork and fair play.

A UN Fund for International Partnerships worked with the UN Sport and Peace Office and with Olympic committees at all levels to broaden the playing field for sports worldwide. Such cooperation enabled athletes from Somalia to pursue aspirations for Olympic Gold in the midst of war, it enabled them to surmount obstacles like destroyed stadiums, sporadic training and little realistic chance of winning.

The opportunity to compete at the top of their game was a compelling reason for those athletes to heal wounds of parents and siblings lost during civil strife. They carried into competition the pride of neighbors back home watching on borrowed televisions powered by generators. That gave them the incentive to perform their best. Competing with equals on the global stage despite all their handicaps provided a huge boost for assuming a role in leading their countries out of their troubles.

HELEN FOGARASSY

From Global Olympics to National Convention – America at World Center Stage

The national conventions to elect the presidential candidates of the two major political parties in the United States flowered right out of the tidal swell created by the Olympic Games in Beijing. Among other distinctions at those games, the American Michael Phelps swept up a record-breaking eight Olympic gold medals. The US softball team racked up a loss to Japan in a sport that had been considered too American to be competitive.

A record-breaking 4.7 billion of the world's 7 billion people saw the Games by electronic media. With the audience primed and already aware of the global interest in the 2008 US election, the Conventions were set to harness the tech power that had delivered such acclaim for the Olympics and Beijing. The scheduling strategy demonstrated awareness of audience participation.

The Democratic Convention was set in Denver and the Republican in Minneapolis-St. Paul. By tradition, the Party in the White House held its Convention second, In 2008, the Democratic Convention began the day after the Olympics ended, when global applause still resounded from the Games. The Republican Convention started on Labor Day Monday right after the Democratic ended. By contrast, in the 2004 quadrennial cycle for both the sport and political events, the Olympics took place between the two Conventions. In 2000, both Conventions were concluded a month before the Olympics.

Other concessions to an awareness that interest in American politics was broader than its national boundaries included the inclusion of Spanish in communications of both Conventions. The Republican Convention site was accessible in a Spanish version while the Democratic Convention was simulcast in Spanish, not just for 35 million Spanish speaking Americans, according to the convention website, but for the 300 million-plus Spanish-speakers outside the US.

The Democratic Convention site also outlined ways in which the convention was the most tech-savvy event of its kind ever, It was "transitional" and more inclusive than any past event. New features included live high-definition streaming of proceedings, daily webcasts and a partnership with "YouTube" that gave conventioneers an opportunity to air personal on-site experiences with the country and the world.

America's two political conventions in 2008 were evidence that America was set the lead the world after a period of solo willfulness that had led to a global economic crisis. Of key interest to the world was the presentation of the two candidates who would face off in the November election. Both the Democratic and Republican candidates were equally qualified and both were unconventional in different ways.

The Republican candidate John McCain was a loose cannon maverick with old school ways. The Democratic candidate Barack Obama was a world savvy progressive who had little chance of winning a general election given the country's racial history. The world had its druthers but the choice was up to America, who had already disappointed its women during the primary campaign.

Despite her loss to Obama in winning the Democratic party's endorsement as its candidate for the office of president in 2008, Hillary Clinton had proven to be a formidable candidate. If Obama won the November election, she would be a key player in steering America onto a global path where economy, energy, employment and global migration were all connected and communication was key.

What America Wants in a Woman – as Judged by the 2008 Presidential Line-Up

The first non-white candidate for president of the United States won the right to make history in part because his leading opponent was a woman, described by one news commentator as a "she-devil. " The other major political party then selected its own groundbreaking candidate as a woman just emerging in the media as a throwback to Annie Oakley. Despite appearances and regardless of legislation to achieve gender equality, a persistent decision was being made that Americans wanted their women to be dumb, cute and barefoot in the kitchen.

Michelle Obama, the wife of the Democratic candidate, had an undergraduate degree from Wellesley College and a law degree from Harvard University. Yet the only ambition she mentioned in public as the wife of a presidential candidate was to be a good mother. Perhaps that ambition for good motherhood was the reason she spent eight grueling years getting a law degree from a prestigious institution. After all, a good mother implied a good father and Michelle did demurely joke at the Democratic Convention that Barack was her big bonus for putting in time at a white shoe law firm.

When it came to presenting themselves to the public in the political realm, both women hid their talents under a bushel to safeguard their husbands' political viability. Otherwise, backlash reported in the media was fierce and opinion polls backed up the negative impression that had been made.

In 1992, Hillary Clinton baked chocolate chip cookies to prove she was domestic after criticism that she was too ambitious. In 2008, Michelle Obama faced charges of being bossy. That same year, Republicans chose a woman vice-presidential candidate who had entered politics through the Wassila, Alaska Parent and Teacher Association while raising five children.

Education wasn't everything but in the United States but it was a pawn in the social hierarchy topped by "pale males.". Bill Clinton's Yale law degree and Fulbright scholarship were additions to his stature because of his poor beginnings. Bill Gates was admired for never having graduated from Harvard because he made a ton of money instead. George W. Bush was sold to America as a man of the people because he declined to profit from the learning his family's privilege had earned him at Yale.

It was unlikely that minority member Barack Obama would have become a presidential candidate without his Harvard magna cum laude law degree. And he wasn't likely to become US President if his wife didn't bury her own degree in favor of the woman that Americans wanted to see.

Both Hillary Clinton and Michelle Obama had the smarts to continue the careers for which their education had prepared them. Hillary would assume a role in politics. Michelle would develop projects based on her experience. Meanwhile, Republican VP candidate Sarah Palin appeared to be winning the American popularity contest.

A supreme irony of 2008 America was the topsy turvy image it had of its women. Educated and highly intelligent Michelle Obama and Hillary Clinton were perceived as overly ambitious and overbearing. Annie Oakley mom Sarah Palin was hailed as all American homespun. Yet once brought to light, she was the one who clothed the down home image in designer suits to pursue ambitions that by the end of the campaign earned her the label of rogue by the maverick presidential candidate John McCain who had chosen her as his running mate.

HELEN FOGARASSY

What Drives Palin – Firing a Chef When She Has a Big Job and Five Kids to Feed?

Call me lazy, but I'd want all the help I could get if I had five children to feed and a big state to govern. Sarah Barracuda let go the chef that came with the Alaska governor's mansion so she could feed her own children. She also preferred to drive herself to work, possibly while also doing laundry and cooking.

Piling on more challenges than necessary was a trait that went well with the image of a female frontier moose-hunter. But when right-wing zealotry was factored in, along with the intention to impose it on others, the country and the human right to self-determination, the question of motivation became suspect.

In high school, Palin was nicknamed "barracuda" because of her sportsmanship style. In the political area, the nickname might have been less attractive if Palin had not also been a runner up in a beauty contest. Nancy Pelosi, Hillary Clinton and Michelle Obama had all been judged as overly aggressive. None had ever entered a beauty contest. The combination of qualities made Palin the perfect choice for cheerleader for the 2008 Republican platform.

John McCain was running on a platform of bringing change to the Republican party. His vote record showed that he sided predominantly with incumbent Bush and that he had voted to allow US forces to enter Pakistan from Afghanistan in the Bush self styled war on terrorism. When asked for her views on the matter, Palin said she hadn't paid much attention to Iraq.

The answer seemed flippant for one who was aiming to be a heartbeat from the presidency, even if foreign affairs wasn't a Palin strong suit. In fact, the entirety of her foreign policy experience was based on the claim that she could see Russia from her house in Alaska. That begged the question of why she would want a position for which she was so ill prepared.

Unbridled ambition sprang to mind as an answer. Based on her history of shouldering unnecessary chores, it was possible that she was a control freak in the manner of housebound mothers with frustrated bigger ambitions. That view would accord with her extreme right wing agenda for the party.

In either case, the Republican Party soon took control of Palin to shield the "barracuda" from the circle of piranhas that was the media, as McCain campaign manager Rick Davis described the press. The tactic made sense, not only because Palin was such an easy target for ridicule but because a show of ambition or iron rule would mar the downhome rural Palin image the party was trying to promote.

If Palin was recruited by Republicans to be cheerleader for its agenda, it did not bode well that she needed shielding from the piranha press. Putin would make mincemeat of her.

No Nation is an Island in the 2008 American Election Year

"Country first" was the theme of the 2008 Republican Convention and campaign. The presidential candidate was hothead who as his vice presidential running mate a woman who was a self-described "pit bull" with no foreign policy experience. Judged by her convention speech, she was to be no more than a cheerleader for a conservative agenda. The Republican message to the world was that America would continue its pugilistic loner path with the election of those candidates.

The Democratic theme that year was "securing America's future." The party's presidential candidate was a young non-white activist whose slogans and themes centered on change and on "yes we can." The vice presidential candidate was a seasoned politician with a broad range of foreign policy experience. With an ailing economy, the Democratic message to the world was that election of its candidates would lead America into joining a world that was globalizing for mutual benefit and economic prosperity.

America's global image had grown muddled since it first invaded Iraq in the 1991 Gulf War. The legitimacy of that involvement was questionable since it involved a dispute between the sovereign neighboring states of Iraq and Kuwait. After the horrific attack on 9/11, America had launched another futile war in its campaign against jihad. Based on false charges against Iraq, the campaign proved immensely damaging to America and its image.

America's greed and the hypocrisy of its double-standard were laid bare by scandals involving contractor windfalls, illegal torture practices and abuse of prisoners deprived of basic protections laid down by the Geneva Conventions after the Second World War. In 2008. America did not look good in the eyes of the world and its economy reflected that diminished position in the world, not just because of its foreign policies but its domestic affairs.

The "shock and awe" tactic used in Iraq did its work on America as well. The enemy was publicly identified and attacked. When the information turned out to have been incorrect, America was shocked by the blunder, awed by its own incompetence and left with a faceless enemy lying in wait to strike again. And while America reeled from those onslaughts, it neglected key issues of global communal concern.

Regulations governing staples of international mutual concern were reversed or allowed to lapse. Those included nuclear proliferation, environmental protections and advancement of human rights. Expansion of trade to a global level received little attention.

The 2008 US presidential election was a turning point for the US and the world. The country would either continue putting its resources into defense against faceless enemies or it would join with the globally like-minded to build a better world Americans could not see because of fear.

In the 2008 US election, the contest transcended the obvious polarities of Democrat and Republican, Black and White, experience and youth. The real issue involved openness to the reality of a global world and competence to deal with ensuing changes at the highest level.

America was a maverick to the world. The country was the world's great beacon for opportunity and innovation. Even so, America's fuel, trade, financial institutions, security and well-being were tied in with those of global neighbors. With its 2008 election, America could spend less time chasing faceless enemies and devote more tune to making friends and more leading them in areas development of renewable energy, which would also help create new and exciting jobs for its people.

Better a Black Man in the White House than a Right-Wing Zealot a Heartbeat Away

In the 2008 election campaign, there was little media coverage of race in the American context. Of course it was acknowledged that Obama was black and exotic, but little discussion of that fact as it related to comments heard all over streets, bars and busses. Blacks and whites were convinced that America would never elect a black man as its president.

He had great ideas but he'd never be elected so there was no point in listening, whites might say. "Of course, I'm voting for my man Obama and of course he won't win, but damn, he's running," black men might say with genuine admiration. The perspectives differed but the conclusions concurred. America was not ready to change the racial barrier that had existed since its founding.

In 2008, both candidates running for US president deserved the highest respect. One had proven his loyalty to the country in the traditional manner of military service. He had been tortured as prisoner-of-war in an earlier disastrous misadventure, Viet Nam.

The other candidate offered the revolutionary view that America could step into the global sphere by dramatically structuring its social institutions to increase security for people. That would enable the country to recover from its latest military misadventure in Iraq, complete with redeploying armed services for defense instead of aggression with regard to Iraqi neighbors who had been drawn into the conflict.

In a world where both domestic and international acts of terror were potential realities, the second-in-command of the United States assumed a groundbreaking new importance on the electoral slate. The choice of the person for that role was a reflection of the candidate's qualification for leading the country.

The upstart young Democrat Barack Obama chose the seasoned Joe Biden to be his second-in-command. The maverick Republican John McCain chose the fiery female dark horse Sarah Palin whose policies and style set back progress by a good fifty years in areas such as environmental protections, global sensitivity and family planning choices.

The possibility of a Black man and a Black family in the White House remained remote as the election neared, however compelling the message and image. Yes, America was the world's great melting pot but it's main ingredient had always been white. The sudden change was too great to comprehend. America would need time to adjust even if the alternative was a redneck second in command just a heartbeat from the presidency.

Candidate Families Do Matter in the 2008 US Presidential Election

The cliché that the world was changing fast was seldom more apt than in the 2008 US election year. Just four years earlier, the 2004 election had taken place in a pre-Twitter age. In 2008, the Republican vice-presidential candidate was a self-described "hockey mom" with a pro-life, anti-choice platform. Interest in her five children was bound to appear in the social media gossip arena.

Traditionally, a candidate's family was "off limits" to the press after being trotted out in their Sunday best for campaigns. In a twitter age, their absence created space and appetite for speculation.

Family values were high on both the Palin and Republican party agenda. Those values placed priority on traditional family-based principles such as high standards of morality and discipline. In the view of right wing Republicans such as Palin, lapses in living up to those standards were due to the negative influence of liberals.

Therefore, when an unmarried 17-year-old Palin daughter was found to be pregnant when Palin was already on the Republican ticket, it was decided that the development would be made part of the showcase for family values. Palin made the presentation herself at a news conference.

"Our beautiful daughter has become an adult faster than we expected. We are proud of her decision to have the baby and make a family with the father. They will always have our support."

The astonishing twist on the family values that would have kept the Palin daughter virginal until after marriage stunned the Republican party convention delegates. It was just one of numerous Palin family scandals that ranged from political vendettas to misuse of power. All escaped notice of any significance. There were too many to track and explanations were useless to those for whom the malfeasance was no more than politics as usual.

A Black Family in the White House with the 2008 US Election?

The American perception of politics was the hidden agenda in the 2008 US election. The Republican politicians were the conservative norm, complete with firebrand vice-presidential candidate Sarah Palin and her extreme right wing agenda. A politician like Democrat Barack Obama would shatter the image of public office as an opportunity for self-promotion.

Aside from being black in a society where the history was rooted in racial inequality, Obama seemed too good to be true as a politician. He came across as honestly sincere about the welfare of America and its people. His addresses were intelligent, directed and poignant. He and his wife Michelle seemed genuinely fond of each other beyond the necessary formalities. Few scandals were found in his background and even those didn't stick to him or his image.

No doubt Obama's early cosmopolitan upbringing had a great influence on his ability to adapt, think on his feet and steer clear of pitfalls to his integrity. Those skills helped him navigate the bare-knuckled world of Chicago politics known for corruption, cronyism and reliance on toeing the party line. According to sources, Obama had the rare skill of negotiating his ascent in the party without becoming beholden to any single player.

Independent and charismatic, Obama captured the country's attention and skillfully managed to win the Democratic party's nomination for president over woman rival Hillary Clinton. The broader visibility of his campaign against John McCain brought into greater light the possibility of a black family in the White House. The outlook was mixed.

Barack Obama's political success has been attributed to grass roots appeal and support as well as his savvy use of the internet to attract supporters and field workers for his campaigns. In the press, he was often described as elitist and aloof, two qualities not generally seen as political assets. Likewise, Michelle Obama was perceived as outspoken and opinionated, a label that had dogged first lady Clinton throughout her White House tenure. By precedent, the young Obama daughters were not covered in the press except to show them at public events where they seemed at home on the national stage and in front of cameras.

While the possibility was never stated, criticisms of the Obamas seemed to be a reflection of white racist charges against blacks that they were uppity, bossy, unable to know their place. If Obama was elected president of the US in 2008, America would have a chance to consider those criticism in context of the family occupying the top house in the country.

The Meaning of "White House" in the 2008 US Presidential Campaign

In the 2008 presidential campaign, the conservative New York Post tabloid supported Barack Obama over Hillary Clinton during the Democratic primary. As soon as Republican John McCain won his party's nomination, the Post endorsed McCain over Obama. While those positions were not surprising, the volume of media support brought into question the role of the media machine in the fate of candidates.

In the 2008 Democratic primary, Hillary Clinton conceded her delegates to her male opponent Obama even though she had the support of 18 million voters. She conceded on the basis of voting results, polls and news media support showing that Obama had a strong lead.

At the same time, once Obama won the primary, his media support turned to endorse Republican McCain, possibly because corporate media owners wanted to keep control of the country in Republican hands. They would be banking on the precedent that change at the country's presidential level came only slowly.

Less than 50 years before Obama ran for the US presidency in 2008, John Kennedy was nearly dismissed as a viable presidential candidate because of his Catholic religion. Since then, no ethnic, religious, race or gender candidate had come close to running for the presidency. With the exception of Kennedy, the white Protestant stranglehold on power had remained intact at the highest level of governing the country. The chance that a candidate of any other race would succeed seemed slimmer than remote.

According to the Southern Poverty Law Center, in 2007 there were 888 active hate groups in 16 of the country's states. As reported by the New York Post in 2008, there were 200,000 people nationwide who were active white supremacists and they supported Barack Obama as a way to boost their cause by triggering what they saw as a long-overdue racial backlash.

Those figures reflected the most radical of white supremacist racists. They didn't include the undoubtedly large ranks of the less radical, garden-variety bigots. They couldn't include the quantifiably vague elements of plain old prejudice and bias.

With its 2008 election, America would test itself to see if it would continue to expand its democratic inclusiveness as it had with the election of John F. Kennedy. Alternatively, it would remain mired in a stale strict and literal definition of who was entitled to live in the White House.

HELEN FOGARASSY

Where Does a Palin Family Wedding Fit with the 2008 American Election?

Reportedly, the announcement of an unexpected pregnancy in the Palin family took the 2008 Republican convention by surprise. Global eyes were on the event occurring in the tailwinds of the rousing Beijing Olympics followed by an energizing Democratic Convention. Maverick John McCain had chosen dark horse Sarah Palin to be his running mate. The pregnancy of an unwed 17-year-old daughter was not part of the family values platform that Palin and the Republicans espoused.

Palin, however, came through. She said her daughter had become an adult faster than expected. She was doing right by her decision to have the baby and give it a loving home by marrying the father. The new family would always have the love and support of the Palin family.

The father and groom-to-be was presented at the Republican convention as part of the vice-presidential candidate's family. Questions about teen pregnancies and shotgun weddings did not arise but did reverberate in the 2008 modern American psyche.

At the age of 17, it was unlikely that the daughter Bristol would be getting married if not pregnant. Unless the Palin parents were unusually liberal at the personal level while ultra conservative at the public, it could be assumed they were less than thrilled to hear their unwed 17-year-old was pregnant unless they were avid to continue the family line. In that case, they were willing to let early motherhood prevent their daughter from engaging in challenges like competing for the title of Miss America as her mother had.

Regardless of Palin family dynamics, announcement of the pregnancy and forthcoming marriage created a stronger bond between Palin and her religious right supporters. She became an average mom facing the same challenges as other moms in helping the family to deal with mistakes young people made. Still, the message jarred with the modern social view that early mistakes did not have to seal a youngster's fate.

By 2008 America, a juvenile misdemeanor charge did not hound a young miscreant throughout adult life. A teenage hormonal impulse indulged without consideration of consequence did not have to shackle two youngsters into a life with a mate who was possibly unsuitable.

Republican vice-presidential candidate Sarah Palin stood in stark contrast to such progress. Lipstick became her unofficial brand, a symbol of a time when woman was mere adornment to a man. While that was fine for those who liked it, the image grated on the Republican message of change away from Bush politics to pace-setters for the future.

A woman whose identity was wrapped up in lipstick seemed less than ideal to be a heartbeat from the presidency of a United States caught in an economic crisis unseen since the great depression. The fact that she was chosen by maverick John McCain and nominated by the conservative Republican party spoke volumes about integrity and the lack of that virtue.

Palin repeatedly assured the country that a marriage between her unwed daughter and the father of her expected baby would take place. The affirmations were usually made after news leaked out about the father-to-be, who was sporadically exposed as a party-hearty teen with no intentions to settle down.

No announcement of a forthcoming marriage was made as the election neared. That uncertainty remained insignificant. Integrity had already been compromised by all associated with the announcement of a teenage pregnancy in context of a right wing political agenda.

America Cracks a Global Glass Ceiling with the 2008 Elections

The world's great land of opportunity cracked two great glass ceilings in one fell swoop with its 2008 Democratic primary. A black man and a white woman were contenders for the party's nomination in the upcoming presidential election. Those two cracks in limits to power at the national level were set to resound globally if racial presumptions about hierarchy were overturned.

The Republican Party made election of the Democratic slate mandatory if the country were not to regress. Its presidential candidate was an elder hothead with conventional ideas. He had chosen a running mate so conservative she would undo decades of progress in liberating society from constricting limits. She opposed choice in family planning, belonged to a church that "prays away the gay" and was such a political neophyte she needed a media-shield and concessions in debating her counterpart. She refused to cooperate with investigations into family wrong-doing in her home state of Alaska and she belonged to a political party beset with charges of similar malfeasance.

 After eight years in power, the Republican party was reeling from fallout that stemmed from a cover up of Constitutional violations, including the manufacture of grounds for an illegal war. Lack of transparency and roll-back of regulations had led to a crash of America's financial institutions. In 2008, the tone of the Republican party campaign seemed an appeal to the power of fear, as if assuring voters that in a storm, the devil they knew was better than the unknown.

In 2008, the conservative known devil seemed to be intimidation and the forcing of views onto others, even through war if necessary. The long range view of history. however, indicated that diplomatic discourse achieved greater gains in social and political advances than armed conflict, which enriched only manufacturers and users of arms. Traditional firearms were particularly useful to modern terrorists, whether they were a state or and illicit organization. To achieve their aims, both relied on the colonial "divide and conquer" tactic.

In contrast, a broad view of the problems facing the world in 2008 indicated that "unification" was key to resolving challenges. Global climate change, for example, influenced migratory patterns of fish, animals and humans. The industries and economies of 200 countries were affected as a result. Resolving disputes with arms in such cases was futile, especially since other challenges were immune to armed intervention. Diseases, for example, travelled on airplanes without visas and natural resources such as oil and water did not stop at national borders.

The American invasion of Iraq proved the futility of aggression in a global world. America's image and standing suffered as a result of the attack. America also provided that it had no capacity to distinguish friends from foes. To fix that deficiency, America had no choice but to engage with the world before it sent more sons and daughters to fight in yet another armed misadventure.

Engagement with the world did not require Americans to track every skirmish in each of the world's 200 countries. It did call for an awareness of those countries so that news about them struck a chord with American experience. A flood in Germany and a fire in California or Australia had one thing in common and that was the impact on victims and the various ways in which governments and global aid agencies helped those affected.

As the American misadventure in Iraq had proved, leaders could no longer be passively trusted for news about the world, nor about responses required. In the 2008 global world, choosing the right leader had become critical.

HELEN FOGARASSY

Despite the broad spectrum of age, gender, race and political position, the 2008 election had less to do with those important obvious issues than with old order thinking versus new. The vote in November would decide whether America went forward along the secretive, defensive, blustering path that had led to economic collapse or whether it engaged with the world in a revolution that ousted the historic use of aggression to amass power.

Sink with the old or swim with the new could have been the juice before America in its 2008 election. Choosing the latter would be the biggest crack ever in the global glass ceiling on power.

The New American Revolution with the 2008 Presidential Election

"No taxation without representation!" was the rallying cry of the American revolution in 1776. The declaration was based on a number of measures imposed on American colonists by British royals. They included the 1765 Stamp Act that led to the 1773 Boston Tea Party and the revolutionary war that began in 1775.

The American cry against coercive measured imposed by distant royals was backed by the declaration of independence and elaboration of the American Constitution in 1776. The constellation of those events set off an unprecedented worldwide revolution toward freedom and equality against tyranny.

A dozen years after the first "shot heard round the world" was fired in America, the French revolution sent monarchic structures tumbling across the world from the Russian Romanov to the Ottoman and Austrian Hapsburg empires over the next century. Two world wars and a century after that, America again grew restive when its ruling conservative Party turned out to have enriched the privileged white elite while fleecing working Americans and bankrupting the country's financial institutions.

The American people were told in 2008 to bail out their failing corporate and financial institutions to the tune of a half trillion dollars using their tax money. With "golden parachutes" and record breaking executive salaries still stinging in consciousness, Americans looked to the Democratic presidential candidate to be the leader of their new revolution.

The idea of "entitlement" was not only alien but aversive to America born of its 1776 revolt against the British monarchy. Americans would never openly finance an upper class that ruled by virtue of birth and relied on the work of "lowers" willing to indulge them for the sake of a secure social order. Yet in the eight years leading up to the 2008 election, America found itself in that position without being aware of the condition.

Once Barack Obama secured the Democratic party's nomination for president, Americans began to admit that a racial barrier could be breached if America was to restore the pursuit of the equality ideal promised by its Constitution. As the 2008 election neared, the positions of both parties became ever clearer.

The "shot heard round the world" in 2008 America was the announcement by Republican presidential candidate John McCain that Sarah Palin would be his vice-presidential running mate. The arch-conservative Alaskan woman would take America back to an age when even women were deprived of the equality they had gained. Dubbed by political TV host Bill Maher as "Bush in drag," the Alaskan outlaw governor promised to continue the Bush proclivity for ignoring Constitutional safeguards on democratic values.

Under Bush, deregulation had allowed financial institutions run wild. Lack of transparency had kept hidden the transactions that had led to financial disaster. The claim of executive privilege had prevented investigation. Those traditional means of securing power were the same tactics that Palin had perfected as governor of Alaska on a smaller scale.

Abuse of presidential power aided by political allies peaked with the Bush presidency, starting with his questionable win in 2000 by a decision of the Supreme Court. The offer of another four years under such Constitutional erosion was either an insult to American intelligence or a gamble on good will or gullibility. The alternative would be yet another "shot heard round the world" fired by an America fed up with taxation without representation of its interests in a multinational, multicultural and multiracial world.

It Serves to Remember Rove is Palin's Tutor in the 2008 US Election

The only vice-presidential debate between US Democratic Party candidate Joe Biden and Republican Sarah Palin took place on Thursday of the week in which the Wall Street bailout was a political football. On Monday the House voted down a $700 billion bailout. A campaign stressing urgency led to the passage of a Senate bill on Wednesday, not for $700 billion but for $850 billion.

That same day saw the disastrous airing of an interview between news anchor Katie Couric and Sarah Palin, in which Palin couldn't answer questions about magazines she read or news sources she consulted.

Palin attributed her commonly acknowledged bad performance to annoyance with Couric, according to the Huffington Post. But the bad showing was a prelude to Palin's remarkable comeback during the debate with Joe Biden the next day. The Couric interview set the bar so low for Palin that her flirtatious evasion of answers pre-empted would-be critics.

The strategy was the brain-child of Karl Rove, Republican political strategist who sold George W. Bush to the public in two elections despite calls for his impeachment. In the case of Palin, the media news cycle over her comeback helped bury the massive $700 billion bailout bill that passed in the House on Friday. The following day Palin began her bare-knuckle campaign against Obama, accusing him of "palling around" with terrorists.

The Rove strategy was to find "strong" candidates defined as those who had public appeal. Then he turned weaknesses into strengths.

In the case of the younger president Bush, the weakness turned into strength was the narrowness of his vision. Bush could act on a strongly held view and carry through his goal without regard to the effect of his actions on others. Thus in Rove's hands, Bush's limited intelligence became his strong suit. He delighted in stunning verbal gaffes and boasted about sleeping through college. Those flaws endeared him to the "average" American. It signaled that he was just like common people, a bond so potent he was able to sell the American public on a faked up war. In 2008, that same Bush gift of working the public allowed him to bail out the Wall Street tycoons he had fattened for eight years deregulation of financial markets and instruments,

Sarah "barracuda" Palin bested Bush in the Rove strategy of turning weaknesses into strengths for a candidate who had strong public appeal. With all his limited smarts, Bush was affable, if shallow and flippant with serious matters. Palin's limited intelligence led her to be dismissive of all that didn't fit with her radically right wing vision for America.

Palin at first glance seemed an annoying throw-back to a 1950's anti-progressive woman. In the hands of Karl Rove, she became a potential Weapon of Mass Destruction for the forward-looking, innovative America the world had known for 230 years.

Rove was involved in numerous investigations involving Bush abuse of power, most notably the firing of seven Justice Department attorneys looking into allegations of the Justice Department itself having been politicized. When subpoenaed by Congress, he refused to testify and further legal actions fizzled when the Justice Department declined to prosecute or pursue the cases involved.

In her own right, Palin was familiar with the use of the justice system to pursue both political aims and personal vendettas. Her husband was cited for contempt of court when he refused to testify in a case involving Palin's firing of a family member from the Alaska State Troopers while she was governor of the state.

By 2008 in the 21st century of a nascent tech age, reports of political scandals were so numerous they lost the power to make an impact. They were no longer news, just background noise and the Republican party in power made hay with the development.

Under Rove's tutelage, Palin's limitations were forged into weapons. When faced with a novelty that didn't accord with her view, she lashed out and attacked like the "mama grizzly" she had introduced at the Republican Convention. Likewise, her down-home airiness became a dual purpose tool. It was a self-protective shield that shifted blame for failures onto others.

The tactic was on full display during Palin's comeback debate with Joe Biden after the bar for her was lowered by a disastrous TV interview with Katie Couric. After the debate, media sources accurately cited Palin's flirtatious evasion in answering questions. But the blame fell on black woman moderator Gwen Ifill for failing to pursue the evasions.

Flirty Sarah Palin as America's WMD in the 2008 US Presidential Election

Sarah Palin stormed onto the national political stage in probably the same way she captured the governorship in the sparsely populated state of Alaska. Wasilla, the town where Palin was mayor for six years before becoming Alaska's governor, had a population of under 10,000 and was, according to Wikipedia, the fourth largest population center in Alaska.

In a state where rugged manliness was the subject of a worldwide sensation with Alaska men Magazine, the "you betcha" flirtations of a beauty contest near-winner got attention. Add to that mix a well scripted speech unfettered by the constraints of fact and the formula was complete for success in the Republican party.

The winking, nose-wrinkling and avid air-punching were less effective at the national political level conducted mainly in front of television cameras for mainstream American viewers in the lower 48. Once on the McCain ticket, Palin was upgraded with designer suits and salon-puffed hair complete with flirty bangs. The juxtaposition of down-home and glitzy hip grated on many. Others were taken with the effect, particularly those banking on the religious right to get the party back into the White House for another eight-years term.

In 2008, the Republican party shared priorities with most religious institutions. Those included family values restrictions on abortion and a hard line against progressive measures related to homosexuality and marital unions. While the first amendment to the Constitution stipulated a strict separation of church and state in order to guarantee freedom of religion, challenges to that "foundation clause" had clarified the degree of that separation through Supreme Court decisions. Political organizations promoting religious values had sprung up. Palin straddled the overlap of the two.

The Christian Coalition was one of the largest political groups advancing religious values at all levels of government. It had two million members and 2,000 chapters in all 50 states. That represented a lot of votes and Palin was their darling, an important asset to Republicans.

The 2008 bailout package for $700 billion was an example of why the religious right was so important to Republicans. The elite Senate voted to pass the bill, the House voted to turn it down because the little people voters protested fiercely and their own elections were on the line. The Senate reintroduced the bill for a higher amount, followed that by political drama and got the House to pass the bill that week.

There was no telling what horse-trading went into getting the bill passed, but clearly the little people of America were an important part of the process. They needed to be distracted if Republicans were to enact their conservative agenda.

Palin played her part. The day after the bailout bill passed, she told supporters it was time to take off the globes because Obama was a guy who palled around with terrorists.

A Frankenstein's Monster in the 2008 US Transition

The 2008 Republican presidential candidate unleashed on America a rightwing zealot who overshadowed him like a solar eclipse. In the election, America voted against the Republican slate by a margin large enough to escape court challenges or Supreme Court rulings. But the beauty queen zealot he jettisoned as she rocketed to fame beyond him continued to turn up like the proverbial bad penny after the ticket lost the election.

Back in Alaska after the loss, Palin engineered a Thanksgiving turkey pardon to compete with the official ritual in Washington. Unfortunately, the local TV station covering the Alaska event captured an ongoing turkey slaughter in the background. The footage became an immediate mainstream sensation and an instant YouTube hit. Palin took the media mishap in stride. She'd been greeted as a resounding success the week before at a demoralized Republican Governor's meeting in Miami two weeks after the election.

At that meeting of Republican governors, Palin was touted as the new face of the Republican party. The Alaska governor downplayed the celebrity she had fueled with major network interviews the week before. When asked about emerging challenges in the areas of renewable energy and health care reform, she said those were not areas for government involvement. She dismissed facts about Republican deficits in every region of the country and in every voting group, including minorities and women. Her upbeat take on a bad development gained her more attention.

By the weekend after the unfortunate turkey shoot, the new Republican star was featured in an AOL News story on her rising celebrity status. After that, Oprah wanted her, as did Jay Leno and Letterman. The William Morris Agency had called and she could do an interview with any news agency on the planet, her spokesperson said. And while the media offers remained unconfirmed, only the Anchorage Daily News chided her for carrying on national activities while state issues needed the state leader's attention, including the areas of education and plummeting oil prices.

The superstar who shot to fame when maverick Republican John McCain chose her to be his running mate in the 2008 US election was not about to settle down to mundane state affairs in Alaska. In a number of interviews, she hinted at a run for the 2012 presidency. But in that pursuit of higher aims, one very local issue loomed large on the agenda.

Palin's contribution to the McCain ticket was her appeal to the religious right because of her strong stance on family values. She shot to hero status with that crowd when she turned a family crisis into a living lesson demonstrating that agenda. When her unmarried teenaged daughter turned out to be unexpectedly pregnant, Palin made the announcement in a very public deft twist on expectations.

Like many young people, Palin had said at the opening of the 2008 Republican convention, her daughter had prematurely become an adult. She was doing the right thing. She would have the baby and the parents would marry. A new life was being welcomed into the world. The new young family would always have the love and support of her parents.

The Palin daughter pregnancy along with an upcoming wedding hung in the air throughout the 2008 campaign. Shortly before the election, it was announced that the wedding was planned for spring after the baby was born in December.

At that same time, the father- and husband-to-be was quoted as saying that Palin had to win the election, she was his future mother-in-law. In all that media powered uncertainty about a

HELEN FOGARASSY

Palin wedding in context of family values, the one concrete facts was that a new Palin baby would be born in December. The rest remained suspended in cyberspace to keep hold of America's attention about a Palin role in its future.

Breaking the Bank Before Leaving in the 2008 US Transition

After the 2008 election, the sitting president was technically a lame duck. In fact, however, he was quite busy cementing the legacy that had left him less popular than Richard Nixon at the time of his forced resignation, according to CNN. A Gallup poll showed that when the two presidents met at the White House, the outgoing had a 27% approval rating versus 70% for the incoming.

The unpopularity of outgoing president George W. Bush was a culmination of his entire presidency. He had manufactured a cause for America to enter a war with Iraq. He had illegally detained prisoners at Guantanamo Bay and had approved illegal torture practice to extract information from detainees. Judicial rulings on those matters did not come down until the third week of November, about two weeks after the election. And despite those legal setbacks, the outgoing president Bush delivered on his promise to ensure a smooth transition to the next administration. He and first lady Bush welcomed the new first couple to the White House and the first twins introduced the new first daughters to their new digs.

Beyond those good will gestures, the lame duck president remained as presidential as ever. At a meeting of Pacific Rim countries, he joked about his "forced retirement" and recalled his confusion of the group's APEC acronym with OPEC, the oil producing cartel. He also mistook Australia for Austria in the folksy, gaffe-prone manner that had endeared him to the American public and won him two terms as president of the country. Beneath that veneer, the goals of the real agenda were being finalized.

One example of the Bush legacy was the handling of the $700 billion bailout called the Emergency Economic Stabilization Act. It authorized the US Treasure to buy up to $700 billion worth of troubled financial assets to stabilize tumbling economy. Oversight was limited and the plan failed to address the woes of failing manufacturing sectors such as the auto industry. As the economy continued to tank despite the bailout, the incoming president was asked to step in and he wisely responded that America had only one president at a time.

With that, outgoing president Bush continued cementing his legacy by approving "midnight regulations" being "churned out" before the inauguration. As listed by the Washington Post on November 11, those measures included a proposal to end a ban on carrying loaded guns in national parks, a plan to make it harder to get funding for reproductive health care and easing safety regulations for workers in the chemical industry.

Some 130 such rules were available for action before the sitting president left office, but an overlooked White House memo had stipulated that some action on some rules could proceed outside mandated deadlines. Thus, a new rule would water down the endangered species act. Medicaid would be cut back, mining would be allowed near the Grand Canyon and curbs on emissions from power plants would be relaxed. Drilling next to national parks would be allowed and mining waste would be allowed to flow into rivers and streams.

The range of those measures indicated that everyday lives across the country would be impacted and yet the sheer volume of actions taken were beyond the reach of most Americans. Thus, tracking such information was in the hands of accredited professional experts like ProPublica. But even after discovering such actions in the process of enactment, hurdles were nearly insurmountable in each individual case.

Most midnight regulations could be reversed in court through a dauntingly lengthy process. After approval, the regulations were also technically subject to public comment before passage.

In the case of outgoing president Bush, the regulations were pushed through at a rate that gave the Interior Department only four days to complete a review of 200,000 public comments. That translated into staff reading comments at a rate of seven per minute, or spending less than nine seconds on a comment before action was taken to meet the deadline.

A New Form of "White Flight" in the 2008 US Transition?

With the 2008 election, America voted the first non-white candidate into the country's highest office and into the highest office of any industrialized country. That position was monopolized until then by whites, primarily males, and exclusively so in the United States, founded by Protestant merchant Europeans thriving on slavery and indentured servitude.

The 2008 election in America shot down a 20-odd-year speculation about the "Bradley effect." Tom Bradley was a black Los Angeles mayor who lost his 1982 run for California governor despite opinion polls showing him in the lead. The theory held that voters professed socially desirable views while in the privacy of the voting booth they expressed their true preferences. In essence, the 2008 American election ended the need for white hypocrisy.

Still, the 2008 transition occurred less than 50 years after Rosa Parks sat on a bus and sparked the American civil rights movement. Less than 30 years had passed since America's incoming First Lady wrote a thesis on America's racial divide. The Harvard Law School grad was seen throughout the 2008 campaign in her role as wife and mother. Nevertheless, her husband's presidential run was nearly derailed when she said on the campaign trail that for the first time in her adult life, she was proud of her country.

The simple remark about the experience of being black in America received a torrent of backlash from conservative whites who professed that they'd always been proud of their country. But the aptness of Michelle Obama's comment did not become clear until her husband won the election and the family was taking part in the transition.

In 2008, America and the world were reeling from a conservative, isolationist and patriarchal system of privilege for whites. In America, the system was so stale that the value of intelligence was downgraded during an eight-year administration to the point where ignorance was part of the national identity. With the 2008 US election, American voters returned to rationality by affirming that incompetence was not an effective way to deal with a tanking economy.

The failing financial institutions being bailed out in 2008 with $700 billion of taxpayer money were headed by leaders who were given a free hand to compete without regulation over eight years under Bush. The vast majority were white males, as attested by Annual Report photos. Resumes disclosed impeccable educational credentials and experience gained through school and family connections. They made world-shaping decisions and received celebrity salaries. Their social and financial security was assured by a firm grounding in the inherited instinct and breeding for putting protection of personal interests first.

Ads in high-end publications like the New York Times Sunday Magazine showed the extent of the social divide in America, not just between blacks and whites but between the olde garde and the common people, including the nouveau riche. Financial leaders were preoccupied with personal portfolios and competition. When a crisis hit, they expected to be saved as treasures too valuable to be lost.

The long 2008 election campaign challenged that dynamic. The Democratic primary pitted a woman against a non-white man. The campaign itself gave the country the opportunity to weigh the choice between continuing on the old course headed for a losing global economic spiral or to take a leap into a promising unknown.

Once elected by the American people, Obama was well received by political counterparts, But the real test would not come until the

Obama family moved into the White House after the inauguration in January. Obama himself was half black and half white. The wife moving in with him would all black and descended from slaves. She would be unseating a slave tradition that had haunted America since its European origins.

Amendments had rendered the US Constitution into a living document. In 2008, citizens were no longer defined as land-owning males. Blacks were no longer considered 3/5 of a person for the purposes of the decennial Census. Women had the right to vote and discrimination was against the law. But public sentiment was still a personal holding that could not be legislated. The forthcoming inauguration would usher in a historic development that could prove America to be the beacon of enlightened equality that the forefathers had designed at a time when most people considered to be non-citizens.

The once devalued non-citizens of America were the modern Americans with legal rights who had elected the first non-white head of a western industrialized country. Presumably, the large minority of Americans who had voted for Republican John McCain had not concurred with the historic 2008 electoral decision. Judging by the Bush midnight legislative slate, the losers were far pleased with the progress that the Obama victory augured.

"White flight" was a term applied to a phenomenon in which whites moved from a desegregating neighborhood in anticipation of ill effects expected to result from a drop in "elite" status, according to Wikipedia. Those effects were mere fears until they triggered a large-scale exodus that did result in real damage ranging from a drop in real estate values to reduced services and increased costs of insurance.

The American White House was the country's prime parcel of real estate. With a black family moving in, fretful whites had no more desirable site for relocation. The fight. Flight or freeze model of survival kicked in. Anti-progressive whites were clearing out the publica vaults and putting them into private storage until it was safe to take the valuables out again.

Can an Invader be a Liberator in the 2008 Transition?

The lame duck US president was leaving office intent on selling himself as liberator in the 2008 US transition between his administration and that of the historic first non-white head of an industrialized country. In interviews and press conferences during the waning twilight of his presidency, he stressed the conviction that history would vindicate his actions in office.

The First Lady and the Secretary of State appeared on Sunday talk shows with the message that the President had liberated thousands of Afghanis and Iraqis. The vice-president repeatedly affirmed that all actions taken in the "war on terror" since the 9/11 attack on the US were justified, necessary and successful in preventing another attack.

In January of the of the transition year, the Foreign Secretary of US ally Britain in the "war on terror," issued a statement saying that the term coined by the US president shortly after the 9/11 attack was "misleading and mistaken." He said the concept had united extremists against the West and had invited linkages between diverse groups fighting ethnic battles in countries such as Sri Lanka and Pakistan. Just the day before, the US National Portrait Gallery had agreed to revise the wording on the president's official portrait to eliminate linkages between 9/11 and the wars in Afghanistan and Iraq.

The war in Afghanistan began in context of the Bush-coined "war on terror." At the time of the 9/11 attack on the US, Afghanistan was fighting its own extremist elements, mainly the Taliban that had arisen from the ashes of the Soviet period in Afghanistan. Reportedly, Osama bin Laden as the mastermind of the 9/11 al Qaeda attack on the US, was also operating out of Afghan caves bordering Pakistan. By entering into a war pact in the form of an intervention, mutual enemies would be the target.

By contrast, the only basis for the 2003 war in Iraq was the determination of US president Bush to invade the country, possibly to finish the war his father had begun with the 1991 First Gulf War. That armed attack on Iraq had its own questionable rationalizations.

In his last press conference as president, the lame duck said that not finding weapons of mass destruction in Iraq was a "significant disappointment" to him. In an interview with his own sister, he said that "faulty intelligence" about Iraq was greatest regret of his tenure. Yet by then, numerous sources had found that no "faulty intelligence was involved.

A British Downing Street intelligence memo was leaked in 2005 describing a Bush rush to war. When questioned, the White House made no response either Congress or the press. Not until the president was out of office did the accredited press gather enough information to publish stories like the February 2009 article in The Nation that cited the Downing Street memo as a basis in calling for procedures to hold the president accountable. The Detroit Free Press in January chronicled the blatant untruths about Iraq that the Bush administration had stated as fact.

Most heinous among those misrepresentations was the presentation made to the Union Nations in an attempt to gain international approval for the war and win the support of allies. Satellite images purporting to prove WMD installations were later found to be fake.

Thus, as the sitting president burnished his image so that history would judge him as a liberator, mounting evidence proved him to have been a schoolyard bully while in office who had invaded a sovereign foreign country for reasons unknown. By definition, an invader was one who entered under arms with the intent to control or subdue. A liberator was one who set free. In his campaign to invade Iraq and execute its leader, the would-be liberator never mentioned freeing the Iraqi people,

Rather, he hunted perceived enemies on a pre-emptive basis, deployed mercenary contractors to deal with them and allowed the use of illegal torture to extract information. Meanwhile, the authorization for a president to use armed force without a Congressional declaration of war remained in effect on the books.

In December of the transition year, Bush made a visit to Iraq. At a press conference with Iraq Prime Minister Maliki, an Iraqi journalist hurled his shoes at Bush with the cry that it was a farewell kiss from the Iraqi people. Bush was unfazed. He said it was a sign of the growing freedom that had been won for the country, The journalist never heard that response. He was attacked by security and hustled out to face prison.

A Ticking Time Bomb in the Oval Office as the 2008 Transition Clears?

In his final press conference a week before the historic inauguration of the western industrialized world's first non-white leader, the sitting president wished the new president well. He also warned that the first priority was vigilance against terrorists. "Enemies" out there wanted to inflict harm on America and Americans.

The "mis underestimated" president leaving office with a popularity rating in the low-twenties said he was confident that he would proudly look in the mirror after leaving office. The first half of the $700 billion bailout money had been used effectively. He was pleased that the financial markets were starting to thaw.

Two days later, the Associated Press reported that the U. S. economy started the new year on a weaker footing than expected. The Federal Reserve Chairman stated that the economy was in the midst of a serious recession likely to last at least another two quarters.

That same day, the 9/11 mastermind Osama Bin Laden delivered a new message calling for jihad in wake of a two-week campaign by Israel in Gaza. During that time, the UN estimated that 1,000 Palestinians were killed The Associate Press reported that the already impoverished region had suffered $1.4 billion in damages. Meanwhile, Lebanese militants had begun lobbing rockets into Israel, India was citing military movement by Pakistan in wake of a December attack on Mumbai. The world was restive but the outgoing US president was preoccupied with the upcoming historic inauguration.

A state of emergency for Washington DC had been declared for the event, ostensibly to defray extra costs for the security needed to meet the needs of the large crowds expected to attend. However, while those crowds would be members of the incoming president's political party, the outgoing president's party would pose no security concerns.

Republicans were fleeing Washington during inauguration week, Politico reported in earthly January. Destinations ranged from sunny climes in Florida to overseas locations. Some were leaving to escape the crowds, others to make room for opposite party revelers. One group was holding a Las Vegas "inaugural party in exile" in to "celebrate the last hours of a Bush White House. "

Indeed, the Bush dynasty was making its own plans. Lame Duck's brother Jeb, a former governor of Florida, decided against a run for a US Senate seat. Patriarch Bush, whose unpopularity in the presidential office was eclipsed by that of his son, said he'd like to see another son as president but there had probably been enough of his family in the White House.

In that last press conference as he left office, the outgoing president said he didn't care about popularity. Yet on the same day that bin Laden called for jihad and the inauguration state of emergency became public, it was also announced that the post-presidential office had been launched. It would be staffed by veterans of the current administration, including strategist and Advisor Karl Rove who had resigned in 2007 amid investigations held off by claims of executive privilege.

Those investigations included his role in the outing of CIA operative Valeries Plame for political purposes, justification for the country's invasion of Iraq and voting irregularities in the election of the sitting president to a second term. In the post-presidential office, he would be involved in such activities as a "freedom institute" that would prolong the sitting president's legacy with a "freedom agenda" to promote democracy in the Middle East.

That was the future for the "mis underestimated" exiting president who also said in his parting press conference that he was "getting off the stage" once the 2008 transition was complete since there should be only one person at a time in the klieg lights. His record while under the glare of those lights was stunning.

He had led the country into a war on false pretenses. He had violated constitutional rights. He had let financial institutions run wild with deceptive practices, then had bailed out those institutions because the world economy was in a catastrophic crisis. While there was no accounting for first half of the $700 billion bailout money dispensed by the current administration, strict controls would be imposed on the allocation of the next $350 billion bailout money under the new president. That was the agreement reached with Congress.

With that record amassed in plain sight, George Dubya Bush left the stage with a jaunty "good luck" to his successor. And while the announcement of a post-presidential office being established a week before the upcoming historic inauguration was a reassuring sign that no other wars would be started by the outgoing administration, the question of brazen impunity remained an open question.

"We Had Fun," the President Tells a Tanking America in the 2008 Transition

According to the nonpartisan Center for American progress, outgoing president Bush held the fewest first term press conferences of any modern president. In 2008, six months passed between pressers when he held his last one a week before leaving office, seemingly in keeping with an ongoing campaign to convey the view that his legacy to history was a portrait of him as a "liberator."

The earlier 2008 press conference was held in context of his signing of a new round in the American Competitiveness Act first initiated by Bill Clinton. In his statement to the press, president Bush had said that his initiatives were designed to keep the American economy "the envy of the world. He also said that the "fundamentals" of the economy were strong and then he addressed a string of issues current at the time.

He said there was no evidence of an emergency in Pakistan, a cover-up of Pat Tillman's death by friendly fire in Iraq would be investigated and that those in his administration who had been associated with malfeasance in Iraq had been held accountable. The indicted vice-presidential aide Lewis Libby had paid a high price for the guilty verdict against him and finally, that Attorney General Alberto Gonzales had done nothing wrong before he resigned in the midst of congressional investigations into jis conduct of an apparently politicized Justice Department

Between that earlier presser and the final one to seal his legacy as a liberator of Iraq, lame duck Bush had seen America vote resoundingly to reject the party he had headed. During his eight-year term, America had been attacked, it had entered into an illegitimate war and it had led the world into a global economic crisis that had required a massive bailout with taxpayer money to keep the system from collapsing entirely. And yet in the final press conference, the outgoing president said that every day of his presidency had been "joyous."

He said that for him, the American presidency had not been "the loneliest office in the world." That was because he had built a "really capable team, " a "fabulous team" of "highly dedicated, smart, capable people. And we had fun, " he added, saying that to him, the phrase, "burdens of the office" was an overstatement.

Moreover, he said Iraq was a challenge for future presidents. Mistreatment of prisoners in Abu Graib was "a huge disappointment" and the failure to find weapons of mass destruction in Iraq was a "significant disappointment."

Those comments were in response to a question on mistakes he may have made during his presidency. Elaborating, he said he didn't know if they could be called "mistakes. They were "things that didn't go according to plan." The only clear mistake to which he admitted was the "mission accomplished" flag aboard the aircraft carrier early in the Iraq invasion. because it had "sent the wrong message." He also conceded that some of his "rhetoric" had obviously been a mistake.

The president said he strongly disagreed with the statement that America's moral standing had been damaged by Gitmo, harsh interrogation techniques and American unilateralism during his term in office. Gitmo had created controversies, but when it came time for critics of America to "take some of those detainees," they "weren't willing to help out. " But most people in the world, he said, viewed America as compassionate.

When asked about anger and hostility toward him, he said he wasn't worried about popularity. He said he went around the country and didn't see anger or hostility. So those people were just a few in the population. He didn't know why they were angry or hostile but in time of war, "people get emotional." At any rate, he said he hadn't really spent that much time, frankly, worrying about the "loud voices." He heard them but they didn't affect his policy or decisions.

What he did worry about, he said, was "the Constitution" and how to make it easier to "find out what the enemy is thinking. " In fact, the most urgent threat the new president and those after him would face was an attack on the homeland because there was still an "enemy" out there that wanted to inflict damage on America and Americans.

Asked about discussions taking place in legal circles regarding preemptive pardons to officials in the administration, he said he wouldn't discuss pardons. He wished the new president all the best and hoped that the tone in Washington would be different for him than it had been during his own administration, when it had been "disappointing."

Finally, he said that of course the new president would have his hands full with the economy. It was "tough" out there for a lot of working people.

Asked if he would request the second half of the $700 billion bailout money to be made available so as to make the transition easier for the incoming president, he recalled the historic lunch he had hosted the previous week at the request of the president-elect. With all those gathered, he had realized they had one experience in common. They knew what it meant to withstand the responsibility of the presidency. The president-elect, he said, "is fixing to do that."

Part II.
America with Obama

Privilege Dies Hard, Even After the 2008 US Transition

In the last press conference a week before he left office with the inauguration f the western industrialized world's first nonwhite president, outgoing president Bush said he had seen people on television crying after the election of the new president, saying they never believed they'd see the day when a black man was elected president of the United States. "It's going to be an amazing - amazing moment," he said of the swearing into office of the new president, adding that there would always be work to do in dealing with people's hearts.

Whatever was in the outgoing president's heart could not be known, but his Secretary of State was a black woman and his Attorney General was the first hispanic to hold the position, no matter if he resigned while under investigation for politicizing the Justice Department. Clearly the departing white president was no classic racist, but the contrast between his administration and one shaping up as a replacement was an indication of two radically different mindsets.

The departing president had assumed office through the intervention of the US Supreme Court at a time when the American economy was booming. At that point, America had little interest in the world at large after its abject failure with the 1993 Somalia intervention. Then the greatest attack against America on home soil occurred nine months into the departing president's tenure. The administration's sole aim after that was to make war on the world and issue warnings about "enemies."

At home, a deregulated financial industry ran wild and then aground until the conservative party's policies were soundly routed by the American electorate. To do that, the country jumped its historic racial barrier to choose the right man for a challenging job, even as the sitting president's "inner circle" began a campaign to sell the country on a legacy aimed at transforming the invader of Iraq into a liberator of that country.

By contrast, the man about to become America's first non-white president was assembling an administration unprecedentedly diverse in both gender and race, including "mutts" as the president-elect referred to himself after the election. By the historic inauguration day, it seemed clear that the "racial divide" ripping apart the young US throughout its history had died on 2008 election night and was at last laid to rest on January 20, 2009. Its death had come after a long illness in which America saw its fortunes decline, its standing in the world wither and its economic dominance shrivels. Still, ghosts of the deceased past malingered.

In addition to the legacy of liberator that the outgoing administration was promulgating, media coverage of the transition focused on the "gracious" reception given by the outgoing Bush family to the incoming Obamas. In the first weeks after the inauguration, Barack Obama created a media ruckus by appearing without jacket in the Oval Office. Michelle Obama was criticized for a sleeveless dress worn to her husband's first address to a joint session of Congress, where a Republican state representative shouted "you lie" in the middle of the new president's address.

As was the case with the fall of apartheid in South Africa, racial barriers fell most soundly when necessity forced the change. Global economic pressure had forced the ruling South African elite white minority to cede power to the working black majority. In America, the immoral duplicity of an incompetent administration opened the eyes of the electorate to choose the right path toward progress and prosperity beyond the rutted grooves of outmoded, ineffectual cultural habit.

Still, nearly half of America had voted to continue the doomed policies that had led to conditions so dire that the "racial divide" was seamlessly breached. And yet a good number in America seemed to echo the words of the American Revolutionary war hero John Paul Jones, "I have not yet begun to fight." In 2008, those uttering that 1779 oath were on the wrong side of the American revolution in a globalizing world.

The Emancipation of America with the 2008 Transition

In the historic transition of the 2008 US election ending the "pale male" monopoly on western industrialized power, it was useful to remember that the exiting president was "elected" by the US Supreme Court rather than the American people. That shadow over the administration deepened with a narrow victory for a second term during a time of war he started without legitimate foundation.

In the waning months of the presidency, an all-out media campaign was launched to convince the world that the people of two countries had been "liberated" by the outgoing president. History would bear out that legacy. The tanking American economy and its global impact were largely ignored except for a mention in the outgoing president's last press conference the week before he left office.

"I came into recession and I go out into recession," the president said. The claim was clearly incorrect. In his first report to the joint sessions of Congress, he had announced a budget surplus. He said the reason for that was the fact that the government was charging too much in taxes. He would ask for a refund on behalf of the American people. In-person testimonials described the relief that an additional $2,000 would provide for the average American family.

"Government should never stand in the way of families achieving their dreams, " he said in that first address to Congress and the nation. That was in 2001, when the price of regular gasoline was $1.47 a gallon, according to an Atlanta Journal-Constitution analysis conducted on January 18, 2009. The high point for the cost of gasoline under the departing presidency was $4.11 a gallon in July of its final year.

Further, the 2001 federal budget had a $180 million surplus. The 2008 budget had a $454.8 billion deficit before the $700 billion bailouts began, starting with the financial institutions. In January of the new president's inaugural year, the deficit for 2009 was projected to be $1.2 trillion and the financial institutions were still tanking.

Obama had a full plate when he was inaugurated on January 2009 to grand national and international acclaim. He was quoted as saying that his presidency should not be judged by the traditional first 100 days but by the first 1,000. Nevertheless, a critical accomplishment during the first 100 days was adoption of his Economic Recovery and Reinvestment Act to salvage the ailing economy with a focus on the manufacturing sector grounded in the massive auto industry.

Additionally, Obama took actions on issues such as fair pay, child health insurance, sexual orientation and reversal of Bush administration policies that had rolled back Clinton progressive measures. Notable, he established new ethics guidelines to limit the influence of lobbyists on the executive branch of the government. Finally, he laid the groundwork for health care reform. At the end of his first 100 days, 62% of Americans approved of his performance in office.

The accomplishment was no small feat considering that the first half of the $700 bailout package had been disbursed with no accountability. The message was clear, however. America had chosen well to leap frog over a historic racial divided in order to elect the right man for the job of fixing an America run aground by a history of unethical "pale male" authoritarian rule, a group that was far from vanquished.

Even before the inauguration, radio talk show host Rush Limbaugh said he hoped Obama failed. At the Obama's speech to the joint session of Congress, Republicans were restive and South Carolina congressman Wilson yelled, "you lie" in the middle of the speech.

Eight months into the new presidency, a Baptist pastor in Arizona told his congregation that he prayed for Obama's death. Republican senator Mitch McConnell went on record in 2009 to say that the number one goal of his party was to make sure that Barack Obama was a one-term president.

While none of these white conservative Republican males said they opposed Obama because he was black, none stated a specific reason for why they were so opposed to Barack Obama. That silence spoke louder than words in an America newly liberated from a history of white male dominance.

The legacy of the old order would continue its influence, but the legacy of the exiting president was indeed that of the liberator he had predicted. As was his habit, there was a fatal error in his assessment of a situation. In his first address to Congress he had claimed that he inherited a recession when in reality he had been handed a budget surplus. In the 2008 transition, he posed as the liberator of two foreign countries when in actually he freed his own country from the tyranny of other pale males in his tradition.

Sport and the Olympic Perspective on 2010 America

The 2008 Summer Olympics in China were held just before the American presidential national conventions at a time when the world faced its worst economic crisis since the 1930's Great Depression. The issue of racial identity loomed over the US presidential election.

By the time of the 2008 November election, the global economic crisis was critical and the world was watching America's two major political parties. One was headed by a confident young black man and the other by a nondescript white man who had a firebrand woman running mate. A global cry of relief went up when the black Barack Obama won.

A global glass ceiling had been shattered. Political power was no longer restricted to a white male stranglehold on the right to exercise that power. America had broadened the field by electing the first non-white leader of a western industrialized country. And yet as the 2010 winter Olympics in Vancouver, Canada neared, the historic step America had achieved since the last Olympic Games was over-shadowed by the discord that had arisen in the country in wake of its 2008 victory.

 Having been spared an economic calamity and freed from a cavalier US leader cocked for war at his discretion, the world saw the successful new leader at-tacked in his own country. Conservatives labeled him both as a socialist and fascist for pushing through a people-friendly agenda centered on regulating runaway financial profiteering. Liberals said he was a sell-out for not achieving more dramatic change. It seemed the world appreciated America more than the country itself, glossing over successes to move on to ever greater grievances. Perhaps its customary successes blinded it to the democratic progress enshrined in its Constitution.

A 2010 media feud over two late night show hosts was a case in point. Jay Leno and Conan O'Brien were jockeying for the top late night spot. The NBC network projected viewer shares for both, made a decision, executed contracts and took action. Outraged viewers unhappy with the decision received backing from celebrities to create a tempest that forced the network to reverse its decision. Beyond the complicated issues of corporate bungling and sponsorship interests, the major lesson that emerged was the power of America's little people to influence higher decisions.

That "little people" power was unrecognized in the young America that had never known any other way. Inequality and injustice were rife but they were human frailties to be perfected according in line with stated ideals. Sport was the universal language that could bring that outside view of itself home to the American people.

In 2010 as America's new president came under fire from conservatives and liberals even though he rescued the global economy, the networks took a cue from the 2008 Beijing Olympics to project and track worldwide viewership for sports. Thus, the 2010 all-American Superbowl in February was expected to attract 150 million viewers nationwide and millions more in 230 countries and territories across the world, according to CBS News.

Based on 2008 Beijing Olympics data, the February 2010 Winter Olympics in Vancouver were projected to attract billions of viewers worldwide on all media including television, computer and cell phone. Such surge in viewership for sporting events reflected the power of sport to bring together the disparate interests of the world's societies in a common language of physical competition. Partnerships for the training of athletes, coverage of events and recruitment of volunteers to successfully bring off events were fast-tracked for the June 2010 World Cup Soccer Tournament hosted for the first time on the African continent by South Africa.

America took part in the competition that presented challenges beyond those faced by participants in reality TV shows like The Survivor. The African country of Togo, for example, withdrew from regional competition after its team lost three members during an attack on its sports convoy in Angola.

Those remnants of enmities laid down during the world's colonial period were remote and of little interest to impatient and ambitious Americans focused on progress in the present. But they were a part of the modern competitive world that impacted on America and required its involvement if American values were to be advanced.

America was blessed with a bounty it had come to take for granted. A view of it-self from outside could revive appreciation. The result would be better teamwork for a more secure global world led by a globally savvy leader. Sports was the universal language capable of bringing about healthy competition that transcended national political rivalries.

A Spotlight on American Goodwill in the Obama Era

The world hailed America's election of a western industrialized country's first non-white leader at the January 2009 inauguration. International presses attest-ed to that fact. Obama's first address to the United National General Assembly was a show-stopper, complete with standing ovation.

Despite that world success, America's new President failed in his bid to win the Olympics for his adopted city of Chicago. He later won the Nobel Peace Prize, a distinction dismissed at home as premature for the largely untested President. However, the prize was awarded for the new tone his election had set for international relations. As Obama himself said, the prize belonged to the American people who had elected him.

America would have been proud to see its new leader address his global peers at the United Nations. The majestic cavern of the Assembly Hall was packed to the rafters and every shade of human skin color was registered. His bearing and the message conveyed the fact that he was wholly at ease in the global arena.

At home, however, just steps away from the global refuge provided by the US host country, strife was rampant. A "Tea party" movement of ultra-conservatives fought against government involvement in affairs that political leaders had been elected to carry out. At the United Nations charged with man-aging weighty global issues such as disputes over state sovereignty. Such light-weight domestic squabbles in the affairs of the world's most solid country were no more than negligible flies in the ointment.

After Obama's first address to the United Nations, musician activist Bono wrote a New York Times op ed piece entitled "Rebranding America." In that article, Bono posed the possibility that the world saw Obama more clearly than the United States that had elected him. The view expressed by the Irish European activist was reminiscent of the Biblical saying that a prophet was not without honor ex-cept in his own country. The article concluded with the statement that the world now needed the ideal that America represented as a guideline for going forward in an undeniably global direction that presented wholly new confusions.

America's choice of a world-savvy leader in 2008 was its signal to the world that it deserved to lead. The choice of Obama was a manifestation of America's sub-conscious awareness that the old way of making war on the world was a dead end. National prosperity was inseparable from interaction with the world's 200 other countries through trade, finance, security and legal articulation.

Everyday Americans couldn't know the multitudes of regional and sub-regional organizations cropping up globally to provide avenues for countries to enter global markets competitively. The ASEAN group in the Pacific Ocean, for exam-ple, connected island states, The CIS group brought into alliance the globally un-familiar mid-Asian countries. CARICOM brought Caribbean countries into the global mainstream. Knowing of such connections could help America more easily embrace its rule as the world leader it deserved to be.

Independence, freedom and self-reliance were fundamental ideals for Americans. But law and order tamed the American wild west and a global alliance stopped a modern metastasizing form of tyranny. Individualism was great. Running water from a faucet was better for most.

In America. freedoms and social amenities were reconciled in context of the US Constitution as modernized through amendments. The result was a country that was a template for the world.

America had taken a big step toward racial equity with its 2008 election. It could lead the world in accomplish such progress on a global scale. The only obstacle was domestic refusal to cede a monopoly on power.

HELEN FOGARASSY

Is Obama's Approval Rating Slipping because 2009 America is Myopic?

Barack Obama started his historic presidency with a 68% approval rating, in a Gallup Poll. The ratings remained high throughout the spring as Congress passed his budget proposal emphasizing education and health care. In the third week of November that year, his approval number slipped to 40%, the first time it had dipped below 50%. According to Politico, the low numbers were a product of bad economic news and high unemployment Figures. In addition, the ratings dropped because of unreasonably high expectations of what Obama could accomplish in office.

The week in which the low ratings numbers came out, Obama was in Asia, strengthening alliances to promote American economic interests amid the continuing global economic crisis. According to Politico, that trip also cost Obama some approval numbers. Many Americans felt he should be home creating jobs to cure the economy.

On the home front that same week, losing Republican vice-presidential candidate Sarah Palin launched her memoir, Going Rogue. The title came from an exasperated comment made by a staffer on the losing McCain campaign when Palin jettisoned the campaign policy in favour of self-promotion. Book reviews ap-peared in all major publications and a nationwide book tour followed. The down-home Alaskan soccer mom recast in designer suits was as popular as the day McCain set her on stage at the Republican convention to energize the base.

The press loved Palin. She was a mix of American contradictions rolled into one Christian fundamentalist family values package. When the family-values policies failed in her personal life, she turned the disaster into a parable on why the values were important. She was a lightning rod for attention. the mythic pioneer American folk hero who defied conventions while capitalizing on them to provoke chatter. Manicured and Flashy, she presented herself as a homespun anti-intellectual who was vilified by the elitist media she used to fuel book sales and political ambitions.

New York Times columnist Maureen Dowd urged America's new President to adopt that losing candidate's "straight from the gut" approach. She said he needed to connect with the American people on a visceral level to get his policies across.

Good advice, perhaps, but Obama was busy jump-starting the American-led global economy. Yes, American had the world's most robust economy, but keeping it that way called for engaging with and untapped large swathe of the world. On a brain or computer scan, that area would show up as "uncommitted space."

That was why America's President was in Asia while the popular losing vice-presidential candidate launched a memoir in which she spoke proudly of being a rogue, an individualist unbeholden to the party that had jetted her to national attention. Homespun or not, the losing candidate for the second-top spot in America's government knew that the title of "rogue" held a romantic charm to her country. It fed into the much needed fantasies that helped ease the woes of working Americans until Obama fixed the economy run aground by the previous administration.

The choice of the "rogue" self-description was a fitting image for a sensationalist who had twice finished as a loser in important campaigns, first in a beauty contest and later in the political arena. The title was a conciliation prize for having dared to run and yet had lost. It was a position America had averted by electing the western industrialized world's first non-white president.

Palin had announced plans for a 2012 presidential run but her memoir was a telling sign that she was already a loser again. Rogues didn't create jobs for Americans in a global world. They didn't build that bridges of good will that enabled American products and services to be bought overseas. Glitz and flash were part of the American fabric meant for entertainment but in a global reality those trappings did not bring home the bacon.

That's why Obama was in Asia even though the trip added to a dip in his popularity. He was working quietly behind the scenes so that America remained free to be itself as it grew into its new role as leader of a globalizing world.

The Cure for America's Economy is to Mainstream a Global Mentality

America's financial wizards knew the world was global but America's mainstream lagged far behind. Money news programs affirmed daily that stock markets were interdependent, currencies were linked and commodity price volatility depended on environmental factors tied in with human activity, including political events Those variables crucial to business were not reflected in mainstream news coverage on the presumption that average Americans were not interested in arcane business matters.

Most large city American newspapers covered national and international news in separate sections. Big city tabloids, like small city papers, covered international news only as necessary, in the event of a coup, catastrophe or tragedy that befell a local in a foreign country. As a result, little of the outside world filtered into American consciousness, a lapse that stifled the creative ingenuity that drove American prosperity.

A single day analysis of news in the New York tabloid Post provided an example of the discrepancy between what Americans knew of the world and what actually was going on in early July a single days analysis of in early July 2009. Cover stories reported on the recently deceased Michael Jackson, control of local schools and a Yankees baseball win. Inside stories of international events covered a plane crash off of the Comoros Islands in the Indian Ocean and an affair between an American state governor and an Argentine mistress. A coup in the Central American county of Honduras received six short paragraphs at the bottom of page 19. Editorials covered Afghanistan and Iran. MarketWatch in the business section cited nine worldwide indexes, most European. The Foreign Exchange Hotlist cited 17 majors among the world's 200 countries.

By contrast on that same day, Google News covered news on Israel, North Korea, Iraq, India, Russia, Pakistan and the European Union through its newly elected Swedish president. Other news related to the International Atomic Energy Agency, Sri Lanka, Croatia, an African Summit in Libya, the question of burqas in France and the situation, in the former Soviet satellite country of Georgia.

The most dedicated professionals and news junkies couldn't keep up with all that global news. But awareness of the broad scope to global activity could help with the important economic indicator in America called "consumer confidence."

A low level of consumer confidence was a major contributing factor in the economic stagnation that continued even after the 2008/9 bailouts helped revive the economy. As Obama fought to get Congressional approval for initiatives like his jobs and health care policies, consumers noted the Congressional logjam and expressed their disappointment in Obama's ability to be effective. From a broader perspective, they may have reacted differently.

Interdependence has been an acknowledged market driver since the late 1990's when corporations began to globalize in earnest. Without a rudimentary grasp of such basic economic dynamics, consumers had small chance of being confi-dent in the stability and growth of their own economy.

American consumers were robust purchasers of products that stimulated the economy through imports, exports, corporate expansion and small business investments. Interdependence meant that parts of products were designed, manufactured, assembled and sold in multiple locations in accordance with business plans. After the collapse of their financial and manufacturing sectors in 2009, consumers need more information before they could believe that recovery was on the way.

Providing that information would take time. Meanwhile, the Congressional impasse dented the faith of Americans that their system of government worked. The consumer engines of the economy knew that their tax money had gone to bailouts but there was little evidence of success. Mortgage defaults were still skyrocketing and consumers had no way of knowing where the money went.

Even worse, Americans didn't know that their financial hardships were a result of predatory banking practices allowed by deregulation under the previous administration. Thus, Americans lost faith in "the system" when information could have averted the tragedy.

In olden days, news was defined as "man bites dog." Anything novel was news. In news. the adage still held that "if it bleeds it leads." While those truisms still applied to news, a global world called for greater latitude to transcend traditional boundaries.

Working American would not be tracking daily developments in the world's 200 countries. But a bird's eye glimpse could bolster the confidence of Americans that their country was doing a bang up job in a global world. Such a view would also reassure Americans of a benevolent world outside the borders of their country. That world was made up of people living daily lives just like Americans. They weren't just victims running from an endless series of disasters. As equals, Americans and foreign peers could learn with each other.

The Last Shall be First with the 2012 Election

The conservative backlash to the historic 2008 US election was no surprise. The first non-white leader of the western industrialized world was dissed during his first address to Congress when Republican representative Joe Wilson of South Carolina interrupted the speech by yelling "you lie." The ultra-conservative Tea Party movement that sprang up with Obama's inauguration continued to gain speed during his first term. The issue of race was the big white sleeping elephant in the room that just wouldn't speak.

Conspiracy theories about Obama were born the minute he stepped into national attention. They focused on his nationality and his religion, two socially acceptable areas for casting shade. By 2008 America on a national scale, laws had made racism a hot button issue that was either unstated or relegated to outposts outside the mainstream. Conspiracy theories thrived in the subconscious cellars below the socially acceptable public persona.

Conspiracy theories flourished in the empty space of the unknown. They dispelled the tension of not knowing, a stressful state akin to the complex dynamic identified by physicist Werner Heisenberg as the uncertainty principle. Basically, conspiracies were a quick fix for the anxiety of a changing world.

The socially taboo subject of racial bigotry was fertile ground for conspiracy theories. So were foreigners, professionals, experts and scholars, all members of groups the everyday American didn't understand. When it came to Obama, he straddled the gamut.

By a classical definition based on the percentages of racial blood in a person's genealogy, half white Obama was black. He was exotic with a multicultural upbringing and he was well educated, even disparaged as elitist. Those globally impressive characteristics in America found a foothold for a most conspicuous conspiracy theory known simply as "birther."

The "birther" rumor was started by a failed Illinois politician who first suggested that Obama was ineligible to be president because of his complex early life in Hawaii and Indonesia. The rumors were distant whispers until New York sensation Donald Trump seized on them, no doubt in part to further his own political ambitions.

The 2010 midterm elections came out as expected only in greater measure. With a Democrat in the White House, the Republicans gained handsomely, winning seven seats in the Senate and a whopping 63 seats in the House of Representatives, the biggest gain since 1948. Despite that huge loss of Congressional support. Obama continued to unroll his progressive agenda as hobbled as it was by Republican opposition and obstruction. His approval ratings fluctuated with successes and failures, but basically they remained fairly high as Trump began actively promoting the "birther" conspiracy.

A business showman of the con artist variety, Trump was e caricature of the chest thumping white Anglo-Saxon protestant male whose most highly developed skill was domination through awe and terror. His history of discriminating against those outside his genetic circle went back to early apprentice days with his father. The father was reportedly detained at a KKK rally that turned violent in 1927 Queens. The duo also settled a federal lawsuit brought against them for screening potential tenants based on race. That portfolio on racial attitudes served as the back story for the "birther" movement in Trump's hands.

Trump had formed an exploratory committee for a 2000 presidential run. While he declined to pursue that avenue at the time, he continued to publicly talk about his presidential ambitions even as he initiated ancillary projects. In 2004 he launched the Apprentice reality show that shot him to national attention. In that same year, he hatched the Trump University entrepreneurial school that ceased operation in 2010 amid allegations of fraudulent practices. Again in that same year, he began serious planning for a Trump Tower Moscow that he first envisioned in 1989 as the Iron Curtain fell.

In 2013, after Obama handily won reelection in 2012, Trump engineered the procurement of Moscow as the setting for his Miss Universe Pageant. While he failed to find favor with Russian President Putin, the Trump Tower Moscow project remained in the works.

Despite all those activities, a Quinnipiac poll conducted in May 2011 showed that the majority of Americans would not vote for Donald Trump. The same poll showed that most Americans would also not vote for Sarah Palin to be president, despite her 2008 promotion by conservatives as the quintessential rustic rube considered all-American. In Trump's hands, the "birther" movement seemed aimed at restoring the image of America to a mythic status based on a white Anglo-Saxon male citizenry supported by women of a similar description.

As indicated by the Quinnipiac poll, America did not share Trump's view of itself as a monochrome country. America was like global society fighting its way out of historical colonialist remnants. Asian countries were emerging economies, as were American nations forming alliances for social stability and economic growth. The mineral resources of African countries were being unearthed through partnerships. Arab countries were adapting to modern democratic ways to afford greater equality of human rights for all.

In that global world, the key to progress was cooperation across a vast array of diverse cultures, races and political structures. Because of his historic 2008 election, America had the potential to lead that global integration movement. Instead, America became a hotbed for white supremacy and conspiracy theories.

In Obama-era America, the question of race was among the most hot button issues facing the country. Before his first election, Obama broached the subject in a speech delivered at Constitution Center in Philadelphia. He made the speech in response to a cry of outrage over radical racial views expressed by a Chicago pastor. In that speech, Obama stressed that the strength of his campaign came from a coalition of black, white and other racial group supporters. They were working to elect him not because he was black but because he was the best person to meet the challenges of America in a rapidly changing world.

Consequently throughout his first years in office, Obama was criticized for being too black and not black enough to advance racial equality more rapidly. But proof of his effectiveness as a leader of America in a global world came in May 2011 when Osama Bin Laden was annihilated.

The Al Qaeda leader had been an albatross to America since the 9/11 attack on home soil. All America's might and resources had failed to locate the dangerous mastermind hidden in the hills bordering Afghanistan and Pakistan. The Obama strategy succeeded where is his predecessor George W. Bush had failed. Under Obama, the threat posed by Bin Laden was eliminated not through the use of force but through cooperation between US intelligence, armed services and local communities on the ground.

The ultimate proof of Obama's fitness to lead America into a global world was the country's view of him. Despite 2,000 years of human racial bigotry and a ferocious backlash to his election by conservatives, Obama's approval rating among Americans as a whole remained high.

America confirmed its faith in Obama by electing him to a second term without any contention of the result from the Republican party. But the result undoubtedly rankled that conservative party, whose leader had one announced that the number one goal of his party was to make Obama a one-term president.

America Belongs to The World

America was blessed by geography, a short history and a founding Constitution that laid the basis for optimum freedom within the safeguards of law. Native Americans paid a big price for the forceful establishment of this experiment in a promised land still working to fulfill the ideal Immigrants have kept the engine chugging forward toward the goal.

The first marauders on a pristine land were Brits who could afford the journey alongside indentured servants who had nothing left to lose back home. Slaves were then imported to remain in that status for 200 years before they were freed by a brutal civil war to preserve the Constitutional premise that all humans were created equal. Waves of immigrants were next. Mostly from Europe and Asia, they came to escape crises at home and to augment America's growing needs for building an infrastructure across a vast stretch of land. Then after all that growth, America faced the brand-new challenge of a global world.

For the first time in its relatively short history, America in the 21st century could no longer sit back to monitor newcomers to its home turf. The 9/11 attack intruded brutally on America's self-containment. It was a wake-up call for America to extend is Constitutional ideals to a global world.

If all people were created equal, then the challenge before America in a global world was gargantuan. While it was possible that all people were created equal, the same could not be said of nations. Yet nations were comprised of people, who certainly were no longer equal in adulthood however they were born that way. The call for America to engage with a global world seemed daunting at first glance. A closer look revealed the groundwork that America itself had already laid down.

The ideal of equality had numerous components. Those were enumerated in the 1948 Universal Declaration of Human Rights, championed by Eleanor Roosevelt, America's First Lady at the time. The nonbinding United Nations document had attached to it nine binding treaties on issues ranging from political and economic rights to prohibition of racial discrimination and protection of children.

By the 21st century, all countries had signed and ratified the declaration. The United States had signed three treaties, one on civil and political rights, another against torture and a third against racial discrimination. During its war on Iraq, the United States had violated its obligations under the torture treaty it had signed.

Rule of law was the foundation for civilization itself. People and countries entered into agreements. Consequences for breaking compacts were potentially severe. Alas, nations were no more honourable than the people who populated them.

America, the land of immigrants from countries all across the world, owed itself the confidence of knowing what was going on in the world it deserved to lead. Its Constitution was the blueprint for world betterment. Its leaders had wisely entered into agreements that helped America keep its word to make it trustworthy. Those agreements also helped America to identify countries and people who didn't play by agreed-upon rules.

Increasingly in a unifying world, America has been caught flat-footed by a conflict between its big generous heart and a situation that proved America to be in over its head. America was eager to help famine starved Somali children. It jumped in with no cultural preparation and the result was a lasting global catastrophe. Likewise, when an earthquake hit Myanmar in 2016, America did not know how to deal with a junta government that refused to let global aid agencies into the country to help.

America was important to the world, not just because of its grand ideals, economic prowess and military might but because of its ability to lead an emerging issues that affected the entire world and needed global cooperation to resolve. Those included management of the environment, controlling new diseases arising from interaction and regulating the exploding information boom in global communication. During eight years with Obama in the lead, America had proved its ability to step up to those challenges.

Part III.
America 2016

Master Con Don

When Barack Obama left office in January 2017, he had an approval rating of 60% according to BBC News. However, that number reflected a rating of 95% among Democrats and only 18% among Republicans.

In the Democratic primary leading up to the 2016 election, Hillary Clinton handily won over her socialist rival, Bernie Sanders. Republican Donald Trump mowed down a slew of opponents primarily by garnering free media coverage with outrageousness.

In the 2016 general election, Donald Trump was the fifth consecutive candidate to win without a majority of the popular vote. Democrat Hillary Clinton won 65 million popular votes to Trump's 62. Trump, however, won 304 electoral votes to Clinton's 227, largely due to upset wins in the Midwestern rustbelt states that had previously voted for Obama.

A January 2017 intelligence report concluded that Russia had interfered in the election to boost Trump and denigrate Clinton. No direct tie between the Trump campaign and Russia could be established. Trump entered office with a 40% approval rating and a general consensus that he was unfit to be president.

Trump was a master of international chicanery when he stepped onto the presidential stage. His great skill was in eluding justice with an arsenal of weapons that ranged from delegating shady dealings to outright lying and shapeshifting. Like the mythical sea-God Proteus, he adapted to the needs of convenient escape.

During the entire 2016 presidential campaign, nearly a third of Americans believed everything Trump said despite glaring videotaped evidence that contradicted him. He recruited questionable dirty-trick specialists and claimed he barely knew them if they were caught. He denigrated those he didn't favor and blasted the press he relied on to propel his ambitions. Nearly a third of America bought the Trump show hook, line, and sinker. The rest of America and most of the world looked with dismay at the uncomfortable dynamic.

A large chunk of America believed in Trump just as a smaller number had believed that the bogus Trump University would teach them the art of making a killing in real estate. That Trump base thrived on faith in delivery on a promise made by a trusted magician only waylaid by enemies. Having pledged allegiance and absolutely certain of promises soon to be fulfilled, the base came to believe in Trump as staunchly as the faithful of any religion. It was of no consequence to the base that Trump bore no resemblance to any reputable religious figure.

Catholics, for example, believed in the Church dogma and they took the Pope at his word. But the Pope was infallible only when he speaks ex officio, not when he tweeted, although, by his Catholic standards, the Pope would never have posted a tweet that was false or offensive. Certainly, the Catholic College of Cardinals would not have elected a Pope who was a documented liar and sexual predator. Thus, Catholics had a valid reason for the trust they placed in Church leaders even if some were short of the ideal.

Like religious leaders, cult founders developed ardent adherents. Outsiders saw clearly the lack of foundation for the trust placed in the leader. They could also see a connection between neediness in the members and a master plan to fill that emptiness, mostly through the offering of concrete hopes and membership in a group whose members shared the belief. Outside criticism solidified solidarity to the point where members were willing to perish rather than lose their special status.

Early in the campaign, Trump boasted that he could shoot somebody on Fifth Avenue and he wouldn't lose any supporters. While the observation may have been true, it was doubtful that any Trump adherent would "drink the Kool-Aid" like the followers of Jim Jones did to appease him. It was also difficult to imagine them slaughtering as the Manson killers did at his command.

It seemed clear that politician Trump with his ardent supporters was neither Pontiff nor a cult leader. The only possibility left was the age-old art of "con" artistry, first practiced by tricksters noted in the Bible, such as the snake that pried Adam and Eve out of the Garden of Eden.

The Trump business resume attested to a career path built by a string of failures. Yet the base believed him to be a success because he presented himself in that guise. The image was carefully crafted in the media to magnify his stature. His political attack on America was perfectly timed. His agenda and message were designed to confound.

After the 9/11 horror, America lost standing in a globalizing world by bumbling impotently under a Republican president clueless about the world and not much interested beyond making overseas armed conflict profitable for American industry. The first non-white leader of the western industrialized world fixed the problem as best he could with opposition from those not ready for change. Enter Trump with a master plan built on the premise that America had no use for the rest of the world.

As a presidential candidate, Trump was a clarion for the confused in America. He confirmed their worst fears, proclaiming that hordes of hostile foreigners were invading. He offered security against those ills, starting with a concrete wall and extending to war on immigrants. He sold himself as a proven success, the only one with the experience that enabled him to fix the problems. The hungry base believed, unaware of the real source for the Trump experience.

Trump's experience in the art of grifting began when he was apprentice to his father. Brazenly declaring he could outdo Dad, he made recklessly bold real estate moves and got Dad to bail him out on behalf of the pipedream the son was carrying on for him. During the apprentice years, Trump perfected skills like lying without flinching, speaking authoritatively about matters beyond his grasp, debasing rivals and grooming toadies until they failed to meet his needs.

This armed for battle, Trump took up the mantle of saving America's disheartened. All he demanded in return was the right to command the allegiance that would allow him to pilfer the country's coffers.

Champ Turns Chump with Trump

The land of opportunity had a sterling reputation for giving people a way to rise above their means. That was why they could afford to gamble on Donald Trump, who sold them a bill of goods that had no substance and yet incredibly held them through to his ascendance to the US presidency.

America made history by electing the industrialized world's first non-white president in 2008. Barack Obama saved a tanking economy brought on by eight years of conservative leadership. The pendulum swung back with the election of Trump to prove most telling about the American psyche.

Trump became President quite possibly with foreign assistance based on intelligence reports after the fact as well as previous shady business dealings with foreign powers. His methods of operation were transparent to those not taken in by his antics, like the ones who never signed up for his notorious Trump University. Still, there were enough suckers among Americans to keep the entire country captive to Trump's colossal scam. A peek into the future gave a glimpse of how that happened.

At the end of August 2018, a trade war started by Trump dominated the news and the stock market crashed over the uncertain future of global trade. At a G7 meeting of world leaders, Trump announced that China had called and that talks would resume. Voila! Stocks went up and stayed there even as China denied that any calls had been made. While there was no telling who was scamming whom, Trump claimed that any lie on his part would have been a mere negotiating tactic.

The Trump base, along with the stock market and Republican Trump enablers, seemed eager to buy a confident claim. If delivered well, a boast about a win was as good as an actual win. The proof of that dubious premise remained to be seen, but to those not taken in, the evidence was overwhelming before he assumed office.

During the campaign, Trump proclaimed that a Wall between the US and Mexico would be built and that Mexico would pay for it. Later opinion polls revealed that even Trump supporters never believed that Mexico would pay for the Wall. That was simply Trump's style of hyperbole and those in the base liked the bravado bluster. After his election, Trump assured his base that the Wall was in the process of being built. On-site sources contradicted the claim. Trump issued an order to get the Wall built ASAP. If laws were violated to get the wall built by the next election, pardons would be issued. While most Americans were aghast at Trump's outlaw method of governing, the base expressed admiration for Trump's tenacity in getting done what he wanted.

In 2016 America, one-third of the country that supported Trump seemed to say that they preferred an autocracy to the democracy that was the American hallmark. The view was astonishing when the freedom and opportunity of American democracy were compared to the restrictions of autocracies like those in Russia and China. A knowledge gap could account for the surprising trend.

A similar situation in America was related to Peter Popoff, a televangelist who skirted the law for 25 years with his Miracle Spring Water. Those who signed up for a free bottle of water were told that their stated goal was just a $20 investment away. Those who sent in their twenty received assurance that just another $50 would get them over the hurdle to their goal. Along the way, some received money and provided testimonials on the efficacy of the water. According to Alternet, televangelists like Popoff, Oral Roberts, Jimmy Swaggart, and the Bakkers loved Trump. The aim they had in common was to fleece the vulnerable.

Trump was said to be rabid about getting what he wanted. In 2016, it seemed clear that what he wanted was to sucker the US and the world beyond it by duping enough people to keep him in position to satisfy entities to whom he owed more than he could repay. Making baseless promises and openly dismissive of Constitutional standards, Trump in his campaign for presidency sold the idea of "draining the swamp" as a euphemism for destroying the American infrastructure, not just its system of roads and bridges but the framework that formed the basis for the institutions, protocols and norms that enabled America to buzz along in an increasingly complex global world.

In 2016, emerging issues in all countries ranged from economics, climate immigration and health care. All called for action at the global level. Again to jump forward to illustrate a point, the Amazon forest in Brazil was burning to emit dangerous carbon quantities that affected the world. By rights of sovereignty, Brazil underplayed the crisis. The United Nations that could have served as a forum for resolving the conflict between national priorities and global needs was ineffectual due to neglect.

The Trump approach to global challenges was to build walls against dangers and to fan anxiety about the enemies beyond the walls. But America could not see that obvious point as long as it had Miracle Spring Water in its eyes.

Tempest Trump Riled by Woman Hillary

It was said that words were mightier than the sword. In the case of Donald Trump they were deadlier.

In part because of his words, Trump managed to decimate a woman who could have continued America on a path to global progress. Instead, he targeted the country's vulnerabilities to carry out his destructive will-to-power.

Like a hurricane riding the winds of climate change, Trump blew away 16 Republican rivals in the 2016 Republican primary with the crudest of verbal assaults based on bogus facts that flew in the face of reality. However, his full force as a leveler was only unleashed when he met up with a woman who could beat him.

Hillary Clinton was the presumed successor to the progressive Barack Obama, America's first non-white president and the first non-white head of any western industrialized country. Trump launched his political career by leading the offensive "birther" movement demanding that Obama produce a birth certificate. When it was produced with a patronizing sight, Trump declared the document bogus. Later he kicked off his campaign with an attack on Mexicans he called murderers and rapists. That was the starting gun for his crusade to crush Hillary and the progressive steps Obama had set in motion and Hillary was poised to continue.

By the time Trump and Hillary faced off in the 2016 presidential campaign, he was infamous for attacking women based on appearance or ethnicity. Most targets were professionals. One was a beauty contest winner Trump humiliated for having gained weight. Outrage at his scornful treatment of women was mild relative to the level of offense, but with Hillary he was downright brutal and the reaction was stunningly numb.

One reason why Trump's assault on Hillary was met with such a tepid outcry was the sheer number of blows Trump dealt to America during the campaign. Like fugitives from an actual hurricane, the majority of Americans accustomed to social order were disoriented by the chaos Trump created with lies, insults, calls for fisticuffs and just plain noisy hogging of media space. Trump's conduct was unthinkable in 2016 America but Trump made "bad behavior" his trademark and the base ate it up. The base went wild when Hillary was the object.

The white middle class workers who made up the bulk of the Trump base had a visceral distaste for a woman in the White House, especially one whose husband had already been there and who had already been tainted by politics-as-usual. From that starting ground, Trump tailored his usual attack on women to specifically target Hillary.

There was obviously no point in attacking Hillary on the basis of her looks. She wouldn't care anymore than most Americans did. Hillary was attractive enough, but she was a working woman in trademark pants suits and hairstyles adopted after she gave up headbands once hazed by the press as not elegant enough for a First-Lady.

To place Hillary in the Trump perspective as illustrated by the infamous Access Hollywood tape, clearly Hillary did not aspire to be the "beautiful" woman who "drew" Trump "like a magnet" and who compelled him to "pop tic-tacs" had an irresistible urge gripped him to molest simply because he was a star and they would "let him." Like most women, Hillary knew that Trump manhandled women not because they "let him" but because social forces had ill-prepared them to take actions needed to "not let him."

Hillary's tested confidence based on experience led her to bid for her country's presidency. Such gumption in a woman signalled to Trump that he could never grope her, not even if she adopted the trappings he read as come-ons. As a rival, moral Hillary was brand new territory for Trump.

Trump's only other female rival had been "Queen of Mean" Leona Helmsley, who went to prison for tax fraud in a scheme that involved the Trump Organization. Charges were brought by "crime fighter" Rudy Giuliani. While also indicted the Trump Organization was never prosecuted.

For the large part, women were mostly absent from Trump's narrow male environment of real estate and golf. In Trump's circle, women were mostly wives, amusements or ornaments. Exceptions were emerging but former first lady and Secretary of State Hillary was unique.

Hillary was clearly head-and-shoulders above Trump in qualifications for the US presidency. That fact became ever clearer as he pummeled her and she refused to go down. With every round in the campaign, whether in debate, convention appearance or press, Hillary's outperformance of Trump seemed to re-ignite his well-known lust for a fight. He scored hugely with the base when he branded Hillary as "crooked" and led a chant to "lock her up."

The labels were catnip for the Trump base and the mostly male Republicans sucked into Trump's orbit. "Crooked" and "lock her up" seemed to touch some long-dead connection to the Salem witch trials. That was a category reserved for women who didn't fit categories. They weren't beautiful in the poet Emerson's sense of "beauty is it own excuse for being." They were also not utilitarian vehicles for bearing offspring and managing the home. Women with ambition to lead had no corner in that world. Trump made sure the base would never forget.

In his home life, Trump seemed to demand that his women be both beautiful and utilitarian. While no great shakes in the looks department himself, Trump's three beautiful wives bore him five children with no loss of looks and apparently no gripes about Trump's hands-off approach to raising children. Changing diapers "isn't my thing," he boasted to the media at large. Twice divorced, children were raised in households other than his. He took claim of them when they were ripe to carry on the Trump name.

To the disenfranchised white middle class workers who formed most of the base, Trump may have appealed as the hero of long-lost dreams in the face of reality. They labored now and wives at home expected help with kids, but they whistled at unattainable beauties who passed by as they worked construction. For the college educated white women who voted for Trump, he may have been the vicarious avenger of dreams that had died while they carried out super-Mom roles complete with nagging of spouses to take on a greater role in home responsibilities. Perhaps they resented Hillary.

Hillary was the once in a lifetime super-Mom who raised a daughter while rising to a singular professional level. She remained loyal to her life-partner through publicly trying times and she had grown better with age. She was strong, poised. forceful and at ease. To some, those qualities made Hillary an untrustworthy political schemer. They may have seen Hillary as the woman they would never be. To them, the term "Crooked" would have been hook for the sense that Hillary could only have achieved all she did by cheating.

Hillary was scanned to the bone and no evidence of cheating was found. In all likelihood, she was simply a very capable woman who had met challenges opportunity offered. Regardless of the election result, she paved the way for women the world over to know they could successfully multi-task demanding roles. Trump, on the other hand, was a throwback to the "pale male" monopoly on power, a misfit in the modern world who made his mark by voicing rage at the encroachment of women and minorities onto his historically exclusive domain.

Hillary conceded the election to Trump on a technicality but she won more than the popular vote. She had survived as political chum for Piranha Trump and in that way exposed his ugliness, the stale mindset that found favour with the base and conservative Republicans willing to enable Trump and thereby forestall the inevitable. Sooner or later, the Trumps of the world would have to relinquish exclusive white male privilege and the stranglehold on power that went with it.

Body language and behaviour told the story of Trump with Hillary. He strutted, loomed, bellowed, charged and lied shamelessly. She stood steady under his tirades. She gave him a run for his money in the age-old war of the sexes and in that way brought out the infantile Trump need to show the world just who "the Donald" was. Hillary the woman brought out the "terrible twos" behavior in Trump. Pummeling her to utter shameful defeat was his Holy Grail, like the two-year old who throws a public tantrum to show the power of his turbulence over a rational mother regaining control under the scrutiny of by-passers who stopped to gape.

Hillary was big game to Trump. Beating her was a mighty trophy on his wall even if he had to cheat to get it done. His win over woman Hillary was the ultimate validation of his self-worth, the kill that won him the loyalty of the base and the Republicans who looked to Trump as their salvation from their own doomed futures as exclusively privileged white males.

Of all those involved in 2016 Trump electoral win, perhaps Mother Nature was most invested. In order for the world to progress, she had to disprove the myth that women were more emotional than men, that they were too emotional for serious affairs of the world beyond the home hearth.

The People vs. Ultra-White Trump

On a technicality in 2016, America leapt off the cliff and handed its mightiest powers to known business huckster Donald Trump. His election was the starting gun for proving that the white-male stranglehold on global power was doomed because Trump in the Oval Office triggered the worst excesses of the runaway white testosterone that had ravaged the world for millennia. Proof was no further away than a contrast of Trump with his unstanding immediate predecessor.

Donald Trump emerged as an American cultural figure in a splash of news coverage over the years by making himself a media magnet. He compelled attention by an assault on the usual much as a traffic accident drew a crowd. He made his mark in the cut-throat world of high-end New York real estate by leveraging interests, dodging laws and hawking schemes so successfully that local banks stopped lending him money that he never repaid when ventures failed. The self-promoting deal-wizard then found financing with more fluid overseas sources and diversified into glitzy fields ranging from beauty contests to product branding, TV, entertainment and a get-rich-quick version of education with the unaccredited Trump University.

Class-action lawsuits against the bogus and defunct Trump U were in the works when Trump won the 2016 election and he quickly agreed to a $25 million settlement with the public boast that he did so only for the good of the country. He didn't want a lawsuit to be distraction as he governed. An avalanche of less time-sensational lawsuits and probes fell by the wayside like road-kill, including the questionable status of his Trump Foundation and possible Trump ties to far-flung Russian money-laundering schemes. Six months into the Trump tenure, the Federal Prosecutor in the latter two cases had long been fired, the Trump U settlement money was still outstanding and the FBI Director investigating a Russian role in the election itself had also been fired. Those developments, which amounted to blocking ongoing actions, were mere details in the tornado of Trump blasting through limits on his unparalleled new powers and opportunities.

Trump won the conservative Republican party's nomination for president by bush-whacking 17 rivals with an aggressive savagery that left them numbed as if struck by cobra venom. He then flayed his female Democratic opponent with the same tactics ramped up to the target. He loomed, lurked, threatened, accused and shamed her through her spouse, freely resorting to such dirty tricks as resurrecting his past indiscretions while his own blistering disgraces were buried in media distractions.

From the beginning of the primary campaign, Trump's crude behavior was treated by politicians and media as a trademark splurge of theatricality. His campaign was considered a bogus bid for president until a handful of followers gave his campaign traction.

The first Trump supporters at the media launch of his presidential bid were actors paid $50 to show up and cheer, according to Hollywood Reporter. The practice continued throughout the campaign, augmenting a growing core base that whooped and hooted to the vitriol Trump spewed lavishly. The synergy between Trump and his base seemed a culmination of rage brewing for eight years after America elected progressive Barack Obama, the western industrialized world's first non-white leader.

Backlash to the historic 2008 election was instantaneous and continued to build throughout the eight-year Obama tenure. It intensified whenever Obama managed to win approval for a measure despite Congressional resistance. In his presidential bid, Trump seemed to channel the rage that had fueled the Tea Party, the birther movement he propelled and the Alt-Right, white conservative fervor that exploded when Trump found the sweet spot with the angry, frustrated and disenfranchised rust-belt middle class left behind by a rapidly changing world in which they were abandoned by Washington, coastal elites and the media.

Trump opponent Hillary Clinton characterized the base as a basket of deplorables, a term that actually referred not to the people but to the traits that Trump was able to rouse in them. Clinton was pilloried for the comment but the base wore the title with renegade pride as Trump plied the bitter underemployed group that was easy prey for his well-honed skills in leveraging interests, reading people and selling schemes to win the trust needed for getting people to hand over their money or, in 2016, their vote.

The trademark Trump skill-set was known as manipulation when used for self-interest and numerous other names when exercised for deceit. Whatever his motivation, Trump pumped the base by inflaming deplorable traits to build symbiotic affinity over inflated injustices and a drive to exact harsh, visible revenge by any means necessary. The red baseball cap became the team logo, adorned with the MAGA acronym for Make America Great Again. Trump and other elites wore the cap with tailored suits to make them veritable Pied Pipers in a leverage move to ensnare Republicans.

Like others apart from the base, Republicans started out castigating Trump for ugly behaviors like attacks on family members of rivals. But once Trump clinched the Republican nomination, he seemed to prove the truism that the end justified the means. However ugly his means, Trump achieved his aims, Republications seemed to conclude as criticism of Trump softened. In line with opinion polls that showed even mainstream Americans found Trump's crude candor refreshing. When Trump actually won the election, Republicans came out with full-throated support. Trump had become a redeemer for the near-lost Republican hope that the status quo could be restored after it was disrupted by Obama and threatened by Hillary Clinton.

That status quo was the premise reinforced over two-plus millennia that whites had a birthright to the lion's share of the world's wealth and that white men had the right to manage it. When Trump vanquished Hillary Clinton, who would have cemented the crack Obama had made in that age-old system, Republicans became full-fledged Trump enablers. They not only tolerated but justified a torrent of assaults on American values, laws and norms because he was a bull in the legal China shop, precisely the reason why the base had rewarded him with its vote.

Trump was a renegade hero to the rabid base and a portion of the mainstream, maybe because they got a vicarious thrill from "my man" doing just what they would do if given the opportunity.

Boredom in a dead-end job would make such a fantasy attractive but the level of logical disconnect needed to make that fantasy a basis for electing a president was profound. To think that the qualities needed in a president were divorced from those needed in a decent person defied all common sense. If that were the case. Mafia boss John Gotti would have died in the White House and not in prison.

The disconnect, however, lasted long enough to get Trump elected and the only explanation was that fairy dust had been thrown in the eyes of Trump voters. In that case, Republicans would be forced to straddle an uncomfortable fence it came to pragmatic matters such as health care.

Part IV.
America with Trump

The Trumps Invade the Capitol

From the day Donald Trump stepped into the political limelight with the declaration that Mexicans were rapists and murders, the world knew he would be no president as usual. Indeed, when he left his garish New York penthouse home, he declared the White House "a dumpt." He abandoned niceties like escorting First Lady Melania to the inauguration, darting ahead to take care of business.

The business on hold until he was actually sworn in would require years to unravel in search of infractions and malfeasance. During the swearing in ceremony, for example, foreign guests were reportedly making overseas calls with updates on the status of the proceedings. Another distinctive feature of the inauguration was the staging of worldwide demonstrations, according to numerous sources including Wikipedia.

While First Lady Melania did not relocate from New York for another five months, the new president had plenty of family to keep him company. Skirting the Constitutional prohibition against nepotism, his daughter Ivanka and her husband Jared Kushner were named Special Advisors. Two adult sons were put in charge of his worldwide personal business centered in the Trump Organization.

Transfer of business to family members was not the same as the divesting called for in the Constitution's emoluments clause, but investigation may have been impeded by the firing of the Justice Department head Sally Yates. In addition, the volume of head-spinning outrages drowned out any one single transgression, Trump started a crowd-size feud through Spokesman Sean Spicer, which was branded by Senior Counselor Keellyanne Conway as a matter of "alternative facts." He claimed voter fraud had deprived him of the popular vote, tried to institute a "Muslim ban" and attempted to bring back the illegal torture practice of "waterboarding." Finally, he reshuffled the National Security Council to elevate his alt-right campaign manager Steve Bannon to Cabinet level and forced National Security Advisor Mike Flynn to retire after he repeatedly lied to officials. All that and much more occurred during the first three weeks of the Trump presidency and the pace never let up.

The peaceful transfer of power was a hallmark of American democracy. Inherent in that concept was the idea that the of successive administrations was to build on national successes already achieved despite differences in next priorities. As in other ways, Trump was a departure from that tradition. Way back before Obama was even elected eight years before, Trump had led the birther movement to prove that Obama was ineligible to be president. Similarly throughout his own presidency, Trump seemed intent on removing all traces of Obama, as if he had never been presidency in the first place.

Executive orders issued in his first days showed Trump withdrawing the US from the TransPacific Partnership formed to curb China's unfair trade practices. Other Executive orders were to withheld federal funding from organizations providing information on abortion, to remove regulations requiring financial institutions to put customer needs first and to withhold funding from sanctuary "cities protecting immigrants." Environmental protections were reversed the federal government was to start building the campaign-promised Wall. But a major boondoggle of her tenure was a campaign to remove the Obama health care initiative that had become known as "Obamacare."

Obamacare to Trump was never about reform but about outright repeal, as if to erase Obama and roll back the progress made under him on behalf of the American mainstream. Trump's roll backs on progressive measures from environmental protections to curbs on corporate greed signaled a great social divide but health care was the issue that revealed the real Republican agenda as driven by Trump. Republicans had no horse in the race to better the lives of ordinary Americans lest they become competition like Obama turned out to be.

The attempt to cut Medicaid in favor of tax cuts for the rich was a nakedly miserly move associated with the privileged rich white elite that was a throwback to the bad old days before Obama. It was also a direct contrast to the modern American wealthy of both genders and all races who came into money based on talents and shared earned blessings with those they could help. Trump in the Oval Office embodied the rich white male miser who fit only into the extinct category of marauding conquistador destroying cultures and building empires merely by projecting a ruthless, unstoppable power that overcame because he was unfettered by morals and was backed by an army that relied on him for leadership.

Securing the White House keys seemed to unleash the Trump drive to fulfill his full potential for capitalizing on his trademark skill-set of maximizing profit for as long as the opportunity lasted. Throughout the campaign he had boasted he was rich enough that he needed no one's money, which left him free of being beholden to anyone. Once in the Oval Office, he wasn't shy about having taxpayers foot his bill for a lavish lifestyle full of pricy gold outings where he courted Republican enablers fighting tooth and nail to retain privilege.

When the Trumps first descended on Washington, Republican enablers were largely passive. They turned a blind eye as Trump took his full fill of liberties in lining his pockets and trampling the Constitution. They stood by admiringly as Trump played at being president, brandishing pen and waiting for servants to deliver a health care bill he could sign in a gala Rose Garden event where he photo-opped himself as Commander-in-Chief of America's mighty armed forces. At all costs they avoided the character-assassination suffered by those deemed disloyal, as if unaware that one-way loyalty was despotism and not respect. With time, Republicans came to enable Trump in the worst of his excesses, perhaps because they themselves were lost white men on the verge of extinction in a global world where Trump had backing from the white American heartland having no interest in a world beyond what was already familiar.

The Trump base was an important part of America that would have profited from a broader view visible to coastal elites and the bigger world beyond America's shores. That would have let them see that beneath Trump's refreshing crassness in a politically jaded America, in reality he was a small-town playground bully in a global big-city gang 'hood where leaders had already gone on to legitimate venues. Fairy dust would have cleared from eyes to show Trump uneasy with peer world leaders and eager to rumble with small-time despots to be downright enthralled with ex-KGB Putin, possibly for mutual benefit.

 Some of the base would always cling to Trump as presented by the right-wing media promoting his views, but others would reach a point where they couldn't deny that Trump in the Oval Office was a cornered stallion banging against the paddock fence of America's checks and balances. He was a 16th century Machiavelli in a digital world where the most he could produce was a Tweet, a satisfaction so profound to him that he became a speed demon weaving so recklessly that drivers pulled over to calm.

In essence, Trump in the Oval Office was an American adrenalin rush that sent the whole world reeling, baffled by how Americans could have been taken in by an obvious fraud who touted a "Made in America" theme while having his goods made overseas, who cracked down on illegals while he hired them for his golf courses. As with all his other illogical claims, no one asked him where he intended to get his cheap labor once he deported all those he exploited.

As with Obama, the land of opportunity made history with its courage. In this case, it gave an opportunist a shot at the White

House. It was an extreme version of the pendulum swing between forward progress and a step back for caution. In this case, the gamble on Trump cost America steeply because he took America back to the dark ages while the world moved on despite him. While American conservatives obsessed with pleasing Trump, China made trade deals with the European Union for jobs that Trump had claimed he would bring back to America. Japan found new partners in the Trans-Pacific Partnership from which Trump withdrew America, just two of the global developments that occurred while Trump acolytes played a brutal version of "Survivor" in the White House.

The contrast between the Trump White House and America under Obama was as stark as that between two New York landmarks, the Trump Tower on Fifth Avenue and the United Nations half way across town on the East River. The glitzy Trump Tower offices were a mirrored incubator for all-white elite anxiety. The United Nations complex was a healthy mix of elites and commoners of all colors, nations and cultures. Not by coincidence, Trump built a Trump World Tower across the street to dwarf the UN. The majority of condo units were sold to those from the former Soviet Union. The Saudi Arabian Mission to the UN is located there.

Those geographic details illustrated the lack of Trump coherence and the favour that such chaos found with Trump supporters, both the base and conservative Republicans. Perhaps the American romance with the renegade or outlaw had a bearing. But it was also possible that Trump supporters admired the rogue in their anti-hero, the part that was a scoundrel, cheat and deceitful. In the Oval Office, those qualities were antithetical to the Constitution itself.

More than two millennia of white male monopoly on global power were not unseated overnight. Great strides had been made with cooperation between the white men who still ruled and those within other groups who had become their equals. The Trumps were not of that cooperative white group. Even daughter Ivanka played by her father's outmoded rules. They hogged their power instead of sharing it with anyone other than their own circle, which seemingly would not have welcomed them if they hadn't held their power over them.

According to Time Magazine, Trump strategist Steve Bannon said Trump had come to Washington to deconstruct an establishment build by progressives over the previous 100 years. Indeed, he cut administrative and State departments to leave them denuded. He appointed industry lobbyists to Cabinet and Execute positions. He fired without cause and hired into malleable interim appointments. Quickly the government crawled in its functions, including in the chaotic West Wing filled with leaks. By the 7th month, strategist Bannon was out for high-profile media attention a power share intolerable to the boss who juggled his administration to his liking.

Trump was a social misfit who was 13 when his parents sent him to military school because of his unruly behaviour. He won the presidency by appealing to the same base instincts that had banished him from home in his early teens. He had wives who raised his kids until he was ready to enlist them into family service. Town and Country listed his closest friends as wealthy businessmen with one woman among them. She was the wife of a boxing promoter who became SBA Administrator under Trump. Business Insider listed 14 close Trump friends, all in entertainment or sports.

Clearly Trump could provide a vicarious thrill for those in the base who could never hope for a better life than they had, the adult adolescents who had never gone to the prom and who were schoolhouse bad boys who pulled pigtails for attention. That covered a large swathe of males and women who loved them. Even so, Business Insider reported that within 69 days Trump broke a new record when his popularly rating fell to 35%, the earliest that any president's rating fell below 50.

Trump the business mogul who made pyramid schemer Bernie Madoff seem a piker had a White House agenda that had little to do with governing. His touting of Constitutional constraints and norms indicated he was out to enrich himself and advance the cause of his white male Republican enablers. Should he leave the country in a shambles like he had done with his casinos, he would be in position to move on without a glance back. Luckily for the country, progressives could see he was on the wrong track in a globalizing world.

Modern geopolitics proved the point. Europeans looked askance at Trump, having learned the lessons of history through wars and ill-fated colonialist ventures. Russia had proved that outsiders were useful only as pawns. Following in Russian's footsteps, China pursued its national interests by making satellites of Asian and African countries, cracking down on dissent along with Arabic countries threatened by progress in communication with the internet. Repression had led to a terrorist movement that had turned on America with the 9/11 attack. Trump's business interests in violation of the emoluments clause loomed as a threat over his presidency.

From the start, Trump courted the autocrats in whose countries he had business interests. Yet a portrait of his cabinet was a snapshot of the white male aggression that had turned those countries into the lost nations for whom a dictatorship was at least a welcome stability. The Trump cabinet was a veritable portrait of the American Pilgrim fathers and photos of him with First Lady Melania could have been recreations of the stiff farming couple in Grant Wood's American Gothic. America had moved on but the Trumps of the world had not. The non-Trump small people of the world noticed and missed America under Obama.

White Hot in the Melting Pot

The world's melting pot was boiling under a president who was an inciter-in-chief. He attacked everyone, even his own pick of the "best people" for their jobs. He was an attack dog, a bull that charged at every red flag that came his way. He was rage personified and he grabbed the country by the throat over the primordial fear of losing a centuries old status of primacy over others by virtue of being "white."

The so-called white people of the world weren't always the most dominant. Civilization itself began in Mesopotamia, now known as Iraq. The Persians, now Iranians, were once a formidable force, as were the Egyptians, Ottomann Turks and numerous others now swallowed by history. Whites became dominant in fertile Europe, where they fought each other over centuries while colonizing and imperializing the rest of the world. The United States of America grew out of that period. It was the rebel offspring that remained proud of its roots while building ever stronger branches.

The global world of 2019 was still tainted with imperialistic vestiges even as the internet information superhighway united the world's "little" people who wanted more than mere crumbs from the bountiful world they saw through "devices." Thereby were sown the seeds of a global civil war between the "haves" and the "wants."

"When you are accustomed to privilege, equality feels like oppression," some anonymous pundit said. The observation could not be more applicable than to Donald Trump.

Many were born privileged but few as ostentatiously as Trump. He was given his first trust fund at the age of three and was said to be a millionaire by age 8. Ambition and chicanery guaranteed by a father's indulgence shot him to stardom as a real estate wunderkind in the mostly white New York market, undoubtedly pleasing the father who was alleged to be a KKK member. Perhaps when the doting father died in 1999, the chip off the old block took up the torch.

Perhaps because business ventures failed, Trump begin dipping his toes into the political waters until the sweet spot arrived with America's election of a black man as president, Beginning with the "birther" campaign that challenged Obama's legitimacy as a natural-born American, Trump fumed throughout the eight-year Obama tenure, including by rehashing his belief in the guilt of five black and latino youth who had been exonerated. Then as Obama's second term was near end, he came out with guns blazing to announce his candidacy for presidency with a promise to end the invasion of America by Mexican criminals.

From that start, Trump moved on to Muslim enemies, leaving American blacks to be a self-evident human disaster for the country. He courted blacks by verbally trashing their neighborhoods, tell them to vote for him because "what have you got to lose?" Not until Trump was safely in the White House did his attitudes become clearly evident.

In October of Trump's first year, Reuters reported that advocacy groups had criticized the Trump administration for lack of diversity in the cabinet. Mid-level appointments would show greater diversity, the administration replied. Yet of 1,000 such appointments, 88% were non-hispanic whites and 62% were male. By contrast, those same numbers in the Obama administration were 67% and 47%. Clearly under Trump, America was not progressing in racial and gender equality.

No one can know another's true feelings or thoughts, but to all appearances Trump in the White House seemed perpetually enraged. That quality seemed aside from admitted enjoyment in riling people and getting them worked up. He was an entertainer, he liked attention. But if rage was the driving force, he was dangerous.

The Puzzle of Trump was a big part of his power as a media magnet. He generated so much print and communications feed that analysis left little time to penetrate the jungle and separate edible from poisonous vegetation. With that fixation of attention, it was impossible to gauge the level of toxic energy produced by the fusion of Trump with his base.

Trump was indeed an intriguing enigma. He seemed to thrive on the chaos he produced and yet he was a power hungry control freak who viciously rolled over anyone who got in his way. He seemed driven by no ideal higher than his own enrichment, and yet he rallied his heart out to get all America to back his view that only he could run America properly.

Some would call such a perspective on life by the label of a God complex. In young, blessed and adventurous America, it could not be suprising that a third of the population bought in to the scheme designed for the sole purpose of getting them to buy the sale. Trump managed the transaction with his art of the deal, which had at its heart the common element of nonspecific rage.

Trump and his base seemed to be balls of rage in search of specific targets that could detonate them. The rallies covered the gamut and left all in attendance purged as after a Greek tragedy. But when details of enemies were stripped away, the only one left was rage at losing a privilege that had yet to pay off..

Trump had been born into every privilege and yet his best efforts had all led to failures. Winning with the base was his last chance at vindication and having lost all other hope, they were eager to win at last by destroying the system that had failed them.

Puny Trump in Grand UN

Eight years earlier, Obama had received a rollicking reception when he first addressed the United Nations at the opening of the annual General Assembly session. In his first UN appearance, Donald Trump was a diminutive figure and he seemed to be the only one oblivious to that diminished regard for America's leader.

A gathering of world leaders in an august location like the United Nations in New York City was a global grand event. New York residents grumbled about traffic but most admitted the inconvenience was worth the benefit. Security at all levels mobilized to keep all safe, which required coordination between city, UN and federal agencies, especially at the US host country level and in addition to personal protective details of world leaders. Hotels and the city's hospitality sector geared up for the briskest of business and Missions to the UN hosted the lavish affairs that gave their countries stature in the global mix. The investment in terms of effort and resources was astronomical and well worth the cost for the opportunity it provided for world leaders to help each other sort through challenges in the company of peers.

As his offering to that august body on behalf of America, Trump forwarded his America first policy and urged all countries to protect their sovereignty and put their own interests first. He then said the Iran nuclear deal Obama had brokered was the worst he'd ever seen and that it was a great embarrassment to the US. He said the UN could be helpful to resolving world problems but many regions were "going to hell." He made reference to the "radical Islamic terrorism" although the term had been widely denounced as defamatory to an entire religion.

Finally in his address of global issues facing the world, he said little Rocket Man of North Korea was on a suicide mission for himself and his country. The United States was prepared to "destroy" the country if he had to.

The speech was a departure from the usual address that world leaders delivered to their global peers. In their own countries, of course the leaders were honored personages. On the global stage, however, they were just one of near-200 others, however esteemed the company. Given access to the global audience, country leaders gave a presentation of their particular challenges and offered their views on how such challenges could be met through cooperation. Outright threats were seldom made by leaders of the world's most responsible countries.

Already knowing what to expect, diplomats attached to their country's leaders applauded politely at milder rebukes focused on the need for UN reform and for countries to pay their fair share of dues instead of expecting others to carry the load. Trump made no mention of issues central to the global community, including climate change, migration, global trade and cybersecurity. But in the sidelines of the official meetings that ran for a week, he met with the Ukraine leader at the heart of his domestic woes.

A July phone call between Trump and new Ukrainian president Volodymyr Zelesnky had alarmed a security monitor to the point where a whistleblower complaint was lodged. The complaint charged that Trump had asked the Ukrainian leader to investigate the son of political rival Joe Biden regarding possible corruption activities. In the balance at the time was an aid package to Ukraine that had been held up. Ukraine was in dire need of that aid for its war effort against Russian invasion of its territory.

During a joint press conference, Trump brought up the phone call and Zelensky confirmed the suggestion that he had felt no pressure during his phone call with Trump. In the hands of Trump, the domestic woe was thus resolved despite impeachment proceedings brought against him by the House of Representatives.

He was acquitted after a quick Senate trial in which no witnesses were called to testify as they had in the House that Trump had abused his presidential powers in pressuring Ukraine and then had obstructed Congress by directing White House executives to ignore subpoenas issued by Congress. The entirety of those proceedings demonstrated the contrast between the Trump and UN approach to global relations as measures by cooperation in advancing the rule of law.

Trump the business tycoon made his deals by bargaining with individuals and then skirting laws until success was achieved. Obstruction through lengthy legal procedures were a forte. By contrast, however encumbered by bureaucracy, the stated aim of the United Nations was to streamline the jumbled mass of legal processes that existed on the global scale in order to advance worldwide progress. In short, Trump obstructed while the global world facilitated, however imperfectly.

Notably absent during that first Trump visit to meet with global peers at the UN were the leaders of China and Russia. Neither was known to be a fan of the United Nations. The leaders of Germany and Kenya remained at home due to election issues. Mexico, Myanmar, India, Philippines had urgent domestic affairs to manage. Also absent were the leaders of Syria and North Korea, two leaders who did not rub shoulders with global peers. Boris Johnson of the UK left the week-long UN affair early to return home and smooth complications of the Brexit deal he had engineered to withdraw Great Britain from the European Union.

The absence of those leaders from the UN world leader forum left a great gap. In managing a world where challenges were increasingly global. As illustrated by Trump's interaction with Zelensky, the personal angle enabled in a global arena resonated on the domestic scale. Leaders made use of the results for their own purposes, but the transparency of a public meeting was a concrete start to solving problems. The United Nations as the brainchild of the innovative

United States was the world's best hope for airing differences and resolving them in time to avert another hot war.

In light of the challenges facing countries like Ukraine who were just emerging from autocratic regimes, the Trump bluster on the global stage didn't amount to much. At home in the seat of democracy, that bluster was disastrous.

Moscow Towers Over Trump

Donald Trump was a nonstop hurricane wreaking havoc on the world after his 2016 election. A third of the American public applauded the force of his will based on his word rather than on fact.

Trump said the economy was fine, manufacturing jobs were returning to the rust belt, coal mining was coming back to West Virginia and his adherents believed. In truth, those promises failed to pan out. Fact checkers proved that Trump spoke without regard for truth. He said whatever his audience wanted to hear and just possibly he did all that just so he could build a tower in Moscow.

"I came, I saw, I conquered," Julius Caesar once said. Trump may have seized on that boast when he first visited Moscow in 1987. As usual with Trump ventures, he had the right idea but the wrong conclusion. According to numerous sources, it was Trump who was conquered by the idea of a Trump Tower Moscow.

According to numerous sources, Trump was invited to an all-expenses paid visit in 1986 to Moscow just as the Gorbachev winds of democratization were in the works. Indeed, in 1989, the Iron Curtain started to fall away from Eastern Europe and two years later the Soviet Union collapsed after losing its strangled on half of Europe. No doubt Trump saw Russia as a depressed property he sought to grab at a bargain rate as was his practice throughout his real estate career.

Getting what he wanted by any means was the stated Trump motto. The end goal and its merits were of small consequence. If he took umbrage or he was disappointed, someone was fired without cause or notice and not by him but by some underling. Conquering his heart's desire was a driving force laid bare in the infamous "Access Hollywood Tape" where Trump bragged that he was drawn to manhandle beautiful women because he couldn't help himself and stardom gave him license to indulge impulses.

Trump indulged instant gratification. By 2015, a Trump Tower Moscow had eluded him for thirty years and his desire to have it must have been rabid. KGB-trained Vladimir Putin surely knew the value of such lust. He had dangled the prize for all those years as he reeled in the target for his own ends.

Russia was economically defunct. It had a lot of territory and a large population but few natural resources. In its Soviet Union incarnation, Russia made its living by pillaging the resources of its satellite conquests. By 2016, Putin-designated oligarchs operated worldwide to funnel dark money at Putin's discretion. Those oligarchs were known with little actual proof to the Trump conglomerate and key US Republicans, including Senate leader dubbed "Moscow Mitch." Quite possible, a wide net had been laid for letting Trump at long last to earn the tower he wanted in Moscow.

A Trump Tower Moscow Memorandum of Understanding was signed in 2016 while Trump was running for President. He repeatedly denied any dealings with Russia. and as indictments came down from the Mueller investigation, he asserted that he knew nothing about any of those dealings. He maintained that stance even after his own son bragged that Russia was the major source of the Trump Organization income.

Like father, like son, the Trumps backed up each other with lies so cleverly that there was no telling who was lying about what. From over in Russia, Putin observed, perhaps with scorn, how handily Trump managed the chaos he was able to create for a relatively slight reward like a Trump Tower In Moscow,

In pursuit of that goal, Trump may have stumbled into a morass beyond his wildest fears. He was adept at lying, deflecting, conning, throwing fairy dust and mangling the legal system. He had practiced those skills all his life and he was good at them. But he had never performed those feats in the fishbowl of the US Presidency under media scrutiny.

As of 2016, no one knew where the Trump Tower Moscow project stood. But it was quite clear that Trump promoted Putin on the global stage, for example by trying to get Russia reinstated in the G-7. Russia had been suspended by that group of the world most economically developed countries for its annexation of for its annexation of Crimea. Like most Trump projects, the effort failed but no doubt Putin made note of the failure. Also clear was the fact that Putin did not return any favors for Trump's efforts. As with other dictators of the world such as Xi of China and Kim of North Korea. Trump described a friendship while they stayed aloof.

It seemed that world leaders of every political bent, from democratic to despotic, were able to see an obvious truth hidden only from America. Erratic Trump could not be trusted. His blowhard bravado captivated some in his own country but in the larger world it was barely a whimper.

To KGB-trained Putin, the great effort Trump expended for the mere pittance of a tower in his own capitol made Trump a bargain acquisition. If he managed to trounce his own country simply by keeping the spotlight on himself through outrage, he could be useful indeed transferring his skills to horizons beyond his own shores.

Trump Chutzpah and Russian Gelt

Donald Trump was a master of feeding his ambition by making the most of his country's freedoms. He excelled at skirting the law and delegating criminal duties. When local funding dried up after repeat failures on investments, Trump found unsourced money readily available in regions affected by the 1991 fall of the Soviet Union. The moneyed oligarchs were Trump's links to Russia's Vladimir Putin as his next target for expanding his faltering empire.

The cagey Putin was elusive but Trump courted him with projects such as a boxing match, a cycling event touted as the Tour de Trump and a Miss Universe pageant with an invitation to which Putting did not respond. That was followed by a Moscow Trump proposal that was still in limbo when Trump became the US President. By then, Trump's dealings with oligarchs were so globally convoluted that a two-year investigation by Special Prosecutor Robert Mueller was unable to clarify enough to result in direct Trump convictions. In part, that was because the investigation was hobbled by an archaic US Justice department policy that sitting presidents would not be prosecuted.

Russia had no such policy. It didn't need one. Prosecutors there were hand-picked by Putin and they disappeared if they crossed him.

Early In the new Trump administration, American intelligence agencies determined that Russia indeed had a hand in Trump's election. However, with his new presidential powers, Trump sidestepped the intelligence information by inviting two Russian diplomats into the Oval Office complete with electronic equipment. To impress the visiting diplomats, he boasted about intelligence on Iran that had been received from a third country. When alarms rang out over such security breaches, Trump began ramped up the anti-media campaign already well underway.

"Fake news," Trump declared, erasing in the average American's mind the under pining that made legitimate trustworthy. Stories were verified repeatedly with multiple sources. Stories were fact checked and edited to ensure accuracy. Those stringent standards were not applied to the presidency, who daily broke his own records in the number of lies that fact checkers caught him publicizing with presidential authority. A major showdown occurred in 2019 as the 2020 presidential began to loom.

A phone call between Trump and the new president of Ukraine Zelensky had alarmed security monitors. For some reason unknown, Trump had held up release of aid funds needed to help Ukraine fight off Russian encroachment on its territory. The phone call gave the impression that the funds would not be released until Zelensky committed to an investigation into corruption allegations against the son of his presumptive political rival Joe Biden. Debated raged over quid pro quo and shake down versus nothing wrong. Ultimately, Trump was impeached by the House of Representatives with numerous witnesses testifying to wrongdoing. He was acquitted by the Senate after a cursory trial.

America's scrupulous legal system was geared toward protection of the rights of the accused. Legal safeguards were so stringent that two years of investigation had failed to unearth a legally admissible case obvious wrongdoing by the Trump family inner circle. Likewise in the impeachment trial, any collusion between Trump and Putin to manipulate Ukraine for mutual gain would be near impossible to prove. Neither could the likelihood be entirely erased. The impeachment and then the dismissive acquittal kept the question churning in the national discourse.

Trump had the shameless chutzpah to push his country's generous protections beyond their limits for his own benefit. All evidence indicted that benefit to him meant only one of two things, either self-promotion or money. From within the Oval Office, the world was his oyster. He commanded ultimate attention while Republican appointees were free to fleece the public while eroding their protections by satisfying the lobbied interests of wealthy donors. And all that personal bounty had been enabled by the Putin Russian money that had sustained Trump through six bankruptcies.

Putin apparently approved of Trump's Oval Office mode of governing the freedom loving US. He may even have provided guidance during the impromptu sideline meetings the two held during international high level conferences and at the Russia-US Summit held in 2018 Helsinki. Their tete-a-tetes were closed to the American press and even to American interpreters who would have honored the protocols that kept the American government running smoothly. As a result, only Putin had the records of what transpired between them. The secret in his hands would ensure that his oligarchs continued to operate freely in the US.

Trump/Russia, Hungarian-American Eyes

I was long an adult when I asked my mother an obvious question that had never before occurred to me. "How was Russia able to control all of Eastern Europe for so many years?"

"Simple," my mother answered. "They installed local leaders and backed them with military might."

The Budapest New Public Cemetery was a bucolic park dating back to the late 1800s. In 1989, when the Iron Curtain fell, Plot 301 was recognized by a modern monument to identify the unmarked graves of 260 martyrs who were executed in 1958 for their participation in the heroic 1956 Hungarian revolution against Soviet occupation. The body of then Prime Minister Imre Nagy was exhumed. He was given a state funeral and interred in a private grave. All "martyrs" were "rehabilitated" posthumously 30 years after they were killed for revolting against a doomed Soviet regime that kept a tyrannical grip on satellite countries so that their resources could be siphoned into the Soviet empire that collapsed two years later in 1991.

The Russian oligarchs grew out of that lawless Soviet carcass, as did Vladimir Putin who facilitated their work. Probably not by coincidence, that was about the time that Donald Trump ran into financing drought at home and found alternative financing overseas.

No one knew the secrets of the Trump empire, perhaps not even the Donald himself. He was clever and practiced at legal stalling. Many years would pass before threads of his business mazes were unraveled. By then, the statute of limitations built into the American justice system would have expired. In the meantime, the Eastern European experience under Soviet occupation could possibly provide insight.

The Fogarassy family of four left Hungary in the dead of night in December 1956, part of a small group who trekked through sleet across Noman's land to Austria. They left because they couldn't stay. In the Fogarassy case, both parents were involved in the failed revolution. They were marked.

Under the Soviet Communist system carried out by local Communist party leaders, the father was an X-listed undesirable whose family holdings were seized during nationalization of private property. The mother was a Communist Party member, a privilege granted to those from the working class who could be useful to the party and would not be hired to any job if they refused party membership. The Fogarassy couple was already married when the system of class rotation began. Together they weathered the storm, just as they had faced the hardships of their young lives through the Second World War and the impoverished aftermath that had claimed their first child through malnutrition. The effects of those hardships reached into the safety of the United States where the family eventually landed.

Under Trump, Americans felt uneasy about the chumminess between Trump and Putin. To an American who remembered the terror of midnight raids in her childhood home, the coziness was a blinding red flash.

Homegrown Americans were traumatized by school shootings until the Covid pandemic put an end to school itself. But in postwar Eastern Europe under Soviet rule, schools were shut without notice and students fielded out into barbed wire and armoured foreign tanks around the town square.

Such a sight was unthinkable in America, except to an immigrant who had seen it happen before. That view accepted the possibility that Trump was a foreign install and that Russia was the only country with the ambition to co-opt the United States. That Russia would ever rule the US was highly unlikely, but under Trump it wouldn't have to.

Trump was an opportunist who capitalized on every opening that came his way. When he first won the presidency in 2016, he insistently denied foreign interference in the election that had won him the presidency despite Intelligence reports to the contrary. Devious Putin could easily have pulled his strings without notice, his aims of destroying democracy achieved without effort.

The turbulent Trump era climaxed in the global Covid pandemic that exposed the folly of trying to fence off America from an encroaching world as Trump promised to do. Meanwhile, America began spinning in social equity issues that Trump fought with stabs at dictatorial solutions. Democrats called for vigilance to protect a fragile democracy when actually, America's democracy was solid unless Trump was a Putin install or merely in Putin's pocket.

The US Constitution was a time-tested broad platform to resolve disputes about emerging issues. It was a legal framework that absorbed crises into the grand safety-cushion of evolving history. Information about an increasingly interconnected world fed into that fundamental bedrock, most reliably through legislation and the accredited news sources governed by evolving editorial standards. Russia, in contrast, had no such democratically elaborated constitution. It also had no mechanism by which to enforce the already weak protections in its Constitution.

By the 1993 Constitution adopted after the 1991 dissolution of the Soviet Union, Russia was a semi-presidential constitutional republic that granted sweeping powers to the president. Constitutional gaps regarding rule of law enabled oligarchs to flourish in close coordination with the central government. In essence, crime paid in Russia and the massive amounts of money earned were channeled into international expansion.

The Russian marriage of business with government was in direct contrast to the American divorce of business from government. The Constitution's Emoluments Clause and the Hatch Act prohibited capitalizing on a position in government. Trump was the first US President to dismiss legal boundaries to his conduct in office. With his massive global private interests, Trump was a global goldmine for Putin.

In the democratic freedom of America, Trump easily accomplished feats that Putin needed force to pull off. Trump boasted of gaming the system, of paying no taxes, and America applauded. Trump flouted Constitutional law and America gave him a pass. To Putin and the global underworld, Trump was a godsend. To America and its 300-year strong democratic system of juggling freedom with the rule of law, Trump was a disaster

Despite his global real estate holdings based primarily on branding, Trump was surprisingly provincial, as if he had no clue about the world beyond the promotion of his successes, including by burying failures. His Panama City hotel project, for example, entailed numerous lawsuit, name changes and an apprenticeship for his daughter Ivanka. He brought no attention to his overseas projects, possibly because of compromising complications. For example, his Panama City hotel complex involved law suits, name changes and a training opportunity for his daughter Ivanka. As US president when confronted with social unrest, he took refuge instead of taking action.

During Trump's tenure, the situation in Belarus was an example of a classic dictator at work, Russia-friendly dictator Lukashenko was in power for 25 years when activists proved that his latest election win was fabricated. Protests arose, news agencies became involved and still Lukashnko declared himself the winner. He also claimed that the Belarus military had his back, even as NATO gathered on one side and Russia sent word it would help from the other.

Meanwhile, international sources reported that Russia's Putin was waiting to see which way the situation resolved before he sent help.

The Belarus situation was still unfolding when the US Democratic Convention got under way in its Covid virtual guise. US President Trump trolled the Convention by barnstorming toss-up states. His mainstay rallies were mere touchdowns near airports since a fiasco in Tulsa where few supporters had braved the Covid dangers to render support.

In Belarus, protests led to a countrywide factory strike. The dictator in turn staged a rally claiming 100,000 supporters when outside sources reported no more than 10,000. The dictator ordered the internet to be shut down.

News reverberated in a global world connected by the info highway. In the glut of misinformation, the truth stubbornly asserted itself.

Like Trump, Putin needed no subterfuge. Trump made clear that he had no respect for democracy and his base in America approved the message. Putin had made clear that he intended to restore Russia to its former glory and thereby intended to rule the world. By his country's Constitution, he was immune to censure. Schooled by Soviet predecessors and trained by the KGB, he found in Trump as President of the mighty US the perfect ally for defeating the messy ideal of democracy.

Based on a resume unseen when elected, Donald Trump was devoid of integrity, ethics or morals. He made his bones by making a show of clinching shaky deals he dressed up as grand slams. That made him a perfect tool for a ruthless powermonger willing to grant him the ego gratification so desperately needed in exchange for keys to the American kingdom.

Resource starved Russia had no infrastructure to develop the natural resources it did have, at the same time it needed legitimacy for its shadowy oligarch funds in a world increasingly regulated by international action against global crime. With his penchant for one-on-one deals with aversion to multilateral agreements, Trump was the skeleton key to unlock opportunity for Russia.

As if a product of Putin's wildest dreams, Trump had his bounteous country in a twist. He had enthralled some with entertainment. He had captured others with feel-good messages sprinkled into scathing attacks to give the powerless a vicarious cathartic thrill. He had split the country along racial and political lines, alienated the country from global allies, transformed a benevolent American image into that of an unpredictable loon and most importantly had demoted democracy into an outmoded relic.

Reading into open sources, it seemed clear that Trump relished operating in the kind of underworld where Putin thrived. He enjoyed getting over on people and the law. Getting away with infractions gave him a thrill.

Throughout the Trump presidency, the world watched for the direction of America's next election. The beacon of democracy was in a death rattle battle with an incumbent leader who didn't care which way the election went as long a he came out the winner. Perhaps he knew that Putin was watching and expecting that win as a security deposit for future ventures.

If Trump and Putin were to be allied, a great gulf would need to be breached. Opponents of the government in Russia were disappeared, imprisoned or poisoned, sometimes in a combination of those containment measures and at times carried out overseas. In Trump's US, opposition was met by legal resource unless undercut by a presidential Tweet.

The US Presidential Records Act was passed in the 1978 response to Richard Nixon's Watergate scandal. The Act obligated presidents to make public records of their official correspondence. Donald

Trump blew right past that Act with phone calls and Tweets, a major transgression that paled compared to other actions showing Trump flexing his presidential powers.

Seven of Trump's top aides were indicted during his first year in office. He himself would have faced charges had it not been for the legal concession to the Office that a sitting president would not be indicted. Thus he was impeached for wrong doing by the plebeian House of Representatives and exonerated by the elite Senate. He was in perfect position to partner with Putin except that to Putin he was still an apprentice.

Americans in a blessed land were liable to be gullible but they did not like to be coerced or taken for a ride, especially not by a foreign power. A direct tie to Putin would smash the hold Trump held over Republicans through the base. Throughout his presidency, Trump was under watch to see how he would deliver. He was ready.

Trump Tower Apprentice

Donald Trump was 33 years old when construction of the New York Trump Tower began in 1979. It started with the razing of the historic Bonwit Teller building. By then he was well-skilled in working the legal, political, financial and media angles to erect the gaudy tourist trap launched by funds extracted from his father.

Staggered populating of the building began in 1983. Residential units sold quickly but retail and commercial spaces were slow to fill spaces around the cavernous atrium that was a public space requirement for permits and code exemptions Trump had acquired.

By the mid-eighties, the Trump Organization was housed on the 26th floor and a tiny cooperative named On Paper was hired to organize the files still stored in cardboard boxes on an upper floor. The On Paper venture was a cooperative of artists who handled office temp assignments as a group. They spotted each other when one was called away for a musical tour or theatrical gig. They were coordinated, reliable, competent and connected enough to gain entry into businesses like the Trump Organization. They were also keen observers of details irrelevant to the business world.

The group worked with the Organization through the mid-eighties, when dad Fred still popped in to revel in his son's success, when Ivana breezed through glamorously and when younger brother Robert was an executive no less immune to the Trump vitriol than any other employee at any level. The group was on site when women scandals struck. They witnessed the Trump ritual of summoning his men, turning on the speakerphone and letting the woman beg forgiveness as the men chortled.

Trump brother Robert was among those men but he hung back. He was the nice brother, acting as a foil for his brash older brother and as conciliator with those fed up with Donald's ruthless aggressions. In particular need of assuaging were contractors who performed work and were left unpaid. The invoices were held up for some disputed reason. Court settlements would take longer than contractor could afford while also paying court costs. It was Robert's job to ease those disgruntled rough guys out the door.

The wall-sized file cabinets for permanent storage were in a hallway outside Donald Trump's office. From that vantage while performing the work, On Paper organizers observed and made inquiries about the Office. There was a dress code and women were required to wear high heels, a hazard on the slippery sloped marble of the atrium when it rained outside. The custom-built file cabinets were appointed with clumsy draw-pulls that fell off in use and the files themselves were a bramble-bush of projects and off-shoot companies that came and went faster than could be indexed.

"Don't worry about the files," a sympathetic Trump executive consoled. "The real files are safely stored in a private residence off the premises."

Such candor was rare and it broke out when the stress level passed the point of endurance. The bad breath of indigestion was endemic. Antacids were a staple. A summons to the central office caused shakes. A good review from Donald redoubled anxiety. Who would find a pink slip on the desk in the morning for reasons unknown? They would leave with no one spilling a clue about why it had happened or who had brought it to bear.

When it came to Donald and his staff, even Robert couldn't help. Strategic mirrors allowed the boss to see every movement, which kept the entire office on edge. Nervous people messed up, made mistakes. Repression inhibited peak performance. crippled the will to excel no matter what the reason for joining the enterprise. The opportunity was certainly seductive and the environs glamorous. Perhaps most challenging was the urge to see if one would endure.

Even in those early Trump Organization days, Donald was a bulldozing humanoid. There was no stopping his quest to bend the world to his will. If he had a soft side, it was no doubt hidden even from him. Under legal duress, a few blacks were hired and whisked away when Donald neared. A trump war was waged on disabled vets with special peddling permits operating on Fifth Avenue near the Trump Tower.

With business equals, betters or underlings, Donald relished toying with those shackled by humanity. Most survived and some even thrived. They were the ones comfortable in the Donald Trump world of cutthroat gamesmanship played by his lawless rules.

Nice brother Robert was not among the spineless. He didn't last past the Atlantic City casino debacle that began with a botched opening night due to cut-rate, fast-tracked construction that skimped on operating regulations. Donald excoriated Robert and demanded he assume responsibility. Robert didn't wait to be fired. He walked out on Donald and never looked back.

Apprentice Donald never stopped honing the skills already perfected in the early Trump Tower days. By the time he ran for US president, he no longer bothered with nice people who made sense in dealing with the rest of the world. He went straight for the jugular in everyone who crossed his path. He played those skills with agility never before seen once the grand US presidential powers were in his grasp.

If any nice people were left to still believe in Donald Trump once he assumed the presidency, their major skill was to ignore karmic reality for the country. Trump trampled the Constitution, bilked the country. destroyed its credibility and abrogated his presidential responsibility to protect the American people. Those assaults on American democracy were severe. Those who still supported Trump were avid fans of the corrosive process that had turned Trump the apprentice into a master tradesman.

Toxic Trump

A toxic person may be hard to define but sure was easy to spot. Ssaturday Night Live presented a skit about such people. In it, a couple arrived late for a group dinner and took over the event with boring boasts about their recent vacation, oblivious to the lack of interest in the others Toxic love had the same effect in context of two people. One dominated and the other remained subdued for any of a myriad reasons. That kind of love described the relationship between Donald Trump and his base.

The rational mind played a minimal role in love at its best. In toxic love, the faculty of reason cemented the harmful bond. The more that family and friends objected to the union based on its effects, the more that the special bond was reinforced between the toxified lovers. Outside criticism only served to prove the special connection others couldn't understand. A special soul-to-soul language rendered the union sublime. The connection was a mind-meld, as Dr. Spock of Star Trek would say.

Parties to a toxic love entered into the arrangement as voluntarily as anyone hit with Cupid's arrow. Both people gained from the state of belonging, but In toxic love the joys become drowned by conflict as the needs of one exerted undue pressure on the one who met those needs. The bond of love deepened with every investment made by weathering a storm together until some climatic event seversed the union irreparably. Unfortunately, the rupture often occurred in the form of a catastrophe.

Following such a break and premised on survival, the toxic one either faced legal consequences or went on to new conquests since the driving needs were stronger than the ties that had bound. The healthy partner with no such parasitic needs was left lonely, betrayed, abandoned and often devastated,Years would go into parsing the course of the affair, the forks in the road that had led to continued loyalty instead of an earlier exit. In chastened memory, the beloved would morph from a heroic rebel into a dizzying control freak. Through a bruised and wounded worldview, the healthy survivor would recognize that toxic love wasn't blind, it wore 3-D kaleidoscopic goggles.

To those not enamored, the toxic love between Trump and his base was obvious. In a healthy love, leader Trump would have soothed and inspired. Outside criticism would have occasioned introspection, not the venom that bound his captives closer into the union. After the rousing rallies, once the spewed vitriol performed its cathartic function, the base went home alone to ponder ways to further strengthen the bond between themselves as the needy ones and the object of their love, the great man who let them love him and with that gave them a purpose in life.

To those not smitten, the rallies were painful to glimpse. Trump insulted and blamed, not just others but his most loyal base.

"Love me or hate me, you got to vote for me cause your 401K is going down the tubes," Trump told supporters at a New Hampshire rally. The threat that may not even have affected the base was a classic toxic love mechanism. "No way I would have come to Erie if I wasn't down in the polls," he told a rally crowd in Pennsylvania. There were no accounts of anyone storming out indignantly.

To all appearances, Trump was undevout to his own toxicity. His gargantuan needs devoured his attention and there was nothing left for others. But for those who were lucky enough to escape from a toxic relationship, they knew that a breaking point arrived sooner or later. The most satisfying, according to many, was the one in which a new love emerged to remind the bruised survivor that healthy love simply felt good. It produced happiness, not the anger that came from humiliation.

No Dangerfield, this Don

Almost 100 years ago, psychoanalyst Sigmund Freud described humor as an outlet for aggression. About 50 years ago, the insult humor genre came into vogue along with the spread of television sets in American homes. While the genre ran its course long ago, it resurfaced with the rise of Donald Trump.

As a world leader, Trump himself was a joke. By definition in the Cambridge English Dictionary, a leader was one who headed a group based on ability or position. Donald Trump lead by virtue of his position but he was obviously lacking in the ability to perform the duties of his office.

By turns, Trump was either ignorant or dismissive about the significance of historical context. At a Black History Month breakfast, for example, he said the great Frederick Douglass was doing a great job and was beginning to be recognized. The historic abolitionist was dead since 1895.

In other historically challenged matters, Trump pulled out of accords that had taken decades to elaborate based on the vastly conflicting interests of the parties involved. While leaders recognized the chains of experts available to be of counsel to them, Trump increasingly isolated himself with his presidential powers, systematically replacing experts with those who would implement dictates according to his vision.

The Trump vision was limited to the point of anemia. "Nice letters" and "nice conversations" with global tyrants were his criteria for steering US international relations. He was clearly out of his element as a leader in the Oval Office, showing more interest in hiring and firing than in governing. Perhaps the scars of past failures haunted him in the loftiness of his new position, but six earlier bankruptcies had not fazed him as he moved from one to the next. In addition, the fact that he now gambled with taxpayer money instead of his own should have been a factor that should have boosted his confidence. Perhaps it did, but now he had oversight to contend with.

Trump captured the Republican party and with its acquiescence he set about implementing his agenda, Including construction of the promised southern Wall and the proclaiming of a Muslim ban. The courts got in his way and after losses in the 2018 midterms, he was plagued with attempts at oversight from the democratic Congress. Equally bad was the piercing, prying eye of the pesky American Constitutionally protected right of a free press that he claimed had treated him well until he became president. From the frustrations that leaked out of the Oval Office to the press, it seemed that Trump was enraged. He had all of America's mighty powers at his fingertips and yet he was thwarted by safeguards. When he vented in public, any dangerous insults were written off by staff as humor.

Insult humor was a form of entertainment popular in the 1960-70's when televisions in American homes had quickly become common in a mere 20 years. The basis of insult humor was self-deprecation. The comic admitted a flaw in himself and then took an adversarial position with a target in the audience. As equals, the comic and the mark carried out a ritual of "festive abuse."

Rodney Dangerfield made a career out of working out his aggressions through the insult humor that revealed underlying inferiority afflictions. "I was so ugly when I was born that the doctor slapped my mother," Rodney began before he insulted anyone in the audience.

Donald Trump could never be a Rodney Dangerfield however he insulted people in the outmoded Dangerfield tradition. Trump could be self-deprecating but only to uplift his own image, not to engage in mutual self-discovery with another. The Trump trademark form of humor was gasconade, an elaborate boasting about abilities he didn't have. As with other Trump communications, the two forms of humor blended with uncertainty about intent to create controversy.

"I'm a very stable genius" was an example. Whether the comment was made in earnest, was self-deprecating humor or gasconade depended on the audience. The base saw it as an endearing nod to their perception of him. Liberals saw it as a blowhard brag that begged for ridicule. All were dumbstruck and worried about a future in which no one could agree on anything.

The Pathetic Prez

You might feel sorry for Donald Trump if he weren't destroying the country and damaging a new generation by tearing immigrant kids from parents at the southern US border. Soviet communists in their 1950's experimented with raising kids in communal homes instead of traditional nuclear families. The results were disastrous. Developmental thresholds that were not met by parental nurturing led to lifelong emotional and psychological deficits.

Perhaps Donald Trump didn't know that bit of history when he approved his administration's family separation policy. But it was also possible that he wouldn't care even if he knew because he himself had deficits that left him unable to experience a full range of emotions. Once in the Oval Office, he wreaked havoc because nobody of consequence gave him credit for feats he considered worthy of endless accolades. His inside/outside barometers seemed out of sync.

Donald Trump was said to have friends but it was questionable now many would not happily throw him under the bus if conditions were right. Trump's rage and his thirst for vengeance seemed to override any need for the basic human form of bonding based on emotions that made up the concept of love. Those closest to him through family kinship seemed plastic props on autopilot set to boost the Trump ego when posed near him, They reacted on cue when he referred to himself or his self-touted deeds. Family members who didn't fit the mold were unseen, including a brother and a sister. Trump seemed driven by some force beyond basic humanity.

Two emotions that registered in Trump's expression were derisive smugness and utter rage. Any more subtle emotions behind those extremes were impossible to decipher, perhaps by design. He played for effect in the media lens. Some feeling may have been masked by his trademark ploy of fanning outrage with a war on decency. But whether real or fake, Trump presented an of a ticking time bomb about to explode with rage.

The underlying causes of rage were varied and subject to constant study because of inherent destructive potential. But one cause that could apply to Trump because of its intensity was inconsolable pain, the worst of which was thirst for love from someone who couldn't give it. Throughout history, rage over unrequited love had toppled kingdoms and destroyed families. While seldom followed back to its roots in history or literature, rage over unrequited love to the point of violence could reasonable lead back to the mother. Without speculating hopelessly about Donald Trump and his mother, it seemed a fair assumption that there was a mismatch. Judged by his modern need to inflict humiliation and pain on others, it was a good guess he wasn't loved in early life like he needed in boundless measure.

Sigmund Freud dealt at length with the libido, the life force that battled the death instinct. Loosely understood, the theory translated into an either-or situation. Either I got what I wanted or I would destroy what I couldn't have. The theory explained the "terrible twos" of children learning self-control. The theory also explained the fall of Lucifer in the Bible. The principal archangel challenged God to supremacy. He lost and ended ruling his own domain in the underworld.

In his position as President of the United States, Donald Trump was the world's most powerful person for the moment. Instead of promoting good will and cooperation in a complex world full of challenges, he destroyed the well-structured democratic system that had built for 350-odd years. Whether he was a white nationalist or a mere territorialist guard dog protecting his turf, the level of his vehemence suggested a force much deeper and more visceral than mere thirst for power. Someone at some point in his life had wounded him and his life's goal was retribution for a wrong he could never assuage.

No one could know what had hurt Donald Trump so deeply, especially not the man himself who admittedly had no use for introspection. Maybe his mother didn't give him enough of the enormous amount of attention he needed. Maybe his father was disappointed that Donald couldn't perform better with the enormous family bounty handed him. It was even possible that Donald was irredeemably wounded by first wife Ivana leaving him to fall into a short-lived second marriage.

Whatever deep-seated wound drove Trump to destroy instead of construct like the "builder" he purported to be, it was a good chance he was a miserable human being even when getting his thrills from rotating humans like pieces on a chessboard. The world could only hope that he was deposed before he nuked the world when he didn't get what he wanted, his own life extinguished in the process.

Twitter Trump

The English writer Aldous Huxley wrote Brave New World in 1931 as a dystopian science fiction view of a mechanized future saved by a heroic human. Under Trump near the end of the first quarter in the 21st century, the world was definitely new but certainly not brave.

In the late 1700's the US Constitution took years to formulate. In the late 21-teens, US President Donald Trump rocked global markets with a vexed tweet and then settled them with a new tweet containing fabricated numbers, facts and boasts, all because media feedback had revealed that the first tweet had misfired.

Twitter Trump had the world sitting on a sandbank waiting to drop into the abyss. Democratic alliances were in danger, global dictators were courted by the US. Global climate change was at a crisis point, the US President denied any such change was happening. Perhaps Trump really was ignorant of facts but the world would probably never know.

The US presidency was arguably the most important position in the world. The 1978 Presidential Records Act ensured that an accurate account went down in history as to official actions taken. Donald Trump ripped up those records during his administration. He used his personal unsecured phone to make calls to foreign leaders and in his favourite form of communication, he Tweeted and deleted with no nod to record keeping. He was emblematic of the flighty, fleeting tech reality that opened the world to the chaos of too much bad information easily erased.

Even ardent Trump supporters admitted they'd like fewer Presidential Tweets. But Trump seemed unable to step himself. He seemed addition to spewing off the cuff thoughts as they occurred for the instant gratification of Likes and Retweets from his growing lost of followers. Unlike the inauguration contention that his numbers had been the largest despite all evidence, Twitter numbers didn't lie. To Trump, all the better that casual Tweets were indistinguishable from semi-official Tweets informing cabinet members that they were fired.

Twitter was a great avenue for self-expression. It was a sloppy medium for official business at the level of the US Presidency and that situation was ideal for Trump. He Tweeted declarations that left the administration scrambling to damage control. He retweeted racial posts to which he could apply plausible deniability from his presidential station.

In short, the Trump presidency was commonly called "unprecedented." Twitter proved Trump to be utterly "unpreSIdented." During his four year term, Trump destroyed the US presidency, its dignity, integrity and reliability in a complex world. While politicians were known to lie in the interest of protecting constituents from bad news, Trump admittedly lied as a negotiating tactic. "I just heard from China," he declared to quell jittery markets about a US-China trade deal. China later confirmed in response to press queries that no calls had been placed.

Twitter Trump scrambled the important distinction between the president as a private citizen and the man who represented the greatest power in the world. America's position on issues was muddled in a fog of words blending official statements and quasi-official threats Tweeted in insomniac spasms.

America's Founding Fathers did a great job in exercising wisdom and forward-thinking to ensure that their experiment in democracy endured. They did not foresee an elected leader bereft of the most basic morality who would exploit a worldwide web of Information to sow discord. And while the forefathers could not foresee the Twitter age, they did see into the human soul to declare that all people should be free to pursue happiness. The question for America under Trump in the 21st century was whether it was possible to be happy under a leader who muddled the complexities of a globalizing world instead of easing the adjustment.

Twitter was the ideal platform for Trump during a presidency that masqueraded as a reality show while he carried out a broader conservative agenda aimed at undermining democracy in the interest of a wealthy class poised to capitalize on an increasingly interconnected global world. Twitter enabled Trump to spin the image of himself as a potent success while sidestepping the reality that he was nothing more than a practiced conman.

For the Trump who made deals by gaslighting and obfuscating, Twitter was ideal. Twitter was always at hand, available 24/7. The short Twitter feeds required no thought and carried few consequences. He could fire, hire, castigate and excoriate enemies. If he changed his mind, he could always delete before Tweets got to the National Archives. As for historians, there would likely be a huge gap in the record for the period when Trump occupied the Oval Office.

Blow Them Whistles

America was the world's land of freedom and opportunity guided by laws developed in line with a founding Constitution that served as a model for emerging democracies. By that path, America in the 21st century was a country where a person in trouble could call 911 to get help. After the 9/11 attack on American home soil, NY Transit adopted the slogan, "if you see something, say something." Public safety was worth extra effort.

During the days of Trump, the complex US government had no such handy tool to sound an alarm. All it had was the 1989 Whistleblower Protection Act, which called on federal employees to report suspected misconduct.

Government employees were either elected, appointed or dedicated career professionals. Those who were elected reflected the voice of the people in theory. In reality, they attained office based on money raised for campaigns in tandem with visibility reached either on air or in person at rallies. Appointees were chosen by elected official based on donations to campaigns, often through ties of mutual contacts. In contrast, career professionals entered the government to develop skills in service to the country.

The ingenious US Constitution entrusted government to three co-equal branches to act as checks on each other. Congress was made up of the House and Senate that together made laws by getting agreement on any law before it was passed. The Executive branch headed by the President then put the law into practice. The Judiciary as the third branch ruled in the event of conflict.

For example, if the President wanted a wall built on the US southern border and the Congress representing the people didn't want to fund the venture, the courts would decide on how to proceed.

The courts, however, had many layers, up from state courts and appeals courts to district courts and on up to the Supreme Court.

That interaction of the government's three branches had been refined for more than 250 years. Since the 2016 election of President Donald Trump, that Constitutional foundation of the United States came under challenge.

Donald Trump came into office as a maverick. He was already notorious as a dicey business tycoon known for distressing the law. He fashioned that questionable skill into entertainment with a TV show where the trademark was the devastating verdict of "You're fired!"

Audience interest in terms of ratings lasted long enough for Trump to jump into politics with a splash based on the same qualities of audience capture that had landed him a TV gig when his businesses were tanking. Once in the Oval Office, Trump turned his well-honed skills into shredding the US Constitution and the world order that was based on global development of legal norms primarily based on international treaties brokered by the UN and regional organizations that had evolved under its umbrella.

Throughout his tenure in office, Trump made clear that he would defy Constitutional limits. Instead of divesting his personal business, Trump put the business in charge of two sons. When Congress refused to fund the southern border wall that Trump wanted built, he diverted money from military funds to get the job done. However, when he withheld aid funds from a foreign country fighting Russian aggression until his own political rival was investigated, the House of Representatives put its foot down and impeached Trump.

The precipitating event for the impeachment was a whistleblower alert that some suspect activity had occurred during a phone call between Trump and the president of Ukraine. During the impeachment process, nuances of law centered on such questions as quid pro quo and possible extortion. Trump's major concern as betrayed by Tweets, was the identity of the whistleblower. Whose identity was protected by federal law.

Republicans took stabs at naming the whistleblower and security measures were implemented to protect the persons named. Key witnesses were also threatened and given protection. But the hounding of loyal career diplomats was jarring to the American democracy geared toward a more perfect union.

Whistleblowers had nothing to gain by reporting educated suspicions and everything to lose. Even if their identities remained publicly undisclosed, they would never be the ordinary government employees they had been. No doubt agonized uncertainty went into a decision to blow the whistle. The decision was made when the perceived threat became too imminent to dismiss.

The Trump administration devoted to self-enrichment divorced from governing responsibilities was no doubt fertile ground for whistleblowers. The grueling process, however, no doubt deflected them, To go through the bureaucratic gauntlet was bad enough. To withstand the Trump Tweets of "Who's the whistleblower, I want to know who the whistleblower is," was a chilling ice bucket on any desire to take the risk of ensuring injustice under the system as it existed under Trump.

The White House Born Loser

Donald Trump seized power in the US on a technicality at a time when a minority in the world's only superpower saw him as refreshingly outspoken and as a man who got things done. That view of him endured with a baseline of Trump supporters despite the fact that Trump was a born loser who parlayed a few flashy wins into a blazing brand as a winner.

Terms describing Donald Trump as unfit for the office he held ran the gamut from narcissistic, ignorant and lawless to reckless, corrupt, despotic and racist. Incompetent and dangerous were added later when he mismanaged the Coronavirus global pandemic. Those attributions were accurate based on his history. The very form of his reactions confirmed the charges. In the White House Oval Office, he grew beyond compellingly outrageous to deadly dangerous.

An objective Trump resume showed a skimpy record. He renovated the New York Central Park skating rink in record time and drenched the local media with newsflashes about the feat. Then he moved on, leaving upkeep to others and the smack of ill-will in his wake. Unpaid bills were the tip of the iceberg. Regardless, Trump next shot to national fame with a TV show featuring the glamour of his ruthlessness. with the famous "You're fired" as its brand mark. When audience interest in the nastiness faded, Trump moved on to politics.

The Trump version of his own resume would simply state that he was the best ever in whatever he undertook. He succeeded beyond belief with casinos, vineyards, neckties, steaks, golf courses, resorts and magnificent big buildings all over the world. The dizzy panoply would omit the status of the project, whether defunct, ailing or forfeited. The notoriously censured Trump University of success would be nonexistent in the Trump version of his footprint on the world. Nor would there be mention of the Trump charity defrauded by Trump himself.

Donald Trump was undoubtedly accomplished in defrauding the world, maybe because objective reality and Donald Trump had little in common beyond the most deceptively superficial. Big glitzy buildings in the world's biggest cities were synonymous with the Trump brand. Left out of that picture was the fact that those buildings were located in the developing world of dark money and far from A-list status in the global hierarchy. It took a global pandemic to demonstrate definitively just how shallow was the Trump claim to significance.

The US presidency was arguably the most powerful position in the world. It was traditionally attained through a combination of personal and political skills. Donald Trump took a shortcut by fabricating both ability and success.

Trump may have been born with a self-concept already formed and numerous accounts indicate that family funds enabled him to barrel headlong after ambitions without a look back. Failure led not to introspection and course correction but to increased brazenness in exalting himself. A portfolio of bankruptcies, failed ventures, cutthroat deals gone awry, contract violations and legal litigations all attested to success through failure, except that secrecy and aggressive legal actions thwarted discovery of whether Trump ever learned from failures.

A healthy ego incorporated outside information. It grew and increased competence to deal with the outside world. Defense mechanisms interfered with process. Anna Freud, daughter of the famous Sigmund, first set out those operations of the mind in 1936. She said they allowed the mind to protect itself from the harsh lessons of reality by making up its own version of why an outside event fell short of expectation. The mind then devised its own plan for how to make a correction.

One example was to cast blame on others. The reactive behavior was to exact revenge. Projecting feelings onto others was another example, as was its cousin paranoia. Reactive behaviors denigrated, humiliated and vanquished perceived enemy assailants. In the Oval Office, Trump manifested a master's level of skill in all such defense mechanisms and reactive behaviors except perhaps for one. He seemed not to sublimate feelings for a higher purpose.

Donald Trump's feelings were as transparent as a bank check forged by a five-year-old child and they were just as raw as that child's. Outspoken was the term used by the Trump base. Ugly was the term more accurate based on the effect. He vilified and cast blame instead of offering solutions. His major skill was in selling the idea that he was an accomplished man.

As US president, the Trump repertoire of chicanery was singular. His lies, vilifications, retributions, purges and trade wars would go down in history. Perhaps one day the world would come to see Trump as an adolescent prank played by the puckish young American superpower. In the meantime, America could improve national mental health by recognizing the reality that Trump was a born loser hell-bent on taking down the country that wouldn't grant him the respect he felt he deserved.

Being a man of all show and no substance won Trump the presidency. But since the show was based on ugly defense behaviors that left the ego undeveloped. Trump was a cowardly push over who couldn't fire people unless he did so in the theater or TV. In real life he fired by Tweet or had others do the dirty work. In real life he was a will o' the wisp, a giant oak tree threatening to topple. Perhaps that was why American conservatives lit upon the idea of using him as camouflage while they implemented their agenda in wake of the Obama progressive period.

Trump was a one-man walking threat to American values but containing those values within safe conservative limits was paramount to Republicans. Ensuring pale male dominance against invading hordes of non-white non-males was paramount. Flamboyant Trump with aggressions learned in the cutthroat world of New York real estate turned dark money global was perfect as a useful decoy while the agenda went forward.

Unfortunately for Republicans the Covid pandemic hit and exposed an incompetence in Trump that prompted a backward look at his actions during the entire course of his presidency. As the economy shuddered and another term came into doubt, Republicans, Trump and the base joined forces to ensure that the born loser who had made it to the top did not founder disastrously.

Trump, the American Absurd

The Trump base wouldn't agree but Donald Trump was as out of place in the Oval Office as a colorblind salesman in a haberdashery. Like that peddler, Trump sold his wares by pushing products regardless of suitability. He threw shirts and ties at the shopper with such rapid-fire force that the hapless buyer left with an unfit mélange, perhaps a red striped tie with green plaid shirt. If the grouser returned based on outside advice, the seller couldn't care less. "You bought it," he'd say as he continued selling.

Donald Trump was the proverbial used-car salesman unloading lemons. As president of the mighty US, he graduated to master swindler. Hit with an unprecedented pandemic, he became simply absurd. He became the colorblind salesman pressing more wares on disgruntled buyers as smoke filled the shop. "Just a faulty steam pipe," he assured and hustled to the cash register.

That was the character that Trump brought into the US presidency. He blasted onto the presidential stage by hooking a receptive base with a pitch he had honed over decades. Increasing dexterity kept him in the game despite successive failures as his bravado became polished and family funds ran out. Project became more exotic. A few cohorts became more reliable. Those who fell short were summarily replaced. When the project inevitably failed, Trump had a new source of funding and a brand new roster of aides.

The 1989 fall of the Iron Curtain was fortuitous for Trump. Just when repeat failures deprived him of legitimate funding, he found new infusions from the evolving world's rising needy greedy class. From the ashes of the failed Soviet Union, the underbelly of regulated monetary systems had money aplenty that needed legitimizing. The election of Trump as US president was an untold return on investment.

Trump was notoriously secretive about his finances. In addition to boosting his boast ability, secrecy enabled him to plot ways to confound and obstruct the legal system. That helped to stymie investigation and obscure foreign entanglements. What was not secret about Trump finances was cold hard fact. Legitimate entities had less to hide than those whose dealings would suffer from public scrutiny. That may explain why Trump devolved so obviously once in the Oval Office.

During his first years in office, Trump turned his gift of outrageous gab into an Art of the Scam with the appointment of industry insiders and lobbyists to government positions. Once the pandemic hit and impeachment began, the trademark Trump bamboozle became a full-blown Art of the Absurd.

From the start as US president, Trump trampled the Constitution so egregiously that outrage at any audacity never gained traction before another even more brazen became public. Starting with nepotism and unabashed self-dealing related to his Trump Hotel Washington, he hired and fired with no reservation about doing so to protect himself simply because he could. The base saw maverick Trump draining the Washington deep state swamp. Not until the Covid pandemic hit did it become clear that the swamp was nothing more than that solidly founded and vital part of the might US infrastructure.

Trump was a documented serial failure when he took office on a technicality. The record of losses was already rebranded as proof that he was a superior man of many ventures. His ability to sell that twist on his record won him both foreign support and home base adherence, which solidified his standing with the conservative Republicans. The interplay between the Trump base and the Republicans enabled Trump to thrive like an opportunistic disease, As the base cheered his verbal assaults, Republicans danced to the Trump tune. The result was a chaotic scramble for cover by Republicans, a hapless impeachment by Democrats and a pandemic that proved how helpful a so-called deep state would have been in a national crisis of international proportions had Trump not dismembered it

Trump wreaked havoc on the country and the world during his time in the Oval Office and the most absurd part was that America had let him do it. When seen through the long lens of history it seemed incredible that the mightiest country in the world had hired a P.T. Barnum to manage its affairs. Trump had never held a job, had no resume to present when he won the Republican party's candidacy for the presidency. He had no experience with government, the military, institutions or industry. He had never run anything but a small family business that ruled with an iron first and a code of conduct that shot for the moon and landed in the gutter.

Trump was the colorblind salesman in the haberdashery wanting his contract renewed, despite the fact that he never presented a resume in the first place. His only qualification was a blithe disdain for a coomonly accepted reality when his own version better suited his needs. That was the quality that gave him the chilling gall to claim that he had landed the job and therefore deserved to keep it.

The Runaway Trump Train

The runaway Trump train not only let Trump run over the American Constitution but it also let him skid onto foreign rails. Those were not the state-of the-art rail systems connecting with the evolving European High Speed Raiway System. They were trunk lines in developing countries headed by dictators.

Trump began his run for the US Presidency as a social renegade. He descended the glitzy escalator of his gaudy Trump tower by proclaiming that Mexicans were rapists and drug runners. He fought his way to the Republican nomination by trashing and mocking his opponents. With outside help he won the prize and his track record of nastiness gained speed as the law proved no impediment to his quest for personal gain with the mighty powers of his new position.

American forefathers could not foresee a conman like Trump heading the country. Even so, they set up a system of checks and balances among three branches of government to ensure democracy stayed on track. One branch made laws, another put those law into practice and a third mediated in the case of conflict between the other two. That last provision for ruling on the validity of a law was in and of itself a stroke of genius for a group of white men to whom "all men" referred only to white male landowners. Laws since that time have clarified the intent of the Constitution. New laws would have to further clarfiy Constitutional intent once Donald Trump vacated the Oval Office.

Trump broke new ground with his defiance of Constitutional norms. He did that by exploiting a supersonic world to make his word the end all and be all of what could be achieved with presidential powers. National security was compromised when Trump used his unsecured personal phone to make official calls to world leaders. Secret Service protocols became a battleground when Trump insisted on a role for his own bodyguards and a lock on his bedroom door. He dispensed with the cumbersome process of formal declarations by incorporating the Tweet as a confusing, semi-official decree. That loose and free approach to governing in the world's great democracy caught the interest of dictators around the world.

America was singularly blessed as a complex, diverse, well run society that was still free. Trump grabbed the last of those virtues to trample the others, making himself an outlaw hero in the eyes of supporters who increasingly became as morally flimflam as he was. Once on that track, neither Trump nor his base had any option but to continue on that track. The two were stuck on each other like an info-loop.

 An outlaw could not course-correct without losing status with those who admired the lawless behaviour. That was particularly true of an outlaw whose own self identity was based on that projected image, however false. Trump, for example, called on followers to rough up member of the press. He himself fell victim to a craving for attention that gave the press more information than needed on just how inept and corrupt he was as president. When again in the presence of fans, Trump painted himself as a victim understood only by those who believe.

Thus the runaway Trump train careered headlong down the track toward a disastrous derailment far short of the home depot. Nonetheless, Trump the conductor and the passenger base fortified each other for the ride. They jeered and booed together over every decent but boring target.

The "deep state" that Trump claimed was out to get him was nothing more than the bureaucratic infrastructure that made the United States the powerhouse it was. Its stability derived from its Constitutional framework. Tedious as it was, the human component of the US bureaucracy was dedicated to its job. It had no stake in unseating anybody for political reasons. Of course they jockeyed for promotions but none if any aspired to the presidency. They were civil servants who paid for job security by monotonously adhering to rules and coping with the stress of fulfilling huge demands on tasks that were underfunded and understaffed.

Trump, however, made the system out to be bloated and its staff as superfluous. Not understanding the complexity of a government generally disparaged as inept, the base bought the easier Trump version of the government. That trick of the Trump trade no doubt delighted Vladimir Putin who wanted to make Russia great again by undermining the US.

With Trump as an ally and with an open invitation to interfere in the next election. Putin was undoubtedly comfortable with the way western democracy was faring under Trump. But the Trump train with its conductor had reached a fevered momentum and the speed appeared to have become addictive.

America allocated a long two and a half month transition period to ensure a smooth transition between administrations, The Trump transition team began working before the November 8 election and the team was replaced three days later on November 1. Since he had not won the popular vote, Trump was officially elected until the electoral college voted on January 6 of the following year. By then, Mike Pence headed the transition team. Trump himself spent the transition period conducting a thank you tour of rallies. He followed that with post-inaugural rallies, then 2018 midterm rallies and finally a highly contentious series of pandemic rallies prior to the 2020 election.

The rallies were the lifeline between Trump ad his base. They were a symbiotic unit that fed off the basis of human instincts. They then powered the train making a headlong dash for the home depot where democracy could change its character.

Chill Out America, Kick Trump & Opioids

Ouch! Too much, too fast. That could be the slogan for the social media age with an ADHD Prez in the Oval Office.

Nobody knew what went on in Donald Trump's head, probably not even the man himself. He saw a record crowd at his inauguration when cameras clearly showed empty spaces. From his lofty post, he dispatched a spokesman to back his view. A few Republicans either bought or sold that Trump view to lend reality to the absurdity.

In the superhighway information age of technology, all America seemed drugged under the Trump tenure. With his skewed angle on reality, the president himself could have been influenced by a cocktail of narcotics. The Senate seemed numbed, slavishly backing the Republican party's top renegade. After the midterms in which the Democrats gained a narrow majority in the House despite Trump midterm rallies, Representatives seemed mixed. Half seemed on speed and the other half on downers.

Meanwhile, the American people seemed mired in a Facebook reality with themselves as the stars of their own trivial dramas. Minutiae crowded out the larger picture like weeds overgrowing garden plans. And all the while, an opioid crisis plagued the country.

Until the Covid pandemic hit, opioid overdose was a leading cause of death in the US, right up there with heart attacks and car crashes. According to NPR, in 2017 the estimate was that more than 42,000 Americans had died that year of overdoses related to heroin, fentanyl and prescription opioids. By 2029, the number rose to 50,000.

The epidemic was most marked in the battleground states that Trump needed to win the election and on the campaign trail he promised the base in those states that he would eradicate the crisis 100%. Once in office, he allocated more funds for the Office of National Drug Control Policy but he also proposed to cut the Office budget by 94%. While that decision was reversed, the Office was subjected to a complete overhaul of its staff. Career scientists were replaced by nonprofessionals such as the former head of Trump's transition team.

Of course America was not privy to such behind the scenes details and few nonprofessionals could have tracked the obfuscation that was a Trump staple. But most Americans could see that something was wrong. The land of opportunity and innovation had become a land of opioid addiction caught on a tech treadmill headed by a president whose intellectual range was limited to the number of characters allowed by Twitter. Amazon's Alexa could turned on the house lights but it couldn't turn on the human common-sense button in the brain. In a tech world, that function had become rusty in a few short years.

Trump advisor Kellyanne Conway coined the phrase alternate reality but most Americans knew the difference between an alternate reality and a mortgage payment due. Likewise, a quick reality check helped clarify the probability of a wild theory picked up on social media. No deep research was required to skim over Google entries and their sources. While overwhelming in volume, ten minutes of effort provided enough information to make a decision on whether to believe or reject a stated claim released into the web cloud.

With regard to Trump and the innuendoes he tossed out to steer his base in the direction he wanted, it was useful to divide views of him into two categories. The first was subjective, whether or not a person liked his style or performance. The second was objective fact in the real world and not in some alternative reality unrelated to the one in which we live. In that reality Trump was a New York real estate tycoon who had lost financial credibility due to serial failures. He was a record breaking purveyor of falsehoods who had made promised that had never materialized,

Those who still believed that Trump had their best interest at heart despite his massive tax cuts to right Republican donor friends, the search for "true north" in a complex changing world was probably fruitless. But others could benefit from delving into the backstories behind the strong economy and jobs numbers that made Trump so popular with his base. Their view of his performance might change if they knew that the healthy jobs numbers were a product of workers holding multiple jobs in to make ends meet.

 America wasn't about to give up its fast moving tech toys just to make life more livable, but it could learn to take a time out in order to sort the overwhelming amount of information disclosed each day. Down-time was a forgotten art that could ease distress, which under Trump was a result of the constant adrenalin rush he produced in those around him. Distress also came from an OCAD dependence on the outside world that could alienate a person from an inner self.

Opioids eased pain and so did the joy of self-sustenance. There was satisfaction in recognizing the obvious truth that Walls could not keep out a globalizing world, that Facebooks "likes" and Twitter "retweets" didn't fill an inner void. For those who felt the emptiness to the point of needing drugs, it could help to face and resolve conflicts so as to better face outside challenges.

Taking time out from the tech ret race carried its own rewards. There was instant gratification in being independent of outside stimulation. Friends were happy to hear from those who hung a "gone fishing" sign on their social media sites from time to time. The time out was most rewarding when the Muse struck with an urge to pick up a pencil or Google a new train of thought. Trips to outer space or the Himalayas were not the only adventures left for humans. Like the ocean, the human soul remained a delightful mystery to explore as the world grew complex with neighbors and problems that called for group solutions.

A New Yorker cartoon once depicted a sleeping visitor and an artiest who sat in front of an empty canvas. The caption read, "watching creativity at work." The cartoon was a variation of watching grass grow or contemplating the navel as advocated in Zen meditation. The contemplation recommended by Confucius was an old remedy but it worked for human peace and fulfillment in a hectic world.

The world's young people could bring about a global revolution for justice climate change, health care and relations with neighbors. According to Politico, support for Trump in the age group of 18-29 dropped significantly from 2016 to 2020. At the same time, opioid use in that same age group remained high in the battleground states.

All those factors suggested a road forward for America. In line with tradition, America would do well if children listened to their elders. It would do even better if elders listened to their children and gave them credit for their wisdom in seeing through the doomed future of politicians like Trump.

10 Things to Love About America on Trump Days

In 2008, America was the first western industrialized country to elect Barack Obama as a non-white head of state. In 2016, the pendulum swung backwards in the election of ultra-white media-made business tycoon Donald Trump. As Trump rolled back progress made under Obama toward global cooperation in critical areas such as climate change and health care, Americans could not be blamed for forgetting what made their country so great. A reminder could help them endure.

1. America had a great foundation. The 1776 Declaration of Independence stated that the new country freeing itself from England was based on an inalienable human right to life, liberty and the pursuit of happiness. The country was a living work in progress ever since

2. The 1786 Constitution set out the rights that would be protected. Those included the right to free speech and freedom of the press, the right to assemble and right to bear arms.

3. Amendments to the Constitution spelled out rights not foreseen by the forefathers in line with their inferred intent as determined by legal scholars. Thus over time, one-time slaves were acknowledged as full citizens. So were women, who won the right to vote in 1920.

4. In America, the ruler was the law. The ingenious part of the Constitution was its separation of the country's governing structure into three branches, one that made the law, another that put the law into practice and a third that mediated when the other two came into conflict. In the end, a legal interpretation of the Constitution was the winner.

5. America provided legal protections for its people. In the 250 years since its founding, America developed a legal system in line with the constitution to insure the rights of citizens as they evolved under law. Thus the 1966 Miranda laws gave unprecedented protections to the rights of the accused. Legislation under current consideration included those related to regulation of gun traffic

6. America was helpful and forgiving. Social aid was available to those in need and bankruptcy laws helped others out of financial troubles. Legal recourse was always available to those who could not find justice under criminal law and to those who sustained serious injuries. When in doubt, lawyers were empty available. Rights organizations also offered legal services.

7. When legal relief for a grievance could not be achieved, the American media offered potential outreach. America presses were fan friendly to those in need of attention to troubling or frustrating issues. The exposure of scams plaguing the land of opportunity was particularly helpful and of interest.

8. America was friendly. Yes, America was a complex nation of immigrants. Violence occurred daily but those incidents were not the norm. Conflicts were inevitable but the local bodega conveyed the accurate picture. The Mexican, Indian or Afghani attendant behind the counter was there to please. That was the real person behind the threatening label of immigrant.

9. America was the land of opportunity for change. Americans had a Constitutional right to assembly. They were free to organize marches, sit-ins, sit-downs and walk-outs. All they needed was a motivating cause, a permit and a starting

spark to recruit others to a cause. America made room for the aggrieved to collectively express needs.

10. America loved to party and have fun. A land of immigrants provided a year full of holidays to celebrate. The all-American 4th of July and Thanksgiving reaffirmed a basic connectedness as Americans. Other prominent holidays included St. Patrick's Day, Israeli Independence Day, Puerto Rican Day and the Caribbean Festival. Other festivals awaited to recognize America's new immigrant groups even as its cherished traditional celebrations endured.

The list could go on and build with the realization of just how lucky were those who lived in America. The path through 2019 continue to be stressful with the uncertainty of just Donald Trump would do to damage the country and its Constitutionally based democracy as protected by the rule of law. But 2020 would bring an election and a Census conducted every 10 years. That would count all those living in the United States without regard to citizenship status. All who lived in America were eligible to enjoy its liberal protections so as to sustain its vibrant greatness as a land of immigrants.

Part V.
America 2020 and Beyond

Stranger than Fiction Trump

The great American humorist Mark Twain was credited with saying the equivalent of the observation that truth was stranger than fiction because fiction had to be plausible. Even science fiction needed a plot and story line that made sense from start to finish or else the reader was left unsatisfied and the author had a short career. Twain wrote his comment in 1898. By the 21'st century, no such restriction held back the likes of Donald Trump.

Adept as he is with delivery, the barrage of his incredible whoppers leaves no room to discern that the lies defy reason.

Global chaos is the outcome of a US presidency that has turned the US topsy-turvy in the world's eyes. For one thing, the world is obviously globalizing and the US has led the effort in smoothing the difficult process. Out of nowhere, Trump turns back the clock, scuttles hard won regional agreements and inserts himself as the lone savior in America's relations with nearly 200 other countries, most of which have learned hard lessons from centuries of conflict capped by two world wars. Even dictators with a stranglehold on their fiefdoms rely on alliances. North Korea counts China as a friend and Russia under Putin sends oligarchs to pick pockets. Whirligig Trump goes it alone in the name of the US, whose people are given a Trump say-so about the outcome. That's a tall order for America about a leader who dances to a drummer nobody else hears and by outward signs doesn't seem to exist.

The thought that I'm right and everybody else is wrong is one definition of insanity. Another is to repeat an action over and over while expecting a different result. Both those views could apply to Donald Trump but in the America he has created and with the position he holds, the notion cannot be proven and if it was, the diagnosis would not stick. Throwing mud to roil the waters is

Trump's forte and his saving grace from a verdict of insanity is that he had a common endpoint called greed.

Avarice was defined as extreme greed. Gluttony was defined as habitual greed. Trump fit both those categories with a show of zeal that belonged in the Guinness Book of World Records once he became US president. The extent of damage such pettiness could produce did not become apparent until a global pandemic crippled the world.

Numerous accounts indicated that neither Trump nor his cohorts believed he would be elected President. He was unqualified and the behaviors he exhibited on the campaign trail were antithetical to American values. Nevertheless, on a technicality and likely with outside help, he became president with the mighty US powers in hand, Like a bank robber in a hurry to clean up before the bonanza of opportunity was lost, Trump started pillaging America's great wealth.

The US Constitution was the first Trump victim of his presidency. He skirted restrictions against nepotism by naming family members to advisory positions from where they could parlay their advantage into profits. He dispensed with the emoluments clause by putting business holdings into family hands. He then began subverting bedrock American institutions by defunding, demanding and defaming targets, firing competent and experienced civil servants to hire inexperienced strawmen. Finally, a crucial component in the Trump plan to flee America was the Justice Department.

An ingenious part of the US Constitution was the division of the government into three equal branches to act a check on each other. The Legislative branch made laws that responded to evolving issues in line with the Constitution. The Executive branch put those laws into practice and the Justice department mediated the pathway between the other two branches. To implement his ambitious plans, Trump needed the Justice Department to rule in his favour and from the start he engineered that structure.

Trump got off to a galloping start in his presidency by the lack of Justice interference in his systematic subversion of Constitutional strictures. He then began his war on immigrants and managed to evade investigations into illegal activities that had promoted his election in the first place. Once in the clear, he proceeded to lay the groundwork for his re-election with an attempt to extort electoral help from a foreign power in exchange for the release of aid funds that had been approved by the Legislative branch. Impeachment ensued and Trump skated thanks to machinations by his conservative Republican base.

That exhaustive process for America and the world was barely finished when the Covid pandemic hit and the bull in America's China shop of democracy was left without cover. The pandemic hit in the election year when Trump expected smooth sailing based on a thriving economy. As the death toll mounted, businesses shut down, society came to a standstill and racial injustice rose to the forefront of attention, Trump resorted to a series of tactics that got him past a lifetime of failures, including six bankruptcies that devastated entire industries and cities.

In dealing with the pandemic threatening his re-election prospects, Trump first denied the existence of danger. Then he called for defiance against the dangers, complete with rejection of scientifically proven methods to deal with a biological threat. Finally, he called on followers to prove their loyalty by daring to contract the disease at a rally that gave them the opportunity to refuel on the sense of victimhood they shared.

If the story of Trump as American president were submitted for publication, editors would want questions answered before the work could be accepted as plausibly rendered. Addressing those gaps in the story line called for a deep dive into deep background.

But whether or not that work was done before the entire story was finished, the ending already called for a satisfying finish regardless of the horror genre that the story fit into.

Quite apparent from a literary angle, Trump could not come out as either hero or antihero in the story. A hero would have led the country on a campaign to defeat the virus. An antihero, like Trump, would use the virus as a political wedge to divide opponents into smaller, more manageable groups. But no antihero was believable if as inconsistent as Trump, who urged followers to defy common sense while he himself surreptitiously took the steps to ensure his own safety.

The Snookered Trump Base

In 1989, "Queen of Mean" Leona Helmsley was sentenced to four years in prison for telling a jury the truth that only little people paid taxis. Members of the jury were obviously not her peers. They were the little people who paid the taxes that got them on juries to decide on the fate of the Leona Helmsley's shrewd enough to evade taxes. But even with those legal safeguards, Leona Helmsley was small potatoes compared to Donald Trump, who fought tooth and nail to keep the truth from the little people, one third of whom didn't care that he was a crook fleecing them.

In his 70-year career starting with his first million dollar trust fund at the age of five, Trump got the best of those best whose goal was to make money. He apprenticed in his father's business and made his bones in the high-end Manhattan world of real estate with a documented ruthless raid on depressed properties. His unbound ambition was backed by the confidence of knowing his father would back him financially regardless of merit or delivery. Ambitious success of the highest order seemed the family creed. Trump embraced the legacy with a focus on selling his persona as a winner who could circumvent the confines of the law.

Trump was supercharged for success and yet ventures failed big time. He destroyed casinos and devastated the economy of New Jersey's Atlantic City. When legitimate banking resources no longer came through, he moved on to shady developing country financing while scoring a TV gig with "The Apprentice" reality show that gave him a chance to showcase his ruthless prowess with the trademark punch line, "You're fired!"

The fantasy of such decimating power over others took hold of the disenfranchised among the US mainstream. When interest waned and ratings faded, Trump took his skills on the road and turned his winnings into a raid on the US Presidency.

With the mighty presidential powers at his disposal, Trump continued his winning trademark creed, barking "you're fired!" to every aspirant in his path. Those included needy immigrants, progressives working to better the world, aides who disagreed with him or news favorites who failed to support him strongly enough. In fact, after he took office, the Trump rage against any evidence of his failure went haywire.

In the audience-rich rallies Trump favored as arranged by his staff, Trump was king of his hateful universe. He could rouse fervor and incite chants to lock up opponents. Whether true adherents, paid attendees or constrained factory workers, the crowd sparked a contagion of ardor that spilled over into the outside world where angry white men expressed pumped-up feelings with assault weapon mass shootings aimed at happy gatherings.

Rage was contagious. So was benevolence, the feeling of well being and wanting to build on the good in life rather than destroying perceived offenders. Benevolence was an evolutionary no-brainer. Civilizations were built on successes, not undermined by attacks against them. But in dealing with the likes of Trump who had captured a large chunk of the American population with the adrenalin rush of hate speech, those on the right side of preserving the worthy country in which they lived depended on trust in their constructive convictions.

Two phrases were capable of summing up the difference between those of good will and those with malicious motives. They were the powerful "You're hired" vs. "You're fired." Both carried a heavy emotional charge on both sides of the interchange. Those who had experienced either or both knew the force of the impact delivered with the utterance. Both also knew the consequence.

Those who were fired without just cause had legal recourses to pursue. Those who fired without just cause were subject to lawsuits and institutional fall-out.

The long arm of the law was no more than the rule of law in action. Legal actions outstripped petty personal petulance in the long run. In the case of Trump exerting power from the lofty post of his US presidency, the perception that his leadership was beneficial to his base was transparently inaccurate as judged by just one small parameter, his reaction to mistakes he might have made.

To err was human, an old saying held. Instead of owning up to an error and correcting it, Trump took a Sharpie to an official map of the US Weather Service to prove he could have been right about the path of a hurricane nowhere near the site he had said it would be. Over the following week, statements were issued by agencies such as the National Oceanic and Atmospheric Administration stating that the winds from the hurricane could have affected the area Trump had mentioned. Numerous investigations disclosed White House pressure behind the issuance of those statements. An investigation by the House of Representatives has been ongoing since the 2019 incident involving the path of Hurricane Dorian.

Taxpayers footed the bill for the years-long investigations into the lengths to which the Trump administration went to bolster an image Trump wanted to have preserved and promoted. But the lengths to which those measures needed to be taken were proof enough that the Trump behind the façade was not just a manipulator but a born loser.

When caught in a lie about a phone call from China that was never made, Trump said his claim about the call was a negotiating tactic to calm a jittery stock market. Even aside from the fact that the market had been set on edge by a Trump trade war, the entire packet of machinations went above the heads of most Americans and maybe even impressed the Trump base. But sooner or later the truth was bound to dawn.

Mistakes were hard to admit. Trump used the entire American intelligence apparatus to hide a trivial off the cuff utterance. But if questioned, it was doubtful that Trump would claim that the ruse was a negotiating tactic aimed at keeping the base devoted to him. That would undoubtedly prove to be the straw that broke the camel's back. He would be admitting to the little people that he had played them for suckers.

While Trump was unlikely to make such an admission, it was possible that he would slip up the way that Leona Helmsley had. One day when he no longer had America's resources to cover his mistakes, he just could tell a jury he took to be his peers that he considered the little people who supported him to be pathetic patsies for paying the taxes that were beneath him to honor.

The Deadly American

The Ugly American was a 1958 book by Burdick and Lederer that talked about shortcomings of American diplomacy in South East Asia. The book led John F. Kennedy to establish the Peace Corps so that Americans would get better acquainted with other countries of the world.

If Donald Trump ever read that book, he would call it fake news about the world. His answer to global problems in his campaign to Make America Great Again was to build a Wall on the UN southern border, separate migrant families to deter others from coming, and ban undesirable Muslims from even visiting. The plan sounded good to a third of Americans but the other two-thirds who believed that the Constitution formed the basis for the best ever form of democracy, the Trump platform was deadly.

Donald Trump was an aberration of American ideals gone wrong. He hijacked the land of opportunity to milk it for all he could get out of it. He was a six-time serial failure in business who had spread his holdings into emerging depressed countries overseas. He shot to national fame with a TV reality show in which he played the part of the successful business tycoon he had never been, with a "You're fired!" kiss-off to those who emulated him. One in the political arena, he redoubled the strategy of profiting from tapping into the ugly side of human nature. Once in the Oval Office, he set about capitalizing on all he'd learned by making use of his immense presidential powers.

Trump began his presidential tenure by subverting Constitutional limits on personally profiting from the opportunities open to him by virtue of holding the office he had been awarded. Then he jumbled the institutions that had been built over 250 years by defunding, cutting staff and replacing experienced civil servants with allies appointed to Acting positions so as to keep them in check with uncertainty about their futures. Finally, he managed to engineer a compromise of the two governmental branches that were meant to act as a check on his executive powers. In other words under Trump, the US government became hamstrung.

About a third of Americans liked the Trump approach to governing. They found his style refreshing. But as his tenure progressed, disturbing elements became increasingly apparent to the other two-thirds.

Trump supporters predominated in the sparsely populated states that had an electoral college advantage due to a Constitution formula devised in the 1770's when the population distribution of America was far different from that in the 21st century. Trump rallies were held in those locations largely off the main track and they were aimed at a crowd unaccustomed to attention. Trump won the support of that crowd with promises of relief that never came to pass, but hope was enough of an offering to those who needed a reason the believe. Trump gave them that gift and with that, he secured support with those in Washington who represented them.

The Trump routine of rousing the base to goad their political counterparts was transparent, but less obvious was the connection between that feat and its end result, the turning of a benevolent society into a lawless gutter of corruption willingly tolerated. The Trump complex stonewalled and obstructed investigation until a global pandemic brought the Trump portrait of America into full focus within the broader global context.

The origin and course of the Covid pandemic were still to be determined, but already it was clear that world leading America could have led to a faster solution than the Trump response initiated. Focused on her personal need for a healthy economy during an election year, Trump at first downplayed the pandemic. When that response proved a mistake, he launched a volley of defensive postures that destroyed the credibility of any person, agency or organization that could have helped either nationally or internationally.

As of July 2021, over four million people had died worldwide from the Covid pandemic. While no correlation was drawn between the biological disease and its management at the public health level, it seemed clear that the Trump effect had spread contagiously.

As part of his campaign to cover up his initial mistake about Covid being a negligible threat, Trump politicized the response. Red Republican states who supported him would tough out the virus. Blue Democratic states who opposed him would hunker down in slavish adherence to rules set down by "deep state" institutions.

Similarly at the global level, countries like Brazil who were led by Trump clones became red macho countries with no use for rules. Those political standoffs were complicated by the logistics of vaccine distribution, which fed into economics and ultimately returned to personal level of the voter who chose the leader.

Dead Duck Dino Don

Anyone who ever fell in love with a "tough" catch knew how to read beneath the lines. Some under-layer in the hardened person reached out and fused a bond with the admirer that was stronger than gorilla glue. That love affair between Trump and his base left America in the position of the concerned other needing to stage an intervention in a toxic affair.

The romance between Trump and his base was off kilter from the start. The flashy Trump with a shady past was courting salt-of-the earth mid-western Americans desperately in need of a hero to save them from an unsettling new world. A non-white president Obama with progressive ideas had destroyed jobs with regulations. The social fabric was unraveling with permissiveness. Trump was the tough guy who would fix all that.

City folks throughout the country recognized the hustle that Trump pulled on the base, but the more trusting in the suburbs took a chance that the glib Trump would deliver on the promises he made. They objected to his bad behavior but that was a mere foible compared to the steely resolve he exerted on their behalf. The nexus of all those smitten with Trump kept the bond of loyalty growing, fueled by criticisms of the hero seen as attacks by an enemy intent on bringing him down.

A huge tax cut for the rich didn't both the little people. They were getting a tax cut too, just more in line with what they deserved until the benefits of the greeted cut began to trickle down. That would have happened, Trump fans explained, only Covid hit and enemies blamed him for the way he handled the crisis. And yet a sliver of doubt crept in.

The knight in shining armor, the leader of the pack, exposed his Achilles heel when a physical virus bested his superb abilities to sell, re-frame, and spin. Trump allies covered for the leader who had engendered such loyalty in his captives. They drowned out the cries of concerned others that the leader was incompetent. They stood firm as Trump made a public fool of himself in the company of experts. Even the George Floyd debacle followed by riots and a failed Trump photo-op couldn't shake an admission of disaster from Trump enablers. Concerned others saw the dawning reality. Trump and his allies were social dinosaurs in a rapidly evolving modern world.

Donald Trump had all the mighty powers of the United States at his disposal and yet he could not bring himself to admit the most basic of simple facts, that he knew nothing about the virus and didn't care to find out. He just wanted it gone. Racial issues were not his concern. He just wanted the crowds to disperse, all the better if he had to call up the military to restore order. A starter course in management would have taught that such an approach was disastrous for building a productive environment.

In a globalizing world, America had an opportunity to lead with regard to both the pandemic and the racial reckoning that was inevitable in an interconnected global society. Tough guy Trump proved nothing but impotence, in both himself and his country in the international arena. To the smitten base, however, Trump continued to be the rebel hero bucking the established order.

That view found a promotional opportunity with Trump allies who counted on Trump to influence his base to vote for them. It seemed never to have occurred to any sector of the Trump orbit that turning America into a global pariah was not the way to make America great again.

It seemed simplistic in the extreme to point out that walls would not keep out viruses and that disinformation aimed at disparaging the accredited press was doomed to a short lifespan. In a global world, the truth was bound to surface as web users consulted each other, businesses expanded and common problems like climate change affected disparate parts of the world. International cooperation to manage those challenges was vital. The Trump approach of walling off America from reality was as obsolete as the once-gigantic extinct dinosaurs who couldn't adapt to a changing climate.

Uncle Sam on Life Support

Uncle Sam was a legendary figure who first symbolized America in the War of 1812, quite an international event. It involved not only the young United States but the European countries involved in the Napoleonic Wars, who at the time had colonies in the Americas. Uncle Sam, whose initials were those of the United States, cropped up to stir patriotism at times of war.

Uncle Sam played a major role in the two World Wars of the 20th century. Those were fought primarily in Europe of behalf of preserving freedom and justice, two founding principles of America from the start. Then In one fell swoop, Trump dealt a series of death blows to those principles and rendered Uncle Sam a vegetable.

Among the first of those blows was the presidential decision to abandon the Kurds who had helped America fight radical terrorists after the 9/11 attack on America. Abandoning loyal allies was a betrayal of responsibilities that came with freedom, an act that fell far short of justice. Uncle Sam caught his breath when Republicans at long last condemned the action, but still he was undeniably bruised.

America was settled by pioneers fleeing oppression and the stroke of genius in the Constitution was the ideal of benevolence. For all its flaws, America welcomed the immigrants who reminded those already here that they did indeed live in a blessed country. It was protected by oceans on two sides, had a temperate climate and plenty of natural resources. It was a vast land that had been populated at a great cost to natives already here and slaves imported at first through the old country. While slow to actualize, the principles of freedom and justice kept the country moving toward application of those principles equally to all.

France recognized America's value to the world by presenting it with the Statue of Liberty, whose formal title was Liberty Enlightens the World. The statue was conceived in 1865, and at liberty's feel were laid a broken shackle and chain to commemorate the recent absolution of slavery in the country. The statue was built in France & shipped to the US in crates. It was not dedicated until 1886 because funding to erect the statue proved difficult in the US. Joseph Pulitzer finally started a drive and received over 120,000 donations, most in amounts less than $1.

The little people who finally put up the iconic tribute to liberty were the ones represented by Uncle Sam. They were the ones who responded to his call whenever America core values were threatened, since in the words of Martin Luther King, injustice anywhere was a threat to justice everywhere. In that spirit, America made two stabs at preventing wars like the two in the 20th century that occasioned Uncle Sam to summon the troops.

After the First World War, America was instrumental in establishing the League of Nations, an international organization that collapsed when nations broke the rules they had agreed to honor. After the Second World War, America led the drive to establish the United Nations, a diplomatic forum for countries to deal with differences, many of which dealt with the core values of freedom and justice. With the establishment of the UN, Uncle Sam could turn his attention to the American hallmark of benevolence, only to be bushwhacked just after great progress was made.

America made history by electing the western industrialized world's first non-white president. That great step toward justice was then sideswiped by a would-be dictator whose grip on power lay in malevolence. Instead of building on hard-won alliances like NATO and other regional groupings established under the UN, America's new president cut ties with allies and promoted global tyrants he blithely labeled friends. He turned back progress on global issues such as climate change and refused to accept responsibility for actions such as inhumanity to refugees fleeing countries due to climate change. In short, after four years of Trump polities, Uncle Sam was bruised, battered, defiled and finally in a coma.

Kept alive on life support while an attempted coup was mobilized in his beloved country, Uncle Sam wept as dreams conveyed the image of all those who had risked and lost lives to defend the country and its honor. He saw in a haze how proudly they walked with heads high in both home towns and overseas, a noble contrast to the suicide bombers out to destroy instead of build. Then in that same haze, he heard a nearby voice.

"Relax, Uncle Sam. We're brought in a new team of specialists. Can you hear me?"

Please Mr. Postman, Count Me Into the Vote

The 1961 hit song by the Marvellettes entitled, Please Mr. Postman, captured the ache of young love waiting for word from a far-away beloved. In pre-tech days, the postal carrier was a central focus of daily life. Despite technology, the postal carrier has maintained that pivotal position as part of the US Postal Service, an iconic US institution under fire from Trump, along with the US Census Bureau. The already complicated US Voting system was nearly decimated by the law-defying accidental president.

Renegade Trump trampled the rule of law and violated Constitutional norms. If his tenure lasted more than four years, those two staples of American culture would all but disappear. It would be like taking salt and pepper off the American table.

The U.S. Postal Service began before the country was founded. The mail and its carriers connected far-flung new arrivals as waves of immigrants spread westward into wilderness. Native Americans have continued to bear the scars of those early days, but that was how it happened back then and the Postal Service was a stabilizing element in America's fast-paced gallop to the present when America was mature enough to redress the wrongs once allowed in the past.

While not as old as the Postal Service, the Decennial Census was mandated by the Constitution. Modern Americans paid little attention to the Census but it was a nerve center of American growth. In the early days, new arrivals were mostly welcome as essential for expansion. More recently, they've been spurned, but throughout that period of growth, America's immigration policies were based on a Census count of people living within the country's borders.

Of course the Postal Service and the Census Bureau changed and adapted over time. the stage coach becoming obsolete but the mail still delivered to the country's most remote addresses. Likewise, American residents were no longer counted by US marshals in public places, but those gathering centers still played a role in getting America counted. In a way, becoming part of American statistics was as concretely satisfying as casting a vote.

An e-mail advising of a college acceptance was great, but confirmation arrived in the US mail. Credit cards and legal documents relied on mail delivery. A greeting card that arrived by mail conveyed an extra layer of thoughtfulness in the sender. Concrete reality gave substance to ephemeral speculation, the service provided by the Census Bureau.

Contrary to popular fears, newcomers to the land of immigrants were not the thugs and gang leaders who grabbed headlines with outrages. Most immigrants were still as they always had been, ordinary folks needing to relocate for economic or political reasons. They left their countries in order to prosper, and those who fit in with their new communities were those most likely to succeed. Those were the people at all stages of their residency who entered into the Census Bureau's portrait of America taken every ten years. The Census Bureau relied heavily on the Postal Service, the only reliable data source on residents with no legal documents.

Then in the 2020 Covid pandemic year, the Postal Service was tasked with taking on the additional burdens of a heavy reliance on vote-related activities carried out by mail. The system was rife for chaos.

Numerous names continued to be ascribed to the form of government in the US. Most commonly it has been described as a federal republic. Democratic was generally included in the description, along with representative since officials were elected by the people. The upshot was a central government presided over 50 sovereign states. Elections at the federal level were conducted indirectly through an electoral college system administered by the states with each state allowed to conduct state and local elections in their own way. With that stage set, enter Trump.

In June 2020, halfway through the Covid Census year, a new Postmaster General was appointed with a 10-year plan to streamline the Postal Service. He cut back on overtime hours, prohibited late deliveries and removed high-speed sorting machines. Those measures were forced to be reversed by October, but the damage done in the interim was incalculable. It laid the groundwork for Trump to promote voter fraud claims against opponent Joe Biden in the presidential election. It also opened the way for skewing Census data for future elections.

A most important role of Census data was in the apportionment of seats in the US House of Representatives. Representation was based on the number of persons living in a district regardless of citizenship status. In 2019, Trump started a drive to include a citizenship question on the Census, a step that was struck down by the Supreme Court in July 2020. Trump then issued a Presidential Memo instructing the Census Bureau to omit counting undocumented residents. Once in Office, Biden reversed the directive but states had to wait for revised Census data before they could proceed to redistricting based on a 2020 portrait of America.

Trump attained the US presidency and the support of his base by vowing to "drain the swamp" of America's institutions. He fanned animosity by castigating the "deep state" that was nothing more than the sturdy America constructed over a period of more than 200 years. The result was a framework of democracy that was the envy of the world. Trump's goal seemed clear. He seemed undoubtedly out to destroy as much of America as possible within the time allotted him.

As a hothouse product serviced by staff, Trump had probably never opened a letter himself and his Census form had been completed without his awareness. His skill was to convince a large swathe of Americans that he cared about their concerns. According to the Brookings Institute, the number of immigrants who were undocumented in 2019 America was about 12 million. Given the raids conducted by Immigration and Customs Enforcement agents under Trump, an accurate count of those folks was questionable.

Throughout its history, immigrants had refreshed America and kept in check a natural tendency of prosperous countries toward self-complacency. Immigrants, regardless of citizenship status, kept America in touch with iconic institutional basics such as the Postal Service that kept track of them, the Census that included them in the country's portrait, and the voting system to which they aspired once they were citizens.

Speak Up, Dems, the Ruskies R Here

Birds of a feather flocked together, most Americans knew with no idea that a man named William Turner first used the phrase in a 1545 written work. In the first two decades of the 21st century, the phrase still applied to America's flighty president Trump whose covey of friends stayed stable for no longer than a photo op. His penchant for dictators alarmed many freedom-loving Americans, but his naivete with regard to Russia's Vladimir Putin was striking because it was so enduring.

Putin was a record for plans to dominate the world as in reality it never had. It had a large territory and a population to match, but its ambitions fell short of its achievements. Its monarchal history was overturned by a 1917 revolution that the country across a violent path that enabled it to dominate neighbors and half of Europe in a Communist experiment that flopped after 40 years but not before it laid waste to countless lives and the natural resources of others. That resume appeared to captivate Trump.

A massive failure like that of Soviet Communism would have daunted some but Russia recouped by restructuring into an oligarchy. The transition was a natural expansion. The aim of both systems was the same. That was to plunder the natural resources of other nations because Russia had none.

Whether ignorant of history or simply not caring about anything beyond his current moment in the media spotlight, Trump wooed Putin. He invited his representatives into the Oval Office without Security protocols in place and he held unofficial meeting with Putin at the sidelines of international affairs. Again, US Security measures were suspended. Russia monitored the interaction and directed its release to global media.

Like China, Russia was known by accredited global press to sanitize events in accordance with the desired projected image. China doctored details of its 1989 Tienanman Massacre, the same year that the Iron Curtain fell away from Eastern Europe. Likewise, years of denial by Russia followed the 1986 Chernobyl nuclear disaster with a full accounting never forthcoming. Those manipulations of events presented to the public seemed fine with Trump. For all the sensationalism of its own press, America was accustomed to better reporting than that and its Constitutionally established free press was determined to do its job as the fourth estate, the independent part of society that kept a check on the government's three official branches.

Under the Trump administration of the Executive branch, the press was hobbled but still able to work through laws such as the freedom of information act. It also uncovered stories like the "Floating Chernobyl" power plants Russia was launching its power and electricity source. The first of those was stationed off Alaska and while Russia assured the world that the reactor was safe, its record of truth telling was not reassuring.

America had no jurisdiction over the actions of other sovereign states, but it did have the right to bring attention to misdeeds. While the United Nations forum for discourse was largely toothless until reform, it could provide a record of transgressions. Similarly, America could call out Russian misdeeds through its press but that would not happen under a president who approved and maybe even abetted underhanded activities.

Laws in America focused on human rights. Those were low priorities in the laws of both China and Russia, two countries whose leaders believed in the use of force to maintain social order. Trump seemed to find affinity with those leaders but a misfired trade deal plus a pandemic soured him on China. His short lived bromance with Kim Jung Un of South Korea seemed to have vanished without a trace and other despots in places like the Philippines and Colombia seemed too insignificant to merit his attention. Only Russia with its KGB-trained leader had the ability to hold Trump captive, possibly for no greater gain than the personal goal of building a Trump Tower in Moscow.

Throughout the Trump presidency, Putin seemed to be the big game hunter who conned the American master con. As the presidency unfolded, it seemed he had succeeded beyond his wildest expectations when he installed Trump, who masterfully sold the scheme to his gullible base and with that hooked the country's power-brokers. To Putin, the Trump presidency would appear to be a set of Russian nested dolls. When the big outer doll was in hand, the others became available with a simple twist.

A third of America made up the smallest nested doll behind Trump and they were at the heart of his plan for Russia to dominate the world. In the freedom of America, Trump's lawlessness was a bold statement to his base. It seemed to signify an affirmation that the impossible was attainable, that walls could keep away outsiders and that cruelty could vanquish contenders for power. But only, Putin knew, if America could be kept distracted from issues that mattered in a democracy.

America was fond of conducting public opinion polls. Pew and Brookings invested a fortune to find out how Americans felt about candidates and the economy. Those polls omitted the most basic question to be asked.

How would respondents feel if prison were the consequence for backing a candidate not already in the White House? For Democrats, the answer would cut through a lot of misinformation. It would identify those who believed in a government by the people and separate them from those who liked the guy in the White House.

Dems and the Status Quo

Stated simplistically, Democrats pursued social justice while Republicans sought to preserve personal rights. That distinction took a dramatic turn when the law-defying Donald Trump began grabbing all he could from both sides with the great powers of the American presidency at his disposal.

As Trump with his Republican enablers trampled Constitutional norms and values, Democrats splintered over which values were the most urgent to salvage. Racial justice, rule of law, press freedom and voter rights were all under fire, exacerbated by a politicized Covid pandemic response. Caught in its daily stew of Trump outrage, America was unable to step back for a view of its social issues in context of a global hierarchy of values.

Freedom was an American hallmark, in part because of its Constitution-based stability. The result of that freedom was a social order of whole cloth, like a cake that in theory was available for all to enjoy. Due to the combination of historical precedent and human nature, the American ideal of equality was skewed from the beginning. Big chunks of the cake went to well-placed go-getters while the little people were tasked with serving the prosperous in exchange for cake crumbs. Under Trump, the big guys got all the cake they wanted in any way that suited them while the little guys fought each other for crumbs because a third of them were in love with the Old West romance of the renegade hero.

Jesse James became such a legendary hero. Along with his brother, Frank. he led a gang of robbers for 16 years throughout the Midwest. He was killed by one of his own men as the law closed in, betrayed in exchange for amnesty and hope of a reward. While seen as an economic lawless figure of the time, he and his gang were offshoots of the defeated Confederacy after of the civil war. They were part of the Wild West that was tamed through the law, a phenomenon that occurs routinely in the global world that remains in conflict with the romance of crime as a way of life.

Democrats intent on advancing the social good had yet to address the global phenomenon that some in every society preferred lawlessness to order. That of course included conflict profiteers who benefitted from the arms industry on all sides. It included Robin Hoods who committed crimes for a greater good and it included the Bonnie and Clydes who enjoyed wreaking havoc. Few in any of those categories ended with a happy ending, but they played a significant role in both global and American social life.

Under Trump, Washington became the new American wild west of lawlessness. Once the pandemic hit and Trump politicized its management, the reengage fever spread throughout the country like the Covid virus itself. And throughout all that, it was impossible to decipher the motivation for the social chaos.

Trump and his Republican enablers were obviously interested in keeping and monopolizing power by any means. The base was hooked on Trump for any number of reasons. Some he duped with bilking techniques perfected over a lifetime, the identification of vulnerabilities and needs, persuasion of a cure, and an ongoing reminder of his own seeming success. But a fair number of the Trump base must have been attracted by the sheer outrage with which he tortured the media and the Democrats of the country.

Hybristophilia was a term derived from two Greek terms, hybris also known as hubris, and philia, to love. While it was difficult to imagine midwesterm farmers sexually attracted to Trump, their ardour could arguable be the equivalent of such a deep passion. The possibility applied even more aptly groups like the Proud Boys and conspiracy theorists like QAnon. Under Trump, America and the world came to see just how perverse everyday people could be. But also clear was the fact that such people did not belong in leadership positions of any country.

A quick glance around the world's near-200 countries gave a glimpse into a basic principle that the complexity of America seemed to have glossed over since its early Wild West days. The difference between good guys and bad was clear. Certainly, no good guy of any historical period would brag that he could shoot somebody on Fifth Avenue just to showcase his prowess. Likewise, no good guy would ride into town just to separate residents and set neighbors upon each. Bad guys did that, the way that Trump did.

Every country in the world had its own particular challenges in part because of history. Even America had that challenge despite its short history. The practice of slavery introduced at its birth blended with the barbarism inflicted on America's native people. In its 250-year history, America had made great strides in addressing the racial inequity inherent in those practices condemned by the Constitution that all people were created equal. In a global world, America had much to offer the world in terms of best practices and lessons learned about advancing racial equity on a global level.

First, however, America needed a new sheriff in Washington town. After running its experiment with a renegade leader like Trump, America the adventurous was ready to resume its leadership role in the global status

Kamala's Busing Scars

Kamala Harris floored Joe Biden in the first Democratic debate leading up to the 2020 presidential election. In that debate, Harris brought up an image of herself as a little girl being bused to school as a racial integration measure. She also characterized as hurtful the Biden ability to work with segregationists in order to get equal rights legislation passed.

Caught off guard on an important national stage, Biden defended himself by saying his record had been mischaracterized. The exchange, however, brought into question the kind of candidate who could defeat the evident racist presiding even then in the White House.

Harris was no shrinking violet and she was clearly no victim. No doubt she worked hard but she also had an admirable record of achievement. She served as San Francisco District Attorney and Attorney General of California before she was elected to the Senate in the same year that Trump become US president. Surely in that long career she had learned to sublimate personal feelings into the professional conduct that her offices required.

There was no way to tell whether Harris really was hurt by Biden working with those who held objectionable views or if the charges were rhetorical postures to score debating points. Either way, the tactic seemed a disastrous flip side to the racism ripping apart the country under Trump.

In the land of immigrants, historical scars were nearly a national ID badge. They came in all forms. Some bore the remnants of early starvation, others of tyrannical oppression. Few so marked ever entirely erased the effect of early experience and in the melting pot where such early misery was redeemed, American blacks had a special right to a reckoning.

It was America itself that had inflicted the wounds on African-Americans who not only endured 200 years of slavery but another 150 years of horrendous oppression. The Emancipation Proclamation put a legal end to slavery and still a Civil War was fought over the decision. Hard as it was to believe in the 21st century, scars of that bitter battle over the basic principle of equality among all people still continued. They were picked open by racists intent on reopening a definitely debunked fabrication.

America inherited the slave trade from early forebears. By extension in the 21st century, the country had a responsibility to eradicate the practice on a global scale if its own African-Americans were to be truly equal with other races, most notably the predominating whites. The task was made easier for America by the fact that racial distinctions were breaking down along with other personal demarcations such as gender.

Regardless of progress made, achieving equality of all people would continue to take time due to the social intransigents unable or unwilling to accept change. Mental images of social ideals presided with those folks and no variation sufficed. Same sex couples would seem unnatural, the disabled would be lacking, power was never secure unless in white male hands. Bringing about change in those attitudes could not be coerced, though legislation helped propel the need to adapt. But real change in those attitudes came from the benefits demonstrated through interaction.

Some saw social challenges as burdens. Others saw them as opportunities for growth and development. To both groups, the urgency was for people to work together to resolve problems so as to defeat those who opposed resolution.

In the 21st century, traditional definitions were rapidly breaking down. Climate change, for example, made climate refugees of people in their own countries. White supremacist ideology was toppled by successful unions between high profile mixed race couples, those strong enough and connected enough to demonstrate the fault lines in racist theories.

With regard to race, advances were made most rapidly when blacks gained equality to the point where they could let go of grudges and whites were able to stop being defensive about history. America as the land of diversity worked best when groups came together to unseat the bullies terrorizing the country, thus welcoming new immigrants in an orderly fashion to revitalize a blessed country that without them could become complacent.

In Praise of Age and Biden

Youth was the beautiful springtime of life, full of eager energy. Age in America was treated as a handicap, full of aches and in constant need of help. Even though George H.W. Bush went skydiving for his 90th birthday and Jimmy Carter at age 95 went back to building houses for Habitat after a fall. reality was slower to sink into American cultural psych than the ingrained fear of decline and debilitation.

On the Democratic primary trail, Joe Biden was scrutinized for every physical evidence of age. He was described as slow and stiff. If he stopped to find the right word as he spoke, speculation arose about memory loss and perhaps even the onset of an old-ager affliction. His value as an experienced public servant with a proven track record of trustworthiness received scant notice until Jim Clyburn of South Carolina endorsed him. Then when he won the Democratic party's nomination for president, he became the beacon for recovery after the four-year assault on American democracy suffered under the sitting president still in office after an impeachment that failed to get him convicted because of politics.

In 2020, America was a crossroads with democracy. Democrats were intent on keeping the country democratic in line with the ideas set out in the Constitution. Under Trump, Republicans seemed intent on changing democracy into an autocracy of rule by the elite or even a downright autocracy as ruled by one powerful person. Opinion polls showed democracy winning by a margin of three to one, but that one part rooting for an auto-plutocracy was loud. ugly and dangerous.

A huge slate of 20 Democratic presidential hopefuls entered into the primary campaign. That was three more than the Republicans who had run for president in 2016 to replace progressive Barack Obama, the western industrialized world's first non-white head of state. In 2020, Democrats faced the task of bringing America back into balance after the enormous backlash to Obama

The 20 Democratic candidates offered a huge array of priorities to they would address during the next four years. Many stressed the need for health care reform. Others emphasized immigration, environmental protection, economic growth, criminal justice reform and advancement of racial equity. There was little mention of the 800-lb gorilla in the room that would quash all hopes for advancement if the Democrats lost the election. Perhaps they avoided the issue because his approach to winning electoral votes were so alien to American life.

Trump won the loyalty of the Republican party by ensnaring a third of the US population in a scheme that would one day require a brand new legal definition. Throughout history, American politics has been a free-for-all protected from regulation by the Constitutional guarantee of free speech. As Trump blasted past precedents with lies, vilifications and inciteful rhetoric, fans cheered and opponents were stumped.

Circus maven P.T Barnum reputedly said back in the mid-1800's that there was a sucker born every minute. Based on that principle, he made his mark by getting the public to pay for seeing phony freaks and oddities Trump supporters did the same. They paid with the energy of their attention for the chance to see an American public official spill outrages on a public stage built just for them.

As the primary campaign season went on, the focus on secondary issues in the election took a toll. Instead of attacking Trump, candidates attacked each other. Biden came under attack for positions he had taken years before when the current political climate was just developing. By the sixth debate, viewership was at an all-time low. Then just as all hope seemed lost for Biden, Clyburn endorsed him and the rest became history. Two elders of the Democratic party pooled their experience and wisdom to take on skilled conman Trump.

Wisdom was the art of knowing what to overlook, said William James, brother of famed Henry, back in the 1860's. The advice proved out as other Democratic candidates threw their support to Biden in wake of the Clyburn endorsement to give Biden the impetus to charge forward as Trump blustered with rage.

Like the confident little piggy of folk tale whose house was built of stone, Biden went about with presidential actions while big bad wolf Trump huffed and puffed at his door. When racial incidents broke out, Biden was on site to console and reassure those on all sides of the issue. From his lofty White House post, Trump cast blame on the nebulous Antifa group that Trump had branded to cover those opposed to his authoritarianism.

Experience built the foundation for character at any stage of a life. Trump recognized that fact when he took an impeachable action to keep Biden from becoming the challenger to his incumbency. Then just as he had feared, the contrast between him and Biden during the presidential campaign itself showed up the illegitimacy of a man like him to be president of the paradigm for global democracy.

Trump repeatedly mocked Biden for wearing masks and abiding by CDC guidelines for control of the Covid pandemic. In his turn, Trump insisted that "super spreader" rallies be arranged for him to keep his base ginned up for the upcoming election. A lifetime of public service had taught Biden to respect the guideposts of civilization. A lifetime of hoodwinking had taught Trump to stymie legal procedures.

After the notable Republican Herman Cain died of Covid contracted shortly after he attended a Trump rally in Oklahoma, the Trump campaign took steps to safeguard future rallies. They had Trump fans sign a waiver of liability before they could see their hero.

Do Your Homework, Dems

During the 2020 Democratic presidential primary, the country was reeling from a pandemic so mishandled by the country's leader in Washington that states were left to cope on their own. That leader was also terrorizing the country with Immigration raids and holding rowdy rallies to warn of election fraud while he knee-capped the Postal Service pivotal to the vote by mail effort states implemented to counter Covid infection fears. And yet during primary debates, all the courage that Democratic presidential hopefuls mustered was to attack each other as they jockeyed for the position of who could do better.

Among the first to be knocked out of the running was Michael Bloomberg, the billionaire former New York City mayor who was attacked for his record on workplace gender discrimination based on non-disclosure agreements. No allegations of misconduct were claimed and Bloomberg had a sterling Democratic agenda. He supported both environmental and gun controls. He had plans for urban development and yet despite record spending of his own money on the campaign, he performed poorly in the primaries largely became of his performance under attack from fellow Democrat Elizath Warren.

Similarly, front runner former vice-president Joe Biden was the most frequent target of attack. Kamala Harris floored him with a rhetorical blow regarding race. Several candidates piled on Biden for Obama's record on deportations. Under attack, Biden could do no better than to claim the policy was Obama's and not his.

In reality, Obama did deport more illegal immigrants than either Clinton or Bush, and Trump deported fewer than Obama. But that was because Obama's immigration policy and his success with deportations was due to a successful policy rather than the Trump slap dash policy to just deport everybody. That was an important point that Democrats failed to drive home for voters.

According to a 2019 Washington Post report, Obama deported 1.19 million during his first three years as compared to less than the 800,000 deported by Trump during that same time period. According to sources cited in The Hill, the decreased levels of deportations were due to a number of factors. The illegal immigrants under Trump were families seeking asylum from the Northern Triangle Countries of Guatemala, El Salvador and Honduras. Protected status made those people harder to deport. But according to the Southern Poverty Law Center, the big difference between deportations under Obama and Trump were the matter of a targeted policy.

Obama's deportation strategy centered on clearing out illegals who had a criminal record. That established priorities and streamlined the legal process of removing undesirables. Trump's indiscriminate war on immigrants clogged the legal system, particularly when long-standing members of communities were snatched by Immigration and Custom Enforcement agents in the midst of routine activities. The failure to highlights such significant differences was a serious handicap to winning the White House back from Trump, just one of many blunders in the 2020 Democratic primary campaign to unseat an undemocratic president.

Biden's path to the Democratic nomination as the candidate who could defeat Trump rested on the endorsement of South Carolina's Jim Clyburn in March of 2020. Clyburn's full-throated support for Obama virtually guaranteed that he could rely on the black vote. More importantly, it affirmed Biden as a decent, honorable man who could be trusted in a clear contrast to Trump.

The difference between the two men became obvious during the 2020 campaign year once they were official rivals. Trump aggressed on Biden and Biden stood firm. Ang while the strategy seemed successful for Biden as indicated by opinion polls, the country seemed gripped by unease as signalled by record voter turnout on both sides. The fact that two such disparate candidates could elicit an equal amount of enthusiasm on the part of Americans suggested some defect in the network between messaging, perception, content and values brought to American political communication.

"I hear things. I don't know if it's true but many people say," Trump would say and nobody called him out on the slander he attached to a politician not to his liking. "Lock her up," he led the chant throughout his presidency with no recrimination for the baseless lie with which he smeared a former opponent who was no longer even on the scene.

A dishonorable man had snuck into the Oval Office and had ensnared powerful Republican enablers dependent for political power on voters enamored of Trump's Constitutional transgressions. To counter such atrocities, Democrats could not afford to abide by former First Lady' Michelle Obama's exhortation that "when they go low, we go high." Noble as the semiment was, it hadn't worked in 2016 when she said it and conditions had only gotten worse as a result.

In 2020, there was no need for Democrats to sink into the gutter to unseat Trump. But if the "land of the free and home of the brave" were to survive, Democrats would need more of the bravery needed to research and fire back at the master slinger of fabrications.

2020 Belongs to Biden

As the 2020 presidential election neared, it was hard for non-Trumpers to understand how anyone could vote for him. From the snippets of tape the media aired from the super spreader rallies, the Trump shtick was way past tired. The base still showed but dampened enthusiasm suggested that paid attendees outnumbered true fans. Trump's ominous portents about voter fraud, however, seemed to be based on early suspicions long forgotten that he himself had suspected that his presidency was seen as illegitimate.

According to Politico, Trump recounted his glorious surprise win in 2016 at a "thank you" rally in Wisconsin. Numerous accredited sources reported that Melania Trump cried tears of despair when Trump won the presidency in 2016. Two years later in a book, she denied those reports but the overall scenario of the Trump family response to the outcome of the 2016 election was the same as that in the country and the world. That was disbelief.

Robert Mueller was a distinguished legal luminary who was appointed special counsel to oversee an investigation into Russian interference with the 2016 US election. The two-year investigation uncovered a web of links between Russia and the Trump campaign. Overall, 199 criminal charges were filed, 37 indictments were handed down and five prison sentences were issued. However, a Justice Department memo advised that sitting presidents were not to be indicted. Investigation of Trump were severely constricted. While history would undoubtedly uncover the truth eventually, the lesson for America in the wake of Trump was the need to upgrade its slow-motion procedures in pursuit of justice.

In another situation, Trump attempted to shake down the president of Ukraine. He offered to release aid funds already appropriated by Congress in exchange for dirt on Joe Biden, his newly nominated rival in the 2020 election. The attempted crime was brought to light by a whistleblower and impeachment followed in the House of Representatives. Trump was charged with abuse of power and obstruction of Congress. Witnesses gave compelling testimony but key first-hand witnesses could not be heard because of legal actions taken by the Trump administration. The result was a vote of not guilty in the Trump enabling Senate.

"Witch hunt" was the term Trump applied to every legal investigations into his questionable affairs. The term became common usage when applied to him and that practice only became truly dangerous when he began his voter fraud campaign in April 2020, just as Covid began its rampage.

According to the BBC, Trump tweeted 70 times about voter fraud between April and election day. It became a theme at his rallies and turned into "stop the steal" on election night when it appeared he was losing the election. In between, his voter fraud claims on social media became entwined with conspiracy theories tying Covid restrictions into a Democratic plot to unseat Trump as well as more sinister claims about Democratic debauchery. Since surveillance of social media sites was legally restricted, the chatter remained nonspecific rumor even as Biden largely ignored it and simply went around acting presidential, which was a perfect opening for Trump.

In the US, voting procedures varied widely from state to state and the pandemic had called on states to institute last minute changes to accommodate those susceptible to the Covid virus. A midyear change in leadership of the Postal Service caused delays in the complex process of requesting and submitting ballots by mail. As president, Trump made no effort to ease concerns or to facilitate the process. Rather, he stirred the pot of mistrust to stoke fervor among the base for increased voter turnout.

During the Democratic primary campaign, Joe Biden was attacked for his age and for positions he had taken during the times that had led to the freedoms younger candidates knew as a birthright.

That experience enabled him to absorb onslaughts, particularly the derision that Trump unleashed on him. When it came to the upcoming election, he simply paid attention to voters and nominated Kamal Harris to be his vice president.

His nomination of Harris surprised many. She had dealt him a blow in the first primary debate but as a woman of color, her time had come to represent her strongly democratic voter group in the ranks of higher office. She was also highly qualified, and whether her prosecutorial background was part of the equation remained a mystery in regard to the many offenses for which Trump could be prosecuted once out of office.

Biden's ability to forego grudges that to others would seem warranted was just one aspect of the gravitas he offered the country in the time of Trump when democracy was hanging in the balance. Judging by Trump's behaviour and social media chatter during the presidential campaign, Biden's nerves of steel would be called into play before America was free of the tyrannical circus Trump had made of the country.

The choice before America in the 2020 election was made clear during the debates between the two candidates. Trump blustered, fumbled and threw out occasional zingers to wild applause. Biden stood still, stared down and admonished Trump who seemed to implode on his own venom.

In his fifty years of public service, Biden had never met the likes of Trump within his own circle. But given a boost, he adapted quickly. That skill would come in handy as he cleaned house after the Trump tornado laid waste to democracy and the rule of law.

In short, Trump gave America a taste of the bully bravado that was loud and intended to inspire the fear that sent mortals scurrying to find comfort from the source. The wisdom to tame the bully was quiet and inspired the trust that led to teamwork in resolving challenges. At a crossroads about its Constitutional gravitas, America would cast its vote on election day 2020.

America to Trump, You're FIRED

In 2016, America took a chance on the business renegade Trump. He sold himself as a fighter for the forgotten working class and as a successful man of action who got things done. Three years of obvious self-service, lawlessness, catering to cronies, gas-lighting and defiance of decency failed to cool the Trump fever of the base. Even after a global pandemic exposed his thin facade, stalwarts maintained that Trump was doing a good job and would restore the great economy the pandemic had stolen from him.

More than 200,000 Americans dead from mismanagement of the Covid pandemic couldn't offer an opinion on Trump's performance, but those without Trump fairy dust in their eyes admitted to recognizing chaos when they lived it. By election 2020, Covid under Trump felt like a rudderless ship captained by a mad Ahab in pursuit of an imaginary Moby Dick.

The Trump agenda was clear from the start of his presidency. His goal was to erase all traces of the historic progress America had made with the election of the western industrialized world's first non-white leader. For three years Trump followed the pale male power playbook as liberated by him beyond legal limits. He sailed past impeachment and in wake of that victory, he proceeded to exert the full force of his office to mold the country to his liking. The pandemic derailed the economic plan he expected would sail him into re-election.

Faced with a crisis beyond his control on every level of survival, Trump began to flail. He was like a student pilot caught in a tailspin with no co-pilot and no idea where the autopilot control panel was hidden.

Substance, detail and specifics were negligible in the Trump presidential resume. Alongside experts in their fields, the Trump input was feeble when not downright dangerous to the susceptible.

Bravado and gasconaded either irritated or amused in the theater or even in daily life for a while. But in daily real life with the world's greatest nation tanking because of its leader, the country was called upon to trust the common sense usually attributed to its Midwestern segment.

In his campaign to erase all traces of Obama, Trump rolled back regulations aimed at curbing practices that damaged the global environment. Whether or not the state of the environment had anything to do with the emergence of the Covid pandemic, it became clear that that the pandemic was propelled by the chaos that swept the country when leadership at the top delegated responsibility for management to the 50 individual states. Then to make matters worse as the pandemic galloped and killed, Trump began to politicize mitigating measures, no doubt to energize his base for the upcoming election.

To those not smitten with Trump fever, those actions were intended to camouflage and deflect from the fact that Trump was in over his head with the presidency. Clearly, he was out of his element when flanked by expert professionals, regardless of the feckless who drank bleach at his succession as a way to counter the virus. At a loss and intent on restoring the economy amid haphazard state and local lock-down strategies, Trump rolled out an economic relief package that produced more anxiety than comfort.

The Coronavirus Aid, Relief and Economic Security Act was a $2.6 trillion programme to stimulate the flagging economy. It included direct payments to taxpayers, unemployment benefits beyond those provided by states and a Payment Protection Programme aimed at keeping small businesses afloat during the pandemic. Bureaucratic snags at every turn brought legitimate complaints from frustrated Americans, especially small business owners ill-equipped to file the necessary paperwork while "small" businesses like the Los Angeles Lakers swept up millions.

The Covid pandemic was a singular phenomenon. It most likely began in China, where a government policy of controlled information kept the truth of the potential danger out of global awareness until an interactive world allowed the disease to spread like wildfire. Perhaps because of its global leadership position under Trump, the western industrialized world with the most access to vaccines fell into the trap of politicizing mitigation measures. That possibility was a sobering thought for the 21st century world riding high on technological marvels it had created.

Had America been on a better footing with global allies, sharing lessons learned from best practices might have led to quicker solutions for economic and public health challenges. That matter, however, remained in the balance as election day 2020 neared.

Then after the confusing Covid improvisations were deciphered and cleared through vote-by-mail, and early voting arrangements, Americans stood in lines for up to twelve hours to cast a vote for the candidate of their choice. Relief among many was palpable. Despite unrelenting assaults, American institutions had proven sturdy enough for democratic principles to prevail. On that note, America borrowed a page from the Trump playbook.

Trump relished his make-believe role as the powerful boss who could make or break those vying for his approval. Four years after he was given that opportunity to prove himself, America on November 3, 2020 shouted with one voice, **YOU'RE FIRED!**

The Chucky Trump Horror Show

The 2020 US election was highly unusual due to the Covid pandemic. The vote itself was held on November 3. By them, votes had been heavily cast through mail-in and early voting. Rules about counting those votes varied from state to state. As a result, major news networks did not project Joe Biden and Kamala Harris as the projected winners until November 7. By then, Trump's "stop the steal" campaign was in full gallop after its election night start.

The campaign was led by Trump on Twitter and it resonated wildly on social media, the fervor fanned by lawsuits demanding recounts in battleground states where Biden had won. In sum, the Trump team filed a total o f63 lawsuits in five states. All were either withdrawn or dismissed by the counts. Nevertheless, in swing states led by Republican governors or state legislatures, canvasses and recounts were held for up to three times. In Arizona. Republicans commissioned the unofficial Cyber Ninja group to conduct a recount that tainted the ballots as well as the voting machines. All that took place because Trump refused to accept defeat.

Christopher Krebs was the head of cyber security in the Department of Homeland Security. He refused to declare that any voter fraud had occurred and said the 2020 election was the most secure ever due to safeguards instituted after suspected irregularities in the 2016 election. Krebs was fired and replaced by a Trump loyalist, followed by 12 other top administration officials in the next two weeks. On January 14. state electoral college met and certified the votes in their states to verify that Biden had won the electoral college vote by a margin of 306 to Trump's 242. Trump still refused to concede and when Attorney General Bill Barr announced that he had investigated and found no evidence of vote fraud, his resignation was announced on Twitter by Trump.

Despite all the verifications of a fair election and obvious machinations to cast doubt on the process, 70% of Republicans continued to believe that Trump won the election. The conviction was based on potentialities. Mail-in votes could have been manipulated. Early vote ballots could have been discarded. In that realm of baseless possibilities, emotion ruled like an untethered wild horse with the social media as its playground.

Back in the days of classic theatre, dramas were works of fiction with characters and plot lines that were sensational and yet so skillfully drawn that the story caught the imagination and swept a person beyond reality into a "willing suspension of disbelief." The result was a catharsis, a purging of antisocial inclinations. Othello in Shakespeare, for example, murdered his wife Desdemona so that ordinary citizens wouldn't have to. By the 21st century, however, the boundary between reality and art was all but erased.

The wondrous tool of technology created a twilight experience of reality in which fact and fiction were inseparable and interchangeable. The Loch Ness monster could now be photoshopped and only the most dedicated could ascertain whether the picture was real or fake. Trump stepped into that new frontier and took it by storm to upend American democracy by turning its precepts into a horror show.

Horror was a speculative fiction genre intended to frighten, scare or disgust. Trump fueled his presidential campaign and the presidency itself by warning Americans of marauding immigrants and the decrepid cities they inhabited. A third of the American population was willing to suspend the disbelief that an amoral person could lead a successful society. Once hooked into the narrative, the Trump base bought into the "make America great again" message that greatness would come from walling America off from the rest of the world.

The MAGA slogan was catchy and caught the imagination. Most important, it was easy and required no thinking about an increasingly complex world. It was general enough to let imagination fill in the blank with whatever the heart's desire. The rhetoric that went with it was specific enough to engender rage against targets like opponent Hillary Clinton.

Once caught in the dramatic stream, the Trump base held on ever tighter as resistance mounted. To them, he was exciting, different, breaking new ground, facing down enemies and using amazing tools to vanquish those unable to see his greatness. In fact, the Trump presidential playbook could well have come from Chucky, the fictional horror character who was a serial killer returned to life in the form of a doll to take revenge on the law-enforcement officer who stopped him.

Chucky first appeared in the 1988 Child's Play, where he wreaked havoc on a family and ended on a trash heap. He came back in sequels and remakes, kept alive in between with Chucky caps, mugs and other spin offs. The Cult of Chucky was released in 2017, the first year of Trump's presidency. In 2019, the original Child's Play was re-released with Chucky reincarnated as Buddi. A Chucky TV series was planned for 2020, the year of the presidential election. It was delayed due to licensing complications.

Obviously, the horror genre was a terrific draw in capturing and holding interest in the safe confines of screen or page. In the unpredictable hazards of real life, horror was an uncontrollable nightmare full of chaos. In the case of Chucky Trump, the result was an America afflicted with social schizophrenia.

Trump in the social media age made America a nation with a split personality. The third of the population hooked on Trump believed that legitimate news was "fake" and that unchecked retweeted lies carried the authority of the US Presidential seal. That belief was reinforced by the formal confusion created by Trump issuing statements unfiltered by official channels of verification prior to being made public. That part of America was acting on the right side of the brain, the creative and emotional side that wanted to believe Trump was delivering on promises when he clearly wasn't, Perhaps the perception was mixed with the horror elements of fear or disgust at how gleefully the American way of life was being destroyed.

Not so fast, the other two-thirds of America said to the Chucky Trump Horror Show audience. They were the ones using the left side of the brain, the logical that did not suspend its disbelief when Trump in reality did not make sense in the American context. Disparaging war heroes, dismissing Gold Star families, caging immigrant children and peddling obviously false information in the guise of presidential authority were not elements that logical Americans accepted as reality for the country. That was the part that brought impeachment proceedings against Trump and yet that effort to liberate Americans from their addicted to the Trump Horror Show was unsuccessful due to its pervasiveness.

Republican sponsors were heavily invested in keeping the show alive with its enthralled audience. Thus, liberation would not come until the Trump base learned to distinguish between reality and the fulfilments fantasy delivered.

"You're fired!" was a catchy tag line for a reality show that provided a theatrical catharsis for an American middle class feeling left behind by a globalizing world. For that same audience, hearing that phrase in a real life context could amount to a devastating blow that ended in murderous rage.

That happened to Trump supporters who invaded the US Capitol at the urging of Donald Trump to overthrow an election and to destroy democracy itself. All of the country's investigatory powers and all of Trump's subversions had failed to come up with a shred of evidence for the voter fraud being claimed. And yet those same facts were insufficient to persuade Trump adherents that the vote was fair.

Like Chucky, Trump kept reappearing to keep alive the fantasy and stir ardour for the next sequel. The saving grace for America was that two-thirds of its people were not Chucky Trump devotees.

Debunking the Trump Mystique

The allure that Donald Trump held for a third of America was no mystery. It took no trained psychologist to recognize that he represented the basest of the three elements that Sigmund Freud identified as components of the human psyche.

Donald Trump was the essence of the id, the most primitive part that humans shared with animals. The highest level was the superego, the part that absorbed a culture's most noble values and built on them to move society forward and up. Between the two was the ego that in well-balanced people mediated between the easy greedy id and the greater social needs beyond individual concerns. When the free flow of energy between the three levels was blocked, it seemed the most likely clog occurred between the ego and superego, simply because it was harder to be good with the superego than to be lazy with the id.

In the case of someone like Donald Trump, who seemed to have an overflow of base or libidinal energy and virtually no ideals higher than self-interest, the blockage led to a bloated ego when id forces exploded into the ego with no superego release valve. Even to an amateur, Trump was a choked pressure cooker

A quick overview of global tyrants suggested they all had bloated egos as a result of exploding ids with no safety valve into service for the greater good. Most seemed to have invested their lives in mastering the art of satisfying themselves while mastering the wily craft of using all means of the id to achieve their ends, an impression that made sense.

For starters, a tyrant with a bloated ego using id tactics had an easier path to power than a great global leader. It was easier to intimidate and bully than it was to persuade. Then, a lifetime of devotion dedicated to bending the world to an individual will was bound to produce a charismatic person ever more able to attract admirers who willing to take on odious tasks. Finally, the most successful tyrants seemed to be those who had sprung from native soil to capitalize on social vulnerabilities without the inhibition of morality. They could be ruthless without a twinge, which made them gluttons for control of an entire country or even the world.

When viewed through a wide-angle lens, only America could have bred a Donald Trump. Based on an exhaustive list of sources, he was an opportunist who seized the land of opportunity to wrest from it a free hand to reach beyond limits. When failures outstripped home country tolerance, Trump turned to outside funding unimpeded by law. Those dark sources ultimately catapulted Trump into the American presidency, from where he ran amok with the country's highest powers seemingly just to indulge avarice, the ultimate split between id impulses and superego ideals.

The naked display of id forces at the presidential level in the world's most powerful country was a shock to the country and the world. A core group in America, however, apparently fell into thrall at the audacious breach of propriety that they themselves would never dare. Another group seized on the value of such influence. They hitched a ride on Trump's coattails, openly admitting their belief that some measure of Trump's success would devolve to them, a conviction driven mostly by fear.

Trump was notorious for an insatiable drive to destroy all who opposed him or failed to pay enough homage to his great powers. That terrorist tactic worked in the political circle of the conservative party he had chosen to commandeer. Yet in the greater global world, he was a pariah among leaders with healthy egos aiming to address greater social needs, and he was a piker among global despots more inured to the necessary exercise of id-based measures.

At home in America, Trump played the role of savior to some and destroyer to others. In the greater global world, he snubbed the company of equals. With bona fide tyrants, he groveled, simpered and made an enamored fool of himself when he imagined that his infatuations were reciprocated.

The Trump mystique that captivated a third of America was little more than the big fish in a small pond phenomenon. In an isolationist America supersaturated with irrelevant issues that promoted self-absorption, Trump passed as a diversionary new toy that relieved the monotony of decent social order. In the larger global pond full of real problems like massive hunger and true tyrannical oppression, Trump was a toddler, a small fry regardless of the bloated ego fed by the id that had no relief valve to higher social service.

Uncle Scam Undone

America rejected Trump with the 2020 election but like a cobra he wouldn't let go. He was stickier than the Covid virus still ravaging the world, morphing into variants never before seen. Yet for all the distress, rage and damage that his will-to-power inflicted, his contortions of democracy proved the value of the social system as a superlative form of governance. Given optimal freedom within the limits of law, an opportunist in the land of opportunity was destined to self-destruct.

Donald Trump was a washed-up high power New York conman when he found a new target for his swindler skills. The vast disenfranchised American Midwest met Trump through the sadistic Apprentice TV program that played on fantasies of omnipotence.

On the Apprentice, Trump played the part of a fabulous business mogul who screened avid wannabes and declared "you're fired" with relish when they failed to win his favour at the end of a fierce competitive round. For contestants, bitter disappointment was offset by momentary fame with a vast audience, which gave rise to the hope that some additional opportunity would arise from the one that was just missed.

By the time the Apprentice formula staled and the audience began to lose interest, Trump had made his presence known to Russia's Vladimir Putin It was a bid for higher training beyond apprenticeship in the despotic arts.

Despotism seemed an inherited trait with Trump, who used that native talent to run his businesses. He decreed, diverted, delegated, declaimed independently of fact or merit. He showed no mercy and delighted in shocking through outrage. He played the media so, he got optimal attention until he was able to blast onto the political stage with a dramatic descent on the gaudy Fifth Avenue Trump Tower escalator.

Criticism of his ambition was catnip to Trump, who sailed ahead buoyed by every headwind. Obstacles supercharged him whenever he hurdled one, especially in the areas of social propriety and legal accountability. Once on center stage in the serious world of political power with a solid fan base, Trump became a wizard of desecrating civilized order.

In keeping with the aphorism that success breeds success. Trump crashed through rules with a relish that suggested he did so simply for the thrill. Once he breezed into the Oval Office and skirted impeachment, he switched into high gear with the mighty powers of his office, creating a vortex that sucked in the entire country. As driver of the country's engine with Republicans in tow, he harnessed the Justice Department to advance his ambition of corrupting the entire system to service his needs. He was well on the way to another term of opportunity when a virus blocked his path and his skills proved ineffective in meeting the needs.

As a self-described germaphobe who hated shaking hands, Trump told Fox News in March 2020 that he carried out the practice because he was a politician who wouldn't be liked if he didn't. Trump continued to shake hands even after the Centers for Disease Control recommended the practice be suspended. He turned mitigating measures like masks and social distancing into political tools that sharply divided the country. He proved his own conquest of the disease by succumbing and recovering under a singular treatment protocol only to emerge and claim the virus posed no real threat.

All the while, deaths spiraled out of control in the hundreds of thousands. When vaccines become available, they too were weaponized and the country's political rift deepened. Refusing to endorse the vaccines he had commissioned, Trump himself was quietly vaccinated out of public notice. Despite all those contradictions, the base clung to the Trump stated position, which benefited from changing guidelines issued by officials and disinformation spread by the social media. While some supporters changed their views of Trump when they become ill or lost a loved one, the majority stuck with his position long after he was out of office.

Republican leaders pushed the Trump message in hope of political gain. The base, however, had a more intrinsically human reason for continuing to have faith in Trump. Quite simply, there were victims of a scam.

Scams came in many forms and the smartest people could fall victim. The "inheritance" scam was an example. In that, a large unexpected inheritance would be released upon receipt of a processing fee. To most, it seemed impossible that anyone would fall for the story that a person in charge of disbursing $2.5 million in funds would be $200 short of cash. Yet according to Scamwatch, 580 people fell for the scam in 2019. In a pyramid scheme that lasted for 20 years, Bernie Madoff amassed an estimated $64.8 billion. According to the FBI, there were 33 categories of fraud scams ranging from identity theft to romance to doorstop scams. The common element in all was a dishonest sales pitch successful aimed at susceptibility.

According to the Conversation website, there were specific ways to get people to fall for scams. One was to engage them and draw them into a position of trust. Another was to start a trend that gathered followers. Seeming to be nice was a successful ploy, as was the ability to build up an appetite for the product by presenting it as a "must have." Trump employed all those means plus a singular one no one had employed.

"I know the system and I alone can fix it," he declared at the 2016 Republican Convention. In essence, he was selling himself as God.

Nearly a third of the country bought into the Trump variation of the inheritance scheme in which he would fix all problems in exchange for a small upfront fee in the form of a vote. While less than half the country fell for the scam, its targeted design captured a majority of the country's electoral votes.

From the Oval Office, Trump continued to run the scam with promises that never materialized but still managed to keep the base hooked like the Miracle Spring Water peddled by Peter Popoff for over 25 years. He was sued, prosecuted and put out of business but he always resurfaced with willing adherents buying into the promise he offered. Once hooked and invested in a scheme, victims were loathe to admit they'd been scammed. They needed to believe they'd been smarter than those duped by others.

Thus, the Trump base stayed loyal to the Trump promote even after the Covid pandemic bested him and proved him wrong. To all others, Covid only proved what had been known all along. He was no God and he deserved no votes.

America Comes of Age in 2020

Covid year 2020 was a pivotal point for America and the world. Neither would ever be the same after lockdowns and the four years of chaos that America had launched with its 2016 election of isolationist Trump in an increasingly interdependent globalizing world.

In 2020, superpower America would make a choice. It was elect a new president Biden who would return it to values that had made it great. In contrast, America would keep the renegade leader elected four years before as a backlash to progress made either years earlier with Obama. That backlash had alienated America from friends and had allied it with global despots who failed to respond to American outreach under Trump. They had simply used Trump's narrow vision of wielding power to advance their own aims without his notice.

From the perspective of a globalizing world, Trump's view of power was as obsolete as the famous poem by the British poet Rudyard Kipling written in 1899, entitle "White Man's Burden" in the waning days of the European colonialist period. The poem urged America to "tame" the wild Philippine savages without expecting no thanks in return. The sacrifice of creature comforts back home was the price to pay for glory among peers.

The world had changed radically in the 120 years since that poem was written. Two world wars had established the principle that all nations were equal just as the United States Constitution had affirmed that all persons were created equal. While both those doctrines were still to be actualized; the United Natlons established under US leadership after the Second World War was limping along without the active support of its founding patron. Clearly isolationist Trump would not facilitate the work of a global body.

In a way, the 2020 US election was set to determine the direction of a global civil war in lieu of a third world war that with the atom bomb would prove fatally catastrophic for all humanity. In order to take its place in a democratizing global world, America needed to shed a leader on the verge of regressing the world to precolonial days.

In 2020, the choice before America was stark. The global Covid pandemic had made the options clear, as had the complex international imperative surrounding climate change. The stakes at issue surmounted America's pressing attention to its debilitating racial divide. The use of America's great power was at the heart of the election, though in the case of Trump the contest was skewed to begin with.

Trump was a blowhard with not enough courage to fire anyone in person unless a TV script enabled him to carry out the decision. Even so, he had swayed a third of America with the illusion that he was a wonder-worker who would bring glory to America by banning immigrants from undesirable countries and striking trade deals that would revive obsolete industries. In 2020, America had a big decision to make. It would either continue to support the fantasy of a greatness that never was as peddled by a shady character, or it would step up to the greatness it deserved by embracing the challenge of solving problems in concert with the global community.

With its 250-year history, America was a young culture compared to its near-200 global neighbors. America was an adolescent compared to European founding forebears, from whom it had split in defiance of unfair demands imposed from an imperialist distance. It took America another 80 years to vanquish that age-old practice of slavery with a bitter Civil War that exposed the barbarity of the practice. The 2008 US election decimated all residual sentiments about racial inequality, which only served to redouble the ardor of those who clung to outmoded mental models of the world instead of adapting to changing reality.

America was the big hero in two world wars and then it suffered a series of humiliating defeats on the international stage. The first was Korea, then came Viet Nam. Somalia began as a noble humanitarian effort in cooperation with the United Nations. The clumsy early attempt at working together soured America to further attempts at cooperation with the result that the American ego became bloated and with that invited an attack by resentful radical extremists. America's response was to manufacture a war against the wrong enemy with fallout still ongoing.

Self-absorbed with its wounds, America failed to notice that the brave men and women fighting its distant wars were its lifeline to a global world. Human contact on the personal level made a greater impact than any amount of military and intelligence analysis. If America was to take its well-deserved position in leadership of the world, it would assume adult responsibilities instead of clinging to past glories never achieved in the middle of a global pandemic while global climate change burned and flooded both America and the rest of the world.

Trump won the US Presidency in 2016 by conflating American freedom with tyrannical methods delivered in the style of an expert con artist peddling an array of scams. Four years later, the world was hoping America was finished with its antisocial dalliance. Serious matters needed to be resolved so that a mature America could continue it indulge its penchant for the absurd.

States United by US Election 2020

After Trump lost the 2020 election and refused to concede, America seemed more divided than ever. In one way that was true. A record number of votes were cast for both the Democratic and Republican candidates. But beneath that divide, America was more united than ever.

In 2016, Trump lost the popular vote but took the Electoral College votes of the midwestern states in part because he played to their "forgotten" status in the overall image of America. That image was based on media criteria for covering activities considered to be of national interest. Not only were news networks located mainly in New York but the economic and political drivers of American life were located on the East Coast. Cultural drivers were located on both coasts. The other parts of the country became newsworthy only when crime was horrific or the weather brought disaster. The 2020 election campaign in a Covid year changed that dynamic.

In 2020, all states could become newsworthy at any moment because of the Covid pandemic and the way Trump handled the disaster in an election year. One by one, states like Minnesota, Missouri, Arizona, Georgia, Florida and Texas emerged and entered into the national consciousness of a country forced to pay attention during successive lockdowns. The Trump penchant for holding rallies in swing states that could flip in his favour further brought notice to locales formerly known only as part of a region such as the Midwest, South or Sunbelt. Finally, the crises that ensued in wake of those rallies began a whole new round in the news cycle circuit, particularly in relation to color.

Historically in America, color referred to racial distinctions. Since the 2000 election in which the Supreme Court handed the presidential win to Republican George W. Bush over Democrat Al Gore, Red and Blue have come to indicate the party most likely elected by a state.

According to Wikipedia, most states were technically Purple in that the population overall was a mix of Republicans and Democrats. The Red or Blue designation was based on the all-for-one nature of the Electoral College. All Electoral votes went to the party with the most votes in an election, which brought in a critical urban/rural divide still notable in most states.

Under Trump, racial elements became subsumed into the political make-up of a state. Since most property was owned by whites, blacks and other minorities tended to migrate to urban areas. That urban\rural divide was most successfully exploited by Trump when he first entered politics in 2016. He was an East Coast renegade under the Republican banner who targeted Democratic Blue states with depressed economies. Most of those states still had vast rural areas and major cities with large minority populations, a combination ready-made for a divide and conquer offensive.

Trump won the Midwest with promises that failed to deliver. Jobs heralded as returning were hyped and followed up with a few short-lived early successes while actual jobs dried up and factories closed. Deluded solid urban Midwesterners grumbled along with rural neighbors whose farms were decimated by Trump trade wars. Those stories were covered by the Trump-maligned media, which put a human face on the disappointment even as tax cuts to the super-wealthy drowned the impact of the pittance tossed to the middle class, particularly when trickle-down expectations turned up empty. Meanwhile, the plight of Midwest States blended with newfound challenges posed in the Southern border states where the Trump Wall and his immigration policy created a brand new kind of schism.

Catchy as campaign slogans, the "Wall' and "tough on immigrants" cants were duds in practice. The Wall was an ecological and community disaster. The anti-immigrant policy with its ICE raids ended in images of fathers ripped from families and children torn from parents, sobbing alone in cages with not even attendants to give them comfort. Even anti-immigrants in the nation as a whole were incensed by the barbarity toward Hispanics, which brought attention to the variations in the country's many Hispanic groups. The empathic response to basic human injustice blasted into worldwide outrage when black George Floyd was murdered by a white police officer in plain public view as caught on videotape.

In response to the George Floyd murder, Trump said it was terrible but that more whites died at the hands of police than blacks. Not only was the claim untrue, it was an indication of just how underhandedly Trump assaulted basic human dignity. He gave the expected lip service of his office to betray at the same time his true attitude devoid of empathy. Indeed, throughout the 2020 Covid election year, the level of empathy that a person could summon became the primary characteristic that both divided and unified the country's diverse population.

Way back in about 500 B.C. Confucius outlined the three paths to wisdom. Contemplation was the most noble. Imitation was the easiest; and experience was the most bitter. As a product of all three paths, empathy played a major role in driving the response to Trump's handling of the Covid pandemic. Those able to identify with the feelings of others were apt to comply with guidelines to mitigate effects of the Covid disaster. Those unable or unwilling to feel the pain of others were most likely Trump fans who preferred mode of self-expression was rageful defiance.

By Confucian standards, Trump was not a wise man. He bragged that he did not contemplate. boasting that he knew more than "the generals" and called doctors "morons" who didn't know anything. Those were signs he found no one worth imitating. By all accounts, his experience was limited to wheedling money out of others and conniving press coverage. Thus, by extension of Confucian standards, it was safe to say Trump was devoid of empathy. Explicit evidence backed up the supposition.

While visiting a relief center after the deadly hurricane Maria devastated Puerto Rico, Trump threw paper towels to victims hoping to hear words of comfort from the US president in charge of the US Territory. When reviled for the crass insult, Trump defended himself by saying they were "beautiful soft towels. Very good towels." Such a level of insensitivity could appeal only to those who were already overburdened even before Covid hit. And perhaps because of the strong bond between the embittered and their fantasy redeemer, Trump supporters followed his directives on Covid.

Trump at first downplayed the pandemic, reassuring Americans that it would disappear like magic. When his exhortations failed to jump start an economy brought to a halt by mounting contagion and death toll, he turned the virus and the mitigating measures to control it into political weapons for the forthcoming 2020 election.

Even as it unfolded, 2020 was destined to go down in history as a singular period of uncertainty, isolation, fear and social alienation. Particularly in an over-active America led by a hyperactive president, quarantine was a remedy tantamount to torture. But the enforced solitude leavened by news of the outside world gave occasion for Americans to realize just how stratified was their society, not just in pockets but across the board.

Pandemic lockdowns made clear that Covid affected everyone but that most were more affected than the affluent. "Essential workers" braved the virus to keep society functioning while others stayed safe. In that newly dawned reality, the George Floyd murder was an explosive device that fused the racial, social and political components of government irrevocably.

In the long months after Covid hit, Trump emerged as a desperate man at a loss on how to proceed. Expressing no concern for people or their health, he pushed for markers of economic recovery while downplaying the virus with lighthearted quick fix tips that backfired when delivered with the presidential seal of authority. In response to racial inequity protests, he condemned left-leaning agitators. Those social contortions were downright painful to many, but the base held that he was doing fine and no one could have done better in a situation beyond his control. Taking note of the base, Republicans lined up behind Trump.

Viruses had not been considered intractable since the Middle Ages. The taming of pathogens had been a major focus of science ever since the Black Death killed 200 million people in the space of four years during the 14th century. Since then, smallpox and polio had been conquered. But Trump and his Republican enablers managed to convince a large minority of Americans to simply let Covid run its course. In the Trump crowd, that tactic was a call for hateful defiance.

The number of hate groups had been on the increase ever since the 2008 election of Obama as the first non-white president of the western industrialized world. Into that volatile arena, Trump threw a conflation of freedom with defiance with Covid mitigating measures as the object to be hated and defied to the point of death. "Liberate Michigan," he directed a white nationalist group planning to kidnap and assassinate the Democratic governor of swing state Michigan, one of the many with complex power structures due to principle of states' rights.

America has been widely viewed as a democracy based on the principles expressed in its founding Constitution. Technically it was most commonly considered a federal republic, meaning that a central government held together all 50 states that remained autonomous under the federal umbrella. Thus, states made their own laws about local elections, which included the positions that oversaw the federal elections for president and Congressional representatives. That was the vulnerability Trump targeted in the highly unusual 2020 election.

Throughout the messy 2020 presidential campaign, poll numbers of both candidates dovetailed with updates on Covid, news about natural disasters, racial protests, protests about masks and alarms about supply shortages, unemployment and stimulus stalemates. Not muddled enough, Trump began early to throw shade on mail-in voting and voter fraud. Then came the Postal Service scandal with slow-downs of service, and the unevenly conducted Decennial Census which would determine Congressional representation for the next ten years. Those factors combined with stimulus payments, increased unemployment benefits and small business relief. The result was that Americans began to realize that the larger issues of government had a direct effect on their lives.

To the hatefully defiant Trump crowd, the dependence on the government was the sign of a creeping socialism that would destroy the American spirit of liberty. In the wild west of the loosely regulated web network, they plotted, grew and connected. Meanwhile, mainstream America depended on news from the left, right and free-wheeling social media. But since personal bias selected the source, facts were drowned in skewed coverage. Thus, when Trump spoke from the presidential pulpit, his words were accepted or derided for the views expressed with presidential seal of approval. Thrown into a frenzy by mixed messaging, America provided an opening for the premonance of its fringe extremes.

Ultra-extremists such as Qanon and militias were a small part of the population but they were loud, sinister and deadly with their brandishing of uncontrolled arms. Woven into the American tradition of independence and a romance with the outlaw, America's fringe was convenient tool for Trump planning his own campaign of claiming voter fraud in preparation for losing the election and the presidency he may have felt he had not won fairly in the first place. That suspicion was best proved by the aftermath of the 2020 election.

When Trump became president in 2016. the result was dismay by the American majority followed by four years of protests. When Joe Biden won the 2020 election, the results were contested strenuously by the Trump camp and yet no fraud could be found. When Biden was safely sworn in as new president, celebrations went up not only in America but the world over. During the two month transition period in which Trump refused to cooperate, the absurdity of Trump as head of the United States became starkly clear.

For four years. the greatest democracy in the world was headed by a full-blown demagogue who refused to cede power when defeated in an election that was fair by every electoral and legal measure. Further, he not only refused to leave the office he lost, he hounded the country with frivolous lawsuits while purging those who refused to corrupt the system on his behalf. Worst of all, he was hell-bent on obstructing the path of his successor who was bursting to tame the pandemic and restore America to its core values.

While, independence was an essential component of America's character, so were the interdependency skills that allowed the Pioneers to expand and tame the Wild West Empathy born of wisdom was one of those. Trump and the pandemic had given America an opportunity to contemplate, emulate and experience first-hand the suffering of others. In short, America was growing wise to a rock bottom reality.

Despite all his bluster and distortion of American Constitution justice, Trump lacked one key quality for being either a leader or a hero. Despite his iron grip on the hearts of his adherents, none of them ever said that they wanted their kids to grow up just like him.

Trump the Dumped

The blitz of the Trump tenure obscured the character of the America that elected Obama in 2008. The mangled Trump response to the Covid pandemic foreshadowed his demise, complete with frenzied rallies to pump the threat that the vote would be stolen. Yet nothing prepared America for the actual Trump when he lost the 2020 election to Biden.

Trump never did conceded to Biden and his claims of voter fraud continued way beyond the inauguration of the new president. Those two factors helped to perpetuate the mistaken belief that Biden had chatted to win. Even after repeated recounts and lost court challenges, 70% of Republicans refused to believe that Biden could have won. Based on numerous analyses, it seemed that sceptics about the fairness of the 2020 election held onto that belief merely because Trump fit the image they wanted to see in their president.

"No way in hell Biden could have won. He didn't even campaign," one Trump supporter told Reuters in November 2020. Over four years, Trump had acclimated his supporters to the notion that a leader was loud, brash, theatrical and brutal, even lawless, about getting his way. In short, Trump had normalized bad behavior. The electoral loss and the continued faith of supporters was the green light for Trump to unleash the full force of the vengeance that was part of the behavioral repertoire, which culminated in the unthinkable attempted coup on January 6. While the complex circumstances of the insurrection were still in early stages of investigation, it seemed clear that the normalization of bad behavior had taken a symbiotic form during Trump's four years in office.

Trump was no stranger to failure. After six bankruptcies when he started out as a child millionaire, Trump could arguably be described as a serial loser. In fact, he had made a career of losing.

He had lost casinos, yachts, airplanes and sports teams. He had lost untold numbers of court cases and who knew how many millions of dollars. But he had never lost "face" to the degree that he did with the 2020 election loss to Biden.

Trump was humiliated when he lost to Biden, as he probably anticipated when he tried to extort the Ukrainian president in order to destroy Biden. While he was impeached for that unprecedented abuse of presidential powers he escaped conviction through his stranglehold on Senate Republicans. The victory gave him renewed vigor for abusing those powers starting off by firing two witnesses who testified against him. When he was again impeached for incitement to insurrection and again escaped, he had the country on tenterhooks until new president Biden was successfully inaugurated a week later. His hold on the country, however, did not abate as he considered next moves in his career.

Like the health care plan that he dangled before America for four years that never on the horizon only undermine "Obamacare," Trump threatened to run for president again. Holding the menace of that political menace over the heads of Republicans, he wrested loyalty from them. At the same time, the rallies resumed to keep alive the strongman image that had captured the imagination of Americans unable to adapt to a changing world.

Throughout his career, Trump covered losses with blowhard tactics as he recouped with more brazen ventures. When he took on America and its democracy, he shot the moon with the career opportunity of a lifetime. When he lost the 2020 election, America became a failed project to him. Yet the stakes were high. Out of office, he faced the law that had shielded him as president. Until he decided on his next project, public sentiment combined with Republican obeisance was his liability insurance, in addition to the calculation that Joe Biden could very well fail.

The possibility that his days were numbered might have dawned on Trump when Covid hit and he lacked any clue on how to respond. Laying the groundwork for his legacy, he struck one of his signature deals with the Taliban terrorist group ousted from Afghanistan under Bush. The deal was struck in February as Covid hit, then was honored by Biden in the name of US continuity. The result was catastrophic for both countries.

After 20 years of democracy under the protection of US and Allies, Afghanistan within a week was under control of the harsh sharia Taliban sect allied with terrorist groups in the region. Drawdown of the US presence was chaotic and humiliating to the US dependent on the Taliban for a smooth conduct of the operation. The scenario was fodder for Trump and for Republican's intent on subverting democracy at home.

Lies and beliefs about a fraudulent 2020 election would not have been so successful had American democracy been less complicated. A federal republic like the US was a constant balance between individual and group rights, multiplied in the US by 50 states and their multiple layers of governing districts. In 2020, the central federal government and the states that retained individual rights came into constant conflict to be battled by courts at all levels. Those conflicts continued throughout 2021 with increasing intensity under the multiple onslaughts of Covid mitigation, election security and politics still orchestrated by Trump.

Quite obviously, Trump was intent on holding onto power, even if the government had to be destroyed as it nearly was with the January coup. Presumably, he would keep that power by playing his Republican enablers for positions within the plutocracy that would result. Rule by an elite class was far from the democracy enshrined in the US Constitution, which set out the principles of life, liberty and the pursuit of happiness, in addition to declaring that all persons were created equal and that laws would be elaborated based on the Constitution. Further, no one was to be above the law and all were subject to the law, the Constitution laid out in Article VI, seemingly unbeknownst to Trump.

For four years, Trump shredded Constitutional law by corrupting the Justice Department, one of three co-equal branches of the government established to act as a check on each other. He compromised the Republican party, half of the second Legislative branch represented by Congress. Finally, he ran his Legislative branch, the third of those democratic pillars, with the fitful self-indulgence of a born autocrat.

Trump hired, fired and replaced "the best people" he had brought into Washington with no regard to due process. He denuded the carefully constructed governmental infrastructured that he branded as "the swamp" and he brought disgrace to the dignity of the US presidency. When he left, left, the Constitution was in tatters after a pattern of conduct he seemed intent on continuing at the first opportunity.

By all accounts, Trump rose to the eminence of his presidential position by perfecting skills in knavery that he practiced on successive power-brokers able to be of use to him. When New York opportunities would no longer deliver based on his string of failures, he moved on to emerging capitols in developing parts of a globalizing world. As widely chronicled, Trump expanded into ever broader foreign fields by moving on when opportunistic overreach ran into limits. Success in new ventures may have come from a common interest between him and new partners in brokering deals beneath the radar of prying legal eyes. A boost into the Oval may have come from that growing global enterprise, part of which could be unhappy with his election loss. But regardless of how he landed in the Oval Office, his win was a pyrrhic victory for everybody involved because nobody won.

Elected by the US Electoral College technicality, Trump never achieved majority appeal. He himself was dogged by doubts about his legitimacy. "Can you believe I won?" he shouted at a Wisconsin rally during the 2016 Thank You Tour staged during transition between his administration and that of his predecessor Obama. Foreign leaders were mum about the mighty US powers in such fickle hands, but Trump worked the base and played Republicans to reshape American democracy in his deceptive gaudy style until the 2020 election pulled the plug on marquee ambitions.

The Trump phenomenon in America was destined to be studied throughout history. But to an interested observer in the present, Trump was a master manipulator of the masses who might have become a petty dictator in an environment less lush than the grand United States. And because the US was great because of its democracy, Trump's attempt to seize its immense powers for personal gain was doomed to failure.

Over four years, Trump took hold of the law to prove himself above and superior to its limitations. When Covid hit, he attempted to save the economy that would coast him to re-election by taking hold of the medical profession. In concert with Republican enablers, Trump made every effort to prove himself superior to the virus by speaking with presidential authority to sell the spiel that the virus was inconsequential even as people died. His skills were developed enough to create untold havoc, but in a democracy like the US, he could not control the human mind enough to make it bend to his will. To Trump, the elusive goal was catnip.

When science called for mitigating the spread of contagion, Trump scoffed at masks, encouraged mask less rallies without social distancing and veered between calling the virus a "hoax" and developing a vaccine at "warp speed." The catchy term tainted the vaccination effort with distrust from that day forward. But the biggest challenge to Trump in the 2020 election year was Joe Biden with his unpretentious common sense.

Four years of Trump was a constant adrenalin rush for America. Mellowing back to Biden's easy efficiency reminiscent of Obama just four years earlier took adjustment. When Trump lost the 2020 election, the ugly forces he had fostered burst into a violent backlash against democracy itself.

In retrospect, the US 2020 election was an amazing display of democracy in action. A global pandemic threatened participation in the vote. States with diverse rules for voting scrambled to extend opportunities for voters within Covid guidelines.

Trump defied the outcome of the 2020 election based on those solutions devised to ensure fairness in a difficult time. And while states, as well as duly elected officials pushed back against the Trump assault, enabling Republicans at the state level began pushing for reforms that would restrict voter access in the future.

America was torn and wounded after Trump and the vengeance he unleashed when deprived of another four years to dismantle democracy, and still America emerged as a glorious victor. Democracy in America probably began in the early settler days when pioneers shared chores even before laws were established in the new country. Those simple democratic principles cut through the complexities of the 21st century to enable democratic decency to withstand a hostile takeover attempt by an unscrupulous self-server.

After Trump and the 2020 election, America truly deserved its title as the beacon of democracy. The battle with Trump had proved that however fierce, unscrupulous and untruthful. the old world model of a dictator was doomed to failure.

Biden Buries Trump

Times change but core principles don't. Gravity was able to be defied in space but it was still gravity that drew the vehicle back to earth. Likewise, humans could choose to abandon moral standards but the social drive was toward evolution, which overrode revolution and even more fiercely, the devolution that would take society backwards.

Immediately after the January 6 attempted coup in the form of a deadly attack on the US Capitol, social media giants suspended the accounts of Donald J. Trump. Twitter was the first, followed by Facebook and then a dozen others. The decisions were based on indicators showing that the president's incitements to violence were instrumental in creating the riot. Even if unintentional, the messages were read by followers as a call to war.

The attempted coup was a wake-up call for tech giants, politicians and America itself. For four years Trump was allowed to abandon formalities of the office and offhandedly use its powers to drive news cycles, set policy, move markets, rile his base and issue statements without advice of aides. When those actions led to a coup, the unregulated tech giants took the step of suspending the accounts before investigations proved the need to regulate the powerful social platforms and forums. As one Facebook executive told NBC News in mid-January, "These were extraordinary circumstances. We don't have a policy on what to do when a sitting president starts a coup."

The suspension of those accounts took away the Trump bullhorn sounded from the Oval Office. He tried riling the base by claiming suppression of free speech. Without the social media reach, his outrage failed to catch fire. His Save America website was sparse with a huge red donate button. His blog lasted less than a month in May. Out of office and washed up as a result of his latest business flop, Trump turned to Republicans for his next recovery.

To recap, Trump captured the US Presidency in 2016 with qualities that left much to be desired for human decency in a world growing global. He was angry, spiteful, derisive and downright cruel. He mocked both social heroes and the physically challenged. While repugnant to most, those qualities resonated with enough Americans to win him the election on a technicality.

Trump's relish for airing crude impulses was considered refreshingly honest by core supporters. Reprehensible qualities were dismissed as insignificant relative to his role as the leader he promoted himself to be. Opposition to his behavior was seen by fans as an attack on a rugged individualist fighting for the cause of malcontents just like they were.

For three years the bond between Trump and his base deepened as he shattered Constitutional norms. That agenda won help from career politicians for whom Trump was a meal ticket. For the media, Trump was a reliable source of scandal, which maximized earnings. When the Covid pandemic hit as the next election year began, the dynamics of the Trump machine shifted into high gear.

The basest instincts emerged in Trump when Covid threatened his smooth ride to re-election based on a vibrant economy. Never a leader and ever the solo autocrat, Trump by-passed national plans, downplayed danger and delegated responsibility to 50 states governors while leveraging federal aid. Predictably enough, utter chaos ensued. It billowed exponentially as the virus spiked and Trump grabbed the political opportunity.

Ordinarily, a politician managed a crisis and touted success in easing the situation. As the non-politician he claimed to be, Trump fanned division about managing the crisis, perhaps in an attempt to prove himself as "the only one who can fix il," as he boasted at the 2016 Republican convention. Whatever his reason, he contradicted and undermined public health officials. He mocked mitigation measures, branded masks as signs of cowardice on the part of un-American infidels looking to take away liberties from real Americans like those he supported him. In the country at large, debate turned into violence, propelled by super-spreader rallies that drowned out common sense about a plainly biological pathogen. An equally afflicted rest of the world wondered at the waste of America's great power.

Instead of leading as the world had come to expect of America, the wealthiest country on earth seemed no better off than the poorest. Like others, America had food lines, work-place deaths, health care burn-out, unemployment and homelessness. It was a side of America the world had never seen. Even worse, there was no empathy for the once friendly country that had turned mean and ugly.

To the global world, it seemed that America with all its wealth was unwilling to care even for its own, when violence erupted over the wearing of masks, poor countries saw the same behavior as in their countries when people fought for bread. Thus, the world began to see America with all its wealth as a morally bankrupt place. The suspicion seemed confirmed when Trump lost the 2020 election and his base turned rabid.

Like Covid, rabies was a virus commonly called "foaming at the mouth." It was passed from animals to humans and affected the brain and central nervous system. Apparently, the virus prevented a victim from being able to swallow, giving the virus a better chance to infect another host. Extreme aggression was one symptom, certainly applicable to the base when Trump lost an election they fully expected him to win.

Tuned into warrior Trump on social media platforms that welcomed the traffic he generated; the base was solidly hooked on viral

Trump, unable to swallow heathy water to clear the infectant. As a result, the base fell in line with directives of their illness. They showed when summoned, cheered on cue and booed when an enemy name was mentioned. As the 2020 election neared, voter fraud and Joe Biden elicited the most vigorous boos.

In all fairness, confusion abounded in the 2020 election. The most astute analysts would examine the threads long into the future. But it was the Trump manipulation of those openings for error that predetermined the outcome for a base that would never accept evidence contrary to belief.

Due to the American form of government in which states retained individual rights under a federal umbrella, state rules for voting varied widely. In response to Covid, states customized rules to accommodate voter needs for casting ballots. Mail-in and early voting were two methods enhanced. Trump not only used those as weapons for charging the base with doubt, he arranged for a mail slow-down to further cast suspicion on a response to a crisis that by all accounts was earnest

Certain of his strategy, Trump plied rally crowds with portents about voter fraud. There was no way he could lose unless there was voter fraud by crooked Democrats, he proclaimed too wild applause and cheers. Thus, when Biden won, nobody in Trump's corner had any reason to believe the actual facts.

In an American court of law, the mere shadow of a doubt was enough to overturn the verdict in a trial. In the case of Trump and the 2020 election, the base was 100% full of doubt that Biden could win. He hadn't even campaigned. Trump had campaigned hard. He deserved to win. Trump risked his life to win votes. There was no way that "Sleepy Joe" hiding behind a mask could ever have won.

The perception of the base was both real and deluded. It was the result of a phenomenon many knew as a toxic relationship.

On the surface, believing in Trump took little effort. He sold easy solutions, ignored accountability when promises failed to materialize and he pushed a big agenda to gloss over the lack of detail. Disappointment in Trump was deflected to enemies trying to bring him down. The forceful message suitably delivered was easy comfort but the emotional cost of believing his word against all evidence was steep. After all the work to stick within, the base would never buy the notion that their hero was a fraud who lost to ordinary Joe Biden.

Toxic relationships took many forms but in all. Someone got hurt. With Trump, the injury to the base began when he descended the golden escalator and denounced Mexicans in a generalization that sparked an outsized emotional response in fans that stemmed from many streams. Once he tested the bigotry angle to find traction, Trump took the opportunity provided by the Hollywood Access tapes to find he could get away with dishonoring women. Evading the Mueller Report was a big legal win and skirting impeachment was his coup de grace to the Constitution. With the loyalty of the base secure, no power on earth could stop him whatever he did. The Covid "super-spreader" rallies were the ultimate proof. The rural base was ready to die for him.

Into that madness entered Joe Biden, a seasoned politician who at the age of 78 might have thought of retiring except that his country needed him at a critical time. A character reference by black Congressional colleague Jim Clyburn of South Carolina conscripted him. Low-key, empathic and utterly human, Biden was known for integrity, including through his service as vice president with Obama. That connection alone may have stoked the fury of "Birther" Trump, whose mockery increased as Biden refused to take the bait throughout the 2020 presidential campaign.

Biden was the ultimate contrast to Trump. For America and its democracy, all he had to do was needed to do was to stand his ground as Trump, his enablers and his base unleashed their fury against him.

As Trump fought the Biden electoral win in courts and at state levels in ways that herited investigation, Biden stayed clear of the fray and carried on the transition despite obstruction by the exiting Trump team. In the character of Biden nominees for Cabinet and Executive positions, America was reminded of the moral principles set out in the Constitution. Biden never addressed Trump's refusal to concede he left the coup attempt in the hands of Congress and the Justice Department. The two branches of government tasked with oversight of the falsely contested Legislative branch he headed. Once Trump was vanquished to Florida from where he continued to foment unrest, Biden set to rebuilding an America decimated by a great partisan divide.

During his four years in office, Trump had nearly destroyed 240 years of democracy in America. Apparently, he had done that in an effort to erase all traces of Obama, as in his drive to dismantle Obamacare with no plan for replacing it. Biden seemed intent on honoring tradition and continuity. Thus, though he assured the G-7 group of world leaders that "America is back," he took unilateral action to carry through on a peace plan Trump had negotiated with the Taliban of Afghanistan.

The Taliban was a religious-military movement that claimed power over three-fourths of Afghanistan from 1996 until 2001, when they were ousted in the Bush war on terror after the 9/11 attack. Generally considered a terrorist group internationally, the harsh Taliban retreated to Pakistan and re-emerged as successive US presidents announced the intention to end the decades-long war in Afghanistan.

Perhaps as a political stunt in an election year when Covid was just surfacing, Trump struck a deal with the Taliban in February, by which US-led allied troops would be reduced in exchange for a Taliban promise not to attack. The deal that did not include the US-backed Afghan government, also freed 5,000 Taliban terrorists taken captive during the Bush-initiated war on terror. The reliability of the plan was demonstrated by an earlier deal Trump struck with the Taliban.

In November 2019, Trump jerry-rigged a secret meeting with the Taliban at America's Camp David. Apparently, he was staging a historic breakthrough for the elusive peace that had evaded Afghanistan for 40 years since the Soviets were ousted. The Camp David event was cancelled after a suicide bomb in Kabul killed an American soldier along with 11 others. The plan came to light when Trump boasted by Tweet about the deal he had almost pulled off with no mention of the optics in hosting terrorists at Camp David just days short of the 9/11 anniversary.

That was the deal handed to Biden when he won the 2020 US election. He extended the deadline for troop withdrawal but after 20 years the process of disengaging from a society grown accustomed to democracy proved complicated. With Taliban forces strengthened by the released prisoners and an Afghan government sidelined in the deal Trump made with the Taliban, the Taliban swept the country, the Afghan government collapsed and the drawdown chaos riveted global attention.

Biden received harsh criticism from sides for the rushed exit but America's military carried out its duties with a resourceful compassion that won admiration from all. At the same time, Biden demonstrated the qualities that proved him a worthy Commander in Chief of the world's most mighty military. He assumed responsibility for the decision and its operation. He cast no blame on his predecessors. He informed the public about the conduct of the operation and he left up to history any judgments about the wisdom of his actions. Most of all, because of his time-tested integrity, Biden was able to assure both America and the world that his aim was to achieve the best possible outcome, not to compound obstacles for a personal or political purpose.

Overall, the year 2021 was dreary for America and the world. Covid raged. Climate change wreaked havoc. Economies spluttered. In America, Republicans remained tethered to Trump, outlawing Covid mitigation measures, hijacking electoral processes and refusing to investigate the 1/6 coup attempt they claimed never happened. Meanwhile, Democrats splintered over centrist and progressive agendas, as if those issues mattered so long as the Trump inspired 1/6 remained unsolved.

The media paid scant attention to the multiple investigations conducted by the FBI, Congress and the Justice entities of the Justice Department. Perhaps they were lost, slow to adjust after the four-year adrenalin rush of news scandals provided by Trump. But perhaps there was another reason. The gravity of the offense could not be processed as a real part of America.

Again, to recap a point that could not be overstated, Trump nearly toppled to very concept of democracy itself. That villainous action was an outcome of four years in which he was allowed to use the grand US presidential powers to violate laws and Constitutional norms. He used those powers to break international treaties and threat others. He drained the public coffers for his own personal gain and he compromised the Justice Department so he could accomplish his aims.

In Banana Republics with weak constitutions and legal systems, inquiries into the actions of former leaders were often demonstrably based on politics. In America with its Constitutionally-solid legal structure, it was possible to subjugate politics to the rule of law. With the multitude of tasks before him in rebuilding America, bringing Trump to justice seemed a top priority in the global effort to curb the dictatorial impudence of engineering impunity for themselves.

"Rules are made to be broken" seemed the Trump motto, as if borrowed from Douglas MacArthur, a four-star US General largely disparaged for despotic actions during the Second World War, then in the Philippines and Korea. He lost a bid for the White House against Dwight Eisenhower in part for the position that atomic weapons should be used during the Cold War.

"I know more than the generals," Trump famously claimed during his 2016 campaign. Indeed, he outdid MacArthur in subverting the law. Regardless of mistakes that Biden could make while in office, he buried Trump with the integrity that made him deserving of America's mighty powers.

Where's the Beef in Trump America?

Once out of the Oval Office with social media platforms still suspended, Trump receded but not far. Republican adherents paid obeisance and carried on in his name under lead of the base that after Trump took on a life of its own. As Covid raged and Afghan evacuations dominated the news; Trump held a rally in crisis ridden Alabama and for the first time told supporters to "get the vaccine." He was booed.

In 1945, the year that the Second World War ended in Europe, British author George Orwell published his classic "Animal Farm," an allegorical tale about a group of animals who overthrew the farm's negligent human owner only to end up with an animal tyrant who was downright cruel. Orwell's 1949 classic entitled 1984 painted a picture of a society turned upside down by propaganda and ruled by a "Big Brother" that controlled all aspects of life, including thought.

America under Trump narrowly escaped those two fates. He won election by tearing down the best political system in the world that only needed upgrade. Once in control of the country's mighty powers, he controlled all within his reach through cruelty and knavery, including by convincing them to risk life itself by defying common sense in the face of a virus. Luckily for America and the world, Trump never managed to control more than a third of the country, the gullible part easily swayed by bad influences.

In the real year 1984, the American hamburger chain Wendy's released an ad that questioned the meat portion of products offered by large global conglomerate rivals. "Where's the beef?" became a catch phrase for the value of substance beyond a puffed-up presentation.

Thirty years later, Donald Trump won the 2016 US presidency with a flourish of fluff that over the next four years proved devoid of substance. It took a global pandemic to prove the emptiness of his bluff and bluster, A crisis that might have been mitigated by decisive action ran out of control because of Trump puffery. Seeming to be in control was apparently more important to Trump than the work of the Office he held, which meant there was no meat patty in hamburger Trump despite a third of the country either thinking that there was meat to burger Trump or not caring that there wasn't. In either case, that third of the country was scammed.

A successful scam called for a lot of fluff. The act of cheating by scam had many forms, including swindle, con and fraud. Most forms involved a veneer of having already achieved a measure of success. Also essential to a scam was smooth delivery of sales techniques only tangentially related to the truth of the transaction. The proverbial used-car salesman unloading lemons was a classic example of defrauding by scam. The speedometer was fixed, the spiel was delivered and indemnity from liability was covered by legal small print in the contract. Ultimately, the sale was clinched by persuasion, a communication technique covering a wide range of degrees.

Legitimate advertising was regulated by laws. Gray areas between practice and law were litigated in courts. That legal process was the way that laws evolved over time to close gaps between the many forms of persuasion that were questionable. The law settled disputes by determining the level of truth contained in the persuasive technique used. Facts played a central role in persuasion disputes. So did the question of whether facts were used to support or distort the truth. The field was vast and the legal process involved was understandably slow.

As an example, laws regulating Ponzi schemes dealt with a fine line between legitimate and illegal use of investor funds. If an investor expected to make a projected profit but the facts underlying the projection were possibly false, the claim of a scam was litigated in court. Nuances in the legal process of distinguishing truth from fact in persuasion seemed like splitting hairs to most non-lawyers, but the laborious legal process was the only way to protect the public. Without that protection, society was an open season free-for-all bonanza for crafty scammers out to bilk as many as possible. The legal safeguard forces the unscrupulous to exploit loopholes.

In Trump America, the all-important political arena was a goldmine of legal loopholes wide open to ambitious charlatans. The Constitutional right to free speech and expression seemed an albatross on the natural evolution of law. Gray areas were a vast wasteland between truth, fact and persuasive claims. Thus, seasoned conman Trump entered the political field no doubt well aware of a license to lie, defraud and persuade in any way to his liking and to his heart's content. He set out to mine for treasure.

Like scamming, the related evil art of lying had many forms, from little white lies to whoppers and fabrications all the way up to downright malicious intention. Trump pushed the license to lie beyond its outer limits by the alchemy of mixing the gamut of lies with other persuasive tools such as promises and threats. With those tools tested in the campaign field, he took the 2016 presidency and used the powers of that office to sweep up key portions of the country with so much fluff that they ended extorting democracy itself in the fog of having been gaslighted.

In advertising, fraudulent claims were relatively easy to spot though hard to prove in court. The product either delivered on the promise or failed to do so. The line between truth, fact and claim were fairly straight-forward however much limits were vague. "Puffery" was acceptable, a claim so outlandish it was assumed all consumers would recognize it as such. Thus, it was legal to claim your product was best but not to claim that an expert had declared your product best unless he/she had. Likewise, making unfounded health claims was illegal. Late night infomercial advertiser and Trump supporter

Mike Lindell of My Pillow fame, for example, dropped the claim of health benefits from his pillows but only as a result of a class action lawsuit. All such legal protections applied to minor areas of life were irrelevant to Trump once he was in politics and in the White House.

Trump in the White House changed America and the world forever. Before Trump, the limits of presidential power derived from the natural self-constraints of a person fit for the office. Basic human decency was just the starting line of the standards deemed requisitive for the trust to be placed in a person responsible for the world's most mighty powers. Respect was the measure of a person's merit, including the self-respect attendant with having achieved the position. Trump's bloated puffery while in the Oval Office, along with his need for adulation from a disgruntled crowd, was a sure sign that he was utterly devoid of self-respect, a flurry of fluff with no substance beneath a brash veneer.

Fluff had a tendency to scatter and settle on nearby surfaces. The dust ball of Trump with presidential powers flew like dandelion fuzz sent aloft by the wind. It settled and spread like viral contagion among adherents who clung to their view of Trump as a trailblazing maverick fighting for his right to take the country for all it had to offer. America, after all, was the land of liberty and opportunity. Bankruptcy laws gave strivers a second chance if they failed. Trump was a six-time beneficiary of that largesse. The Trump base admired him, gave him their loyalty, fought for him all the harder when enemies tried to take him down and didn't even mind if they were scammed. They seemed content with Trump except for constant anger.

Trump supporters laid blame for anger on outsiders, blacks who made trouble with their fight for equality and Democrats trying to restrict liberties. But from an outside perspective, it seemed obvious that they were angry because they bought the Trump burger believing there was a beef patty inside the fluffy Trump bun when in fact they were being scammed by a disconnect between fact, truth and claim.

Long before he reached for the ultimate enchilada of the US Presidency, Trump sold himself as a wealthy, savvy business tycoon. The claim was not backed by facts. He had run out of options for the legitimate funding needed to keep his Ponzi scheme afloat and he covered financial dealings affiliate and off-shoot decoys. But the process had taught him the evil art of manipulative persuasion in which the truth was a negligible nuisance to be circumvented at all costs.

It would take years for America and the world to recover from Trump. Historians would parse his sentences to find an astonishing lack of logic in his statements. But once the dust settled from the Trump thumping at the 2020 polls, perhaps America as a whole would review its dusty Constitution like any restaurant periodically updated its menu to reflect changing times.

Such a survey would help America ask the question of "Where's the beef?" and did it matter if there was no patty inside the fluffy bun. The answer could help America avert the fates that George Orwell feared for the world after the Second World War.

Trump sold himself as an easy solution to the complicated challenges of a globalizing world. A third of America bought his sales pitch, sticking with their purchase even after Covid unmasked him to reveal tofu instead of the red meat expected under the fluffy bun. That attraction to easy solutions, instead of substantive problem solving was an American specialty. The dynamic young American land of freedom and opportunity liked the romance of a carefree cowboy life. But Covid in the hands of Trump changed that trajectory forever.

As Covid continued its rampage because of an artificial, totally man-made and unnecessary catastrophe propelled from the

White House through the social media, the age-old question of the relationship between truth, fact and persuasion became newly relevant. Perhaps that would yet prove to be the unifying element that drew a triumphant America into the greater world of democratic ideals once the fluff adventure with Donald Trump was put to rest through America's restored Justice system.

Defusing the MAGA Mob-sters

Trump lost his signature Twitter platform when the mob he incited stormed the US Capitol to stop the vote count verifying Joe Biden as the next US President. The ultimate crime of sedition against the country he headed was obvious. Proving liability was mired in the chaos that was the hallmark of every Trump venture…

Trump found his opportunity to seize the country in the social media havoc that overturned social norms. In that environment of "anything goes," he took the 2016 election by trumpeting the basest of human instincts. That appalled most Americans but it caught fire with enough of a minority to get him into office on a technicality.

Trump's big strike was with the disgruntled in America. Most were white men resistant to rapid changes in a modern globalizing world. As in classic Greek drama, a Trump spectacle had a cathartic effect on those he attracted. He gave voice to feelings repressed in the socializing process taught from earliest days. Trump liberated the beast in those who needed the release. He was a quack who unleashed behaviors based on feelings best worked out on an analyst's couch.

Public validation of base impulses forged a bond of affinity between Trump and his admirers. When he elevated the antisocial attitude to the highest level of the US government, adulation turned into idolatry. That sucked a complementary portion of America's conservative Republicans into the vortex of opportunism. Through Trump, like-minded conservatives tapped into base instincts to get elected. Once in office, they were wired into the Trump machine, a Rube Goldberg type of chain reaction generator that turned a simple task into an indirect and overly complicated process.

Trump first appeared as a 2016 presidential candidate in the guise of a successful businessman offering his expertise to rescue what he presented as a downtrodden America. His pitch was aimed at the working class in the American heartland, where traditional jobs were threatened by climate reality, globalization and technology. All were unsettling to those expecting life to be the same as it had been for generations.

The Trump sales pitch in 2016 was a mulligan stew. of doomsday threats and grandiose promises of restoring a past glory that never was. The baseball cap worn with a suit and emblazoned with MAGA to Make America Great Again became Trump trademarks symbolizing his doctrine, which was to restore America to greatness by building walls against immigrants and bringing back jobs grown obsolete. Along with threats and empty promises that sounded good, the doctrine was replayed at rallies like a sports cheer. Delivered with the authority of the Oval Office behind it for four years, the success of the doctrine with the base became became woven into media outrage at Trump excesses and in turn with the growing defiance of the base against the media even as Trump worked the media in his favor. But Twitter was the crown jewel in the Trump arsenal for owning America like a real estate holding. A Trump Tweet could make or break any Republican. It was the tool by which Trump tightened the ligature between himself, his admirers and the hungry Republicans cashing in on him as a meal ticket.

Loyalty was the price of admission to the Trump train headed for Easy Street. "Can't argue with success," Trump politicians seemed to say, limber in jumping to back him whenever Trump deflected charges against him.

The MAGA mob was the barometer for Republicans. To Trump, the mob was the North Star. They validated him and confirmed his course was set in the right direction. Trump admirers didn't care about transgressions or lies. To them, rules were made to be broken anyway. Trump carried off that sleight of hand with expert agility. Republicans saw the rallies, noted the media outrage over them and were reassured. Trump made followers feel good. That was good enough for the Trump political mobsters dead set on re-election.

Like all structures built on flimsy foundations, the Trump MAGA game plan crumbled when he failed to win re-election in 2020. Trump pulled all his punches to stay in office but nothing worked. He exhausted the entire legal system. He broke the Republican party with threats, failed bribes and recounts that came up empty in his quest. With Twitter still available to him at the time, Trump summoned the mob to Washington for January 6, the day Congress would confirm the Biden Electoral College win for the presidency already certified by states. "Be there. Will be wild," he Tweeted after weeks of calling for supporters to "stop the steal."

Thousands of misfits, malcontents, hot heads, thrill seekers and devotees answered the call. They came from all parts of the country, including distant Hawaii. They coalesced in Washington and on January 6 was fortified by a final call to arms at a Trump gala rally. Representative Mo Brooks of Alabama wore body armor. Trump attorney Rudy Giuliani called for trial by combat. Trump son Don Jr. warned Republicans about reprisals if they voted to confirm the Biden wins. Then Trump called on vice president Mike Pence to overturn the election result. He ended by sending the mob to the Capitol with the promise that he was going with them. The last of the crowd arrived at the Capitol to find the assault already underway. The horde as a whole breached the Capitol and nearly carried out self-assigned assassinations of lawmakers, including vice-president Mike Pence.

The storming of the US Capitol delayed the vote verification process but failed to derail it. As the dust settled over weeks, the roles of mob and mobsters changed places to carry on the Trump legacy after he was out of office but not beyond hearing.

When the MAGA mob failed in its assigned task, MAGA political mobsters took over. The MAGA mob dispersed after the failed coup but Republicans were anchored in Washington. They downplayed and denied the violence captured on videotape from dozens of angles.

Videotape of the George Floyd murder broke through decades of denial about police brutality against America's blacks. The validity of videotape capturing the Capital coup was dismissed by Republicans, perhaps because the insurrection for them was nothing more than a plan that failed.

Senator Ron Johnson of Wisconsin said he wasn't concerned about the pro-Trump mob at the Capitol on January 6. Had the tables been turned and Trump won the election, he would have been concerned about an Antifa or Black Lives Matter protest, South Carolina's senator Lindsey Graham called Trump during the riot and asked him to call off his people. He voted against setting up a Commission to investigate the circumstances related to the deadly assault on the US Capitol and the democratic process of confirming votes already certified by state legislatures. Graham made a pilgrimage to Trump at the Mar-a-Lago resort in February, following in the footsteps of House minority leader Kevin McCarthy, who visited Trump a week after Biden's inauguration to discuss upcoming elections.

The early planning was reminiscent of a decade earlier. After Obama won the 2008 election, 2010 midterm elections gave Republicans a big boost in Washington. Republicans gained seven senate seats and a whopping 63 House seats. While still a minority in the Senate, Republican leader Mitch McConnell of Kentucky said the number one goal of Congress was to make sure that Obama was a one-term president. The ultra-conservative Tea Party movement that sprang up within weeks of Obama's election played a major role in the statewide Republican wins.

Similarly, after the 1/6 insurrection in 2021, Republicans were again, intent on regaining control of both the House and Senate with a strategy more extreme than the earlier Tea Party. By 2019, the Freedom Caucus was even more conservative. It was started by Jim Jordan of Ohio. When he stepped aside for more influential positions first on the Oversight committee during the first Trump Impeachment process and then on the Judiciary Committee, he was replaced by super-conservative Mark Meadows of North Carolina, who was called away to be Trump's chief of staff in March of 2020 election years. After Trump lost the election, Meadows became a chief proponent of the "Big Lie" purporting baseless claims of voter fraud. In wake of the 1/6 insurrection and ongoing inquiries, he declared he would not seek re-election in 2022.

Representatives in the House served two-year terms in contrast to senators elected for six-year terms. Among those who would elect the next round of representatives were the 1/6 insurrectionists of the Trump MAGA mob. Seven months after the 1/6 assault on the Capitol, more than 600 were rounded up nationwide. Many arrests resulted from tips to the FBI and local law enforcement from citizens who recognized familiar faces on the videotapes that Republicans still treated as nonexistent. Meanwhile, the 1/6 Select Committee set up after Republicans rejected a bid to set up a broader Commission, signalled its readiness to seek phone records of those involved in the insurrection, including members of Congress including Kevin McCarthy, Jim Jordan and White House executives.

Regardless of what the investigation uncovered, the assault on the Capitol had ended as an act of sedition. The Constitution clearly stated that attempts to overthrow the government were among the worst offences. To address the situation, Trump political mobsters with legally undefined status adopted the Trump signature tactic. They created chaos to preserve the political advantage gained through the Trump mob….

Trump was impeached for sedition in the House of Representatives while he was still in Office. The ensuing trial in the Senate was politically delayed until he was out of office, which gave Republicans a convenient excuse for not convicting a president no longer in office. The novel connivery brought into relief the interplay between emotional conviction, political jockeying and rational maintaining of social order by rule of law.

The Trump MAGA mob that stormed Washington to defend false claims of voter fraud dismissed by courts was probably convinced that the 2020 election was rigged and that the election was stolen from Trump. There was no supporting evidence for the claim and yet no amount of evidence would convince the misguided that the election was legitimate and that Trump had lost. The key to that disconnect between belief and reality was based in the toxic bond between Trump and his mob to begin with.

Trump sold himself as an avatar of blissful simplicity in a complex world. It was a classic sales pitch used by political and religious movers from earliest days of history. In America, snake oil was the common shorthand for fraudulent claims. But the difference between a legitimate claim and a fake one lay in the simple test of intent.

Trump was a social divider plundering the land of opportunity for the opportunism of personal gain. To him, the MAGA mob was a tool to implement a vast organized crime network. By definition, a mob was a disorganized crowd. a mobster was a member of an organized crime group. Trump managed to arrange a marriage between the two opposites. He harnessed a disorganized mob into the pursuits of an organized crime group at the highest level of the mighty United States.

Many in the MAGA mob were disillusioned with Trump as the rule of law came to affect them directly. They were like the litigants who won a class action lawsuit against the Trump University that failed to deliver on tempting get-rich-quick promises. Bait and switch was a common con in the curriculum. Enrollees signed up for a course, then were persuaded to switch to a more dynamic plan at a higher price. Trump settled the lawsuit when the presidency offered him unlimited opportunities.

In a way, Trump ran a Trump University scam on the entire Republican party with the aid of his mob shills. The irony of the MAGA mob couldn't be starker. They attacked a government that allowed them the freedom to do so. That government was built over a period of near 250-years based on a constitution that formed the foundation for the natural evolution of law as society grew. One branch of US government made laws, another implemented them and a third settled disputes about legitimacy. Over four years, Trump knee-capped all three branches to establish his ambitious organized crime racket.

When Trump called his mob to storm the US Capitol, in essence he directed them to kill the goose that laid the golden egg. In that legend about greed, a foolish couple killed a goose to get at the great store of gold they figured was lying within the goose. The mob took the bait. Trump's political mobsters rode the tailwind of that pyrrhic victory.

In America, the ultimate outcome of the 1/6 attempted coup was the affirmation that the Constitution was a solid foundation for the rule of law. The legal processes that led to the evolution law in order to meet the challenges of changing times would undergo serious review after Trump. Before Trump, the land of opportunity had created the environment that enabled an opportunistic grubber to usurp the system and turn it into an organized crime operation. The MAGA mob and political mobsters were prey for the scam. Upstanding citizens faithful to the law and each other enabled the country to withstand the roguery.

Convicted or not, Donald Trump was unmasked and defanged by the 2020 election that stretched beyond 2020 because of the chaos he created to protect himself. Mobsters carried on after him but the mob was scattered in pieces under the rule of law reality, eventually they would melt back into the American fabric of comfortable decency because the remaining political mobsters just didn't have the level of skill with fraud to hold their interest.

Devil in Disguise Qanon Don Does CPAC

US President Joe Biden was savvy in labeling his predecessor as "former guy." Trump was a master of branding, plastering his name across the world to get into every face on earth. By the end of his presidency, the name was associated with every right wing, white supremacist and conspiracy fringe from Proud Boys to Six Percenters to QAnon, a shadowy worldwide by-product of technology that became a syphon for all kinds of web groups of a sinister nature.

The web presence of QAnon receded after the 1/6 assault on the Capitol followed by the Trump ouster from the White House despite the fact that he never conceded and continued his claims of voter fraud and a stolen election. The Trump base continued to believe the fraudulent claim that the election had been fraudulent. Essentially, Trump had created a house of mirrors for a third of the country. In that space, truth and claim were inextricably entwined, which seemed to be the opening that the wounded Republican party needed.

As a result of two highly contested Senate seats in Georgia that Democrats won on January 5, the day before the Capitol riot, Democrats picked up three seats in the Senate to give them the slimmest majority with vice president Kamala Harris the tie-breaker in an evenly split Senate. Democrats also lost ten seats in the House of Representatives, which kept them the majority but with only the slightest margin, with a number of seats to be determined by vote later in the year. Noting the Democratic fragility, Republicans clung to Trump as their great white hope.

After his presidential defeat, Trump made his first public appearance in Orlando Florida in February as the keynote speaker at the annual conference of the Conservative Political Action Committee, a networking organization to promote conservative causes. A second special CPAC conference was held in Dallas during July, where Trump was again the keynote speaker. Texas governor Greg Abbott did not attend but Trump Junior was there to rally the crowd 3,000 strong. Also speaking was Texas state Attorney General Ken Paxton, who for six years had been under indictment for felony security fraud charges. Rounding out the list of incendiary speakers was Ronny Jackson, the drug-abusing former White House physician who testified that Trump was the healthiest man he'd ever seen. As a representative of Texas in the US House of Representatives in 2021, he called for a mental evaluation of Biden,

At both CPAC conferences, Trump reiterated his claim that the election had been stolen from him. He also threw out the favorite red-meat issues calling for secure borders and freeing the country from the grip of the Socialist Democrats trying to destroy America. The tropes were received to wild applause by the Republicans, who needed the Trump audacity to promote an agenda that in their hands would never attract enough mob members to win an election.

There was no denying that Trump could rally a crowd, whether or not it was orchestrated. The wacky QAnon movement first came to mainstream attention through media coverage of a Trump rally. But it was noteworthy that the events were held largely in small towns not usually graced by personages. Any aspect of the spectacle could have been the attractant, and still it was strong enough to addict adherents to the point where they gladly risked life itself to witness a "super-spreader" spree during Covid. Perhaps they still believed that the virus was a hoax as Trump had claimed during the first months as the disease spread. More likely, the Trump rallies satisfied a hunger for a concrete anchor in a formless, ephemeral world of technology. Both QAnon and "former guy" fit the bill and when mixed together they satisfied like a stiff mixed drink. They also exploded like uranium and plutonium in a nuclear bomb, bringing to a head an ancient struggle between good and evil, fought on the battleground of rationality over base instinct.

Belief in God or devil was not necessary to accept both terms as symbols inherent in their names. God and good, devil and evil were obvious. The difference between the two was set out from the earliest humanoid days even before civilization. By the time of the Bible, for example, there was a God who began with a void that he filled with a universe in an orderly way. When finished, he rested at home in heaven with helper angels. All were pleased with earth below, the special place for plants, animals and humans made in God's image housed in the fertile Garden of Eden. Bliss prevailed until God's chief helper grew impatient with the limits of God's creation and his sole right to make decisions.

The archangel Lucifer challenged God and lost. He was cast out to establish his own domain apposite that of God with earth in between. Thus, the first solid form to emerge from the void became the battleground to determine who would rule the universe. Fueled by fury and convinced he could outdo God, the fallen Lucifer looked for ways to recruit others to his cause. Opportunity arose in the Garden of Eden, where God had planted a tree designed to keep humans in line with earth's limitations.

The tree bore a fruit that revealed the secret of God's exclusive power, which was to know the difference between good and evil. Humans were forbidden to eat of the tree and they were never tempted since they were satisfied with tending God's garden. But in the tenderness with which humans cared for God's creations, Lucifer saw an Achilles heel and began to woo the humans.

The humans ate of the tree and were cast from the garden to learn God's secret the hard way through experience. The rest has been human history on earth. Humans had chosen to learn God's secret the hard way at the behest of the fallen Lucifer, which made them living pawns in a divine chess game between God and Lucifer. In that game, "living" was the operative word. Humans were free to choose between the side of God or that of Lucifer, whose only source of power was the claim that he had plan grander than that of God. With specifics left unmentioned, humans were left with the choice of opting for the world God had already created or taking a chance on a plan that required the destruction of God's world for realization. That choice elevated humans from the level of being mere pawns in the divine chess game and up to the level of being invested go-betweens.

The human journey on Earth reflected the path God took to create the universe. He made order out of a formless void, because concrete substance was better than empty space. Likewise, the outcast humans tamed wilderness on earth in an orderly fashion. But unlike God who finished his work in six days, humans have taken many millennia to make a dent in the chaotic earth they had chosen. From Stone Age tools to the mysteries of Quantum Physics, humans found their way forward by trial and error as they clarified areas of science, culture and art. The journey was a jamboree for Lucifer. Humans were looking for the harmony of God's heaven but Lucifer spiced up his offer with the seduction of excitement.

Follow me and you'll be greater than God, Lucifer prodded as he did in the bed that got him ousted from heaven. On earth, the claim seemed valid. The prospect of controlling all earth was compelling. To clinch the deal, Lucifer took a cue from God and returned to the great void created by technology, seizing chaos to undermine God's order.

The Tech Age rocked humans on earth as soundly as Gutenberg with his printing press in the Middle Ages. In the 21st century, the effect was global. Overnight, more people knew more information than ever and much of the knowledge was false. Lucifer was delighted when "former guy" and QAnon met up in a serendipitous union even he couldn't have planned.

Chaos was the devil's wading pool on earth and QAnon became its sump pump, drawing fringe groups into its fold like a black hole in space. With no concrete truth of God to fill the void, QAnon drew scary hobgoblins that arose in the dead of night. It was an internet sensation that caught the fancy of "former guy" Trump who was an empty vessel desperate to be filled with concrete adulation that never satisfied. The huckster "former guy" and the QAnon web phenomenon was like Tantalus to each other. Both offered grand promises. Neither ever defined the form that the grandness would take and neither ever delivered.

The mystery of the great void has been the driving force throughout all creation. God filled the emptiness with concrete good. Lucifer claimed he could do better without any proof. When humans demanded proof, all he could do was distract by making a hash out of what God had created.

By all accounts, former guy was fixated on glitz, money, glamour and above all the attention that came with the trappings of earthly success. The design of his garish high-rise buildings across the world attested to his preference for the glitter of fool's gold. Likewise, the murky QAnon conspiracy theories likely had their origins in multi-twisted unrelated news about scientific developments such as stem cell research and collagen treatments. In the hands of the careless under influence of the chaos Lucifer liked to throw into God's works, earth seemed headed back into the great void. Luckily, humans weren't done with their task of making earth harmonious like God's heaven.

The devil is in the details, said German philosopher Friedrich Nietzsche more than 150 years ago. God was in the details, said architect Mies van der Rohe among others at about the same time. In truth on earth, both God and the Devil were in the details. Only humans could decide which details to decipher and heed. On earth, God's way was solid, steady and straightforward. Lucifer's was chaotic, uncertain and, horror of horrors for humans, exciting.

As with other aspects of life on earth, excitement came from either of two sources. It came either from following God's plan of continuous creation or the prodding of Lucifer to upend God's design for some nameless but tantalizing fantasy. The only way to tell the difference was to attend to the details that revealed the distinctions.

***

HELEN FOGARASSY

Bonkers America in a Tech-Addled Covid World

In 2021, the world's greatest economic powerhouse had a serious problem. The country was one body with countless split personalities.

The Covid pandemic still raged, as did social hostile about how to handle new variants. Racial reckoning sizzled with critical race theory at odds with white defensiveness. Law enforcement was under fire, violence was spiking, mass shootings were routine and the climate wreaked havoc with fires and floods. Insurrection was in the air as a new President put into practice a lifetime of experience to right the Ship of State in a global world while the ghost of the White House former guy stalked a chunk of the population like heartburn near the end of a bad meal.

The global Melting Pot exploded during a four-year backlash after America elected the western industrialized world's first non-white head of state. For eight years, half-white Barack Obama braved an uphill battle with conservatives bent on blocking him. Near the end of his term, the firebrand hellhound Trump burst forth to erase all traces of Obama and his progressive gains.

Even before he took Office, Trump the destroyer began savaging the US Constitution, hounding immigrants and courting global tyrants while snubbing allies. His tenure ended in a cascade of disasters that eroded civilization itself. He turned a virus into a political weapon, conflating a -straight-forward biological threat into a social rivalry where freedom was at odds with common sense. The end goal became clear when Trump lost the next election, his followers staged a coup and his conservative enablers denied that any coup had been attempted. America in 2021 couldn't have been more bonkers except that it became more so throughout the year.

Despite the loud and even violent support of his base, there was no telling how valid was the 2016 election that gave the presidency to Trump. Evidence of foreign interference was clear and it led to tightening of security for the 2020 election. But once in office, he tightened his hold on conservative Republicans by manipulating the base, a dynamic that escalated to warp speed when the Covid pandemic hit.

The brand-new form of a virus that baffled scientists proved to be a brand-new challenge to Trump. It showed up in the very next election year and its severity was a threat to the booming economy that would secure him re-election. As the virus spiraled out of control, the Trump tragedy seemed to shift from denying the pandemic to daring his followers to at first brave it out and then to defy mitigation measures as a patriotic duty.

In essence, nature threw a spit ball at Trump and he turned the Covid plague into a nuclear bomb that radiated well beyond his tenure. He used the authority of his office to augment impetuous Tweets in a volatile mix that turned the country upside down until it erupted in a coup attempt when he lost the next election. Further with the spontaneous combustion of that coup, he hog-tied Republicans into a rolling black comedy with which to keep himself relevant and viable long after he vacated the White House premises.

No one knew why Trump wanted to be president, perhaps for no greater reason than Mallory climbing Everest because "it was there." Yet once in Office, Trump turned autocrat, ignoring laws and grabbing all the bounty he could. When he lost the 2020 election, the true dictator emerged. He refused to give up power he'd accrued. Had he succeeded, America's masses would have overturned democracy in favor of a Republican plutocracy ruled by Tweet decree, posted between rounds of golf at proprietary resorts funded by tax dollars.

Perhaps that scenario would have satisfied the Trump base but clearly the American masses rejected that direction for the country. Still, it was a close call for the world's beacon of democracy at the mercy of a violent mob intent on seizing the Capitol for their autocratic leader. The irony was that the action was taken in the cause of "freedom" and "patriotism" in the land that allowed the historic liberties.

Trump became president because of the latitude given in America to the personal traits of political candidates. Basically, they could run if they were able to withstand attacks on their reputation and record. Trump blew past all parameters and the base loved alacrity. Republicans rode the Trump coattails to curry favor with the base and the dictatorial traits became blended into other idiosyncrasies, particularly the Trump penchant for pettifoggery.

"It's always good to do things nice and complicated so nobody can figure it out," Trump told the New Yorker in 1997. That attitude in the White House Oval Office led to more than 600,000 Covid deaths by 2021, with armed threats against mask mandates in schools and the menace of body harm to election officials over false claims of voter fraud disclaimed dozens of times over.

With the 2020 election, long-stable America had a close brush with the reversal of democracy experienced by emerging democracies such as that in Middle European countries liberated just 40 years earlier from Soviet domination. Like those newly emerging dictators, Trump targeted the vulnerable and won them over with fear and targeted empty promises. He stirred passions by creating enemies all could hate while he played both sides of the fence to build his presence, as he did with the media he vilified. At rallies he painted himself as an omnipotent god persecuted by inferiors intent on bringing him down. All those tactics used by dictators throughout history would not have succeeded in the world's democratic stronghold without a corruption of the Constitutionally protected liberties spelled out in the very first amendment.

Freedom of speech, expression, press and religion were of primary concern to the founding fathers whose own origins began with a flight from England to escape religious persecution. Over time, the Supreme Court refined that freedom to place limits on a right not absolute in a social context. Areas outside the first amendment were those most harmful to society such as fraud, false advertising and child pornography. So far, hate speech has been protected, however vile. Political speech has been especially sheltered, presumably to avoid infringing on other rights such as speech and assembly. The area of incitement to riot was particularly hazy, a twilight zone where Trump excelled.

Trump kept his base spellbound with ambiguity. A healthcare plan was on the way for four years, as was an infrastructure revamp by the master builder he claimed to be. A historic peace plan with North Korea was coming soon. There were good people on both sides of a clash between neo-Nazi white supremacists and those opposing the villainy. We did nothing wrong, it was a perfect phone call, he said of his attempt to extort the Ukrainian president. In four short years, Trump was impeached twice, exonerated both times based on political considerations. Abuse of power was first, then came the inciting of an insurrection a month after he lost the election and dragged the process through the courts all the way to the top. And even after Trump left the White House and Biden was sworn in as president, Republicans covered for Trump, their reasons wide open for speculation and exploitation.

Republicans clearly did not want clarification of events surrounding the January 6 insurrection or stirrup the democratic process of certifying the Biden win that Trump supporters still would not accept. They nixed a broad-based Commission to investigate, then vilified Republicans with integrity who participated in a more targeted Committee probing the unsettling events, possibly because Republicans were loath to examine the fine legal line between general and specific incitement.

By Supreme Court rulings as understood by a legal outsider, culpability for incitement depended on intent and state of mind, both areas difficult to ascertain and prove. Thus, it was permissible to call on others to rise up against the state but not to send them to destroy the Capitol. That fine line was no doubt intriguing to lawyers at the same time that it was uneasy cover for Trump supporting Republicans. But both the Trump base and democratic Americans at large were caught by that fine line in the broader American issue of rational freedom versus enslavement to force-fed information that backed up already hardened preconceptions.

America suffered from a crisis of trust when Trump and the internet rose in the mid to late 1980's. The Iron Curtain fell by the end of that period to free Eastern Europe and shortly thereafter to dissolve the Soviet Union back into Russia. America during that time was recovering from the Viet Nam War topped by the Nixon scandals. Trust in the government was at an all-time low when the 9/11 attack occurred shortly into the new century. Having courted Russia since its Soviet days, Trump readied himself during the Obama years for a take-down of democracy with classic propaganda amped up to internet speed.

Trump was an expert swindler and a master liar, as evidenced by his response to the Covid pandemic threatening his strong economy in an election year. At first, he called the pandemic a hoax, then he said it would disappear and finally he said it was nothing to fear, the sturdy would endure. While inconsistent, the simplicity of those messages struck a chord with Americans already skeptical of the government and confused by cautious guidelines coming from scientists trying to navigate a new disease through troubled political waters. To those Americans already sold on conspiracies and simplistic social solutions such as white supremacy, Trump was a savior hero born of the social media world.

A world united by technology had plenty of room for both growth and logical twists on reality. Logically enough, the illogical pathways were more alluring than the ones of reason requiring patience to navigate. It was easier and more instantly gratifying to blast an opponent than to arrange and conduct a sit down exchange. The difference between the two approaches was cataclysmic, of course. Fall-out differed enormously. But the internet provided the cushion to blend, mute and manipulate the fallout from head on attacks, particularly when it came to the seriously impassioned American game of politics.

The irony of the Trump presidency was the reverse effect of apparently intended political aims. In managing Covid, for example, he rewarded the red Republican states while denigrating the blue Democratic ones. And while those divisions did become ossified during his tenure, the overlaps also came into relief.

Democratic cities within Republican states had more in common with each other than with their state politics. That situation was apparently the result of an overall demographic shift from rural to urban areas to create the purple zone that came to prominence when Trump lost the election he had rigged while professing all along that he would lose only if the election was rigged. The subterfuge was no different from that which Trump had used since he first entered the political arena as a big city business tycoon out to help America's rural areas. The fallacy of that scenario was clear when measured by the five human senses.

Trump never mingled with fans. He summoned and they obeyed, drawn by the Trump mystique. And many did in fact believe in the lies he sold, led away from reliance on their senses by social media, Republican Trump backers and a news media that failed the needs of everyday Americans from both the left and right of the political spectrum.

The corporate world of the mainstream American news media was behind the eight-ball in comparison with the social media web work. Accredited news sources had numerous layers of fact checking to assure accuracy. A Facebook posting needed no more time than for one reader to read a mere headline before a story was launched to countless contacts. While that emerging area of news sharing went through the laborious legal process of clarification, the basic human function of wise discernment came into question.

A charge of "fraud" had no legal standing without proof, nor did it have any credibility with reasonably solid everyday people in a routine situation. One could claim that a product was a rip-off, but seldom did such an exchange warrant legal action requiring proof. For Trump to claim that the 2020 election was a fraud without any proof and with that to put the country through months of torn agony so severe that it inspired a coup was nothing short of a travesty that made a mockery of the country itself. The logic was the anchor that kept democratic ideals grounded to the real world upended by Trump and allies through the nebulous unregulated realm of social media.

In the 21st century, coups happened in nations emerging from transitional periods between regimes. Fraudulent elections were claimed by emerging democracies against entrenched autocrats. Sitting autocrats put down activists protesting suppression. In democratic America, a would-be autocrat tried every legal and illegal tactic to put down those upholding a legitimate election. It was the inverse reality in which Trump excelled when peddling snake oil.

There was no hint of fraud in the 2020 US election, declared by the head of the Homeland Security Cyber head as the most secure ever because of measures instituted after the confirmed foreign meddling in the 2016 election of Trump. But a big swathe orf America needed no proof of fraud to be convinced that it had occurred simply because that was the result they wanted and it was backed by those they trusted on social media.

In 2021, America was still the global world's beacon of democracy and it was still that world's great innovator. But that lead was shrinking, possibly because Americans spent more time on new acquisitions that on learning how to make good use of them. That was how Trump nearly purloined American democracy with the brazen false claim than he'd been robbed of an election he had never owned, which pointed to yet another irony of the Trump presidency.

Based on numerous reliable sources about his background, it was a good bet that Trump was eager to encourage the white supremacist hate groups that had begun to billow with the 2008 Obama election. Those came alive when the 2016 Trump election seemed to give legitimacy to their platform. They burgeoned over the four years that Trump spread their message with the authority of the Oval Office. When he lost that position, they sprang to grab it back with the help of the conservative Republican party dependent on Trump through his control of the conservative base hooked on social media.

Technology has been a harsh master for the last near-200 years since the 1800's Industrial Revolution. The 50-year-old Web revolution threw a speedball into the social upheaval. When Trump coopted the American conservative party by manipulating social media, he brought America to the tipping point of whether it would remain a democracy or morph into a plutocracy of the wealthy championed by an autocrat just like Putin with oligarchs in Russia.

Judging by history, humans did not take well to subjugation. Revolution such as that of the French and the Americans were proof, as were slave rebellions from Roman times to the New World of America. Yet Trump and his Republican allies tried to impose that barbarity on the seat of American democracy through a perversion of its evolving communication process.

Hardline conservative America no doubt knew what it was doing by accepting Trump as its mascot to consolidate a waning power by capturing a vulnerable segment of American society. In that plan, mainstream America was collateral damage as big city hustler Trump barn-stormed No-name regions of America until Covid brought Big-name America to No-name spots and put them on the map. It was a process that got America to know itself during a quarantine period in which the George Floyd murder could not escape emotionally invested notice. The only ones immune were political operatives aligned with dedicated haters connected by the internet.

In 2021 America, Covid continued to rule as America struggled toward a 70% herd immunity with vaccinations. The idea was that not all needed to be vaccinated, just enough to carry the whole to safety. Likewise on the political front, it was not necessary for all Americans to be convinced that democracy depended on personal discretion to sort truth from falsehood. Herd immunity against tyranny began when America faced down an insurrection and persisted in sorting through a glut of information to arrive at wisdom by finding out just how the insurrection had happened.

In 2021, America was caught in a deep well of misinformation. The only way out was to slow down and assess a complex global situation in which the temptation of simplicity was alluring. Anywhere in the world, a tyrant promising security turned out to be suffocating to those used to freedom and justice, even to those who just tasted it. That led to America's next step in emerging from the well of misinformation, which was to reach out for clues through global others.

America became involved with Afghanistan through a misguided war on terror after the 9/11 attack. Twenty years later, America withdrew from Afghanistan with no awareness of how beneficially it had affected that country regardless of earlier aims. But a sober recognition of the current situation suggested the wisdom of calling on a global mechanisms set up after the last World War that had been abandoned in a fledgling state.

The Second World War ended in the 1940's with the dropping of the atomic bomb, a signal that any future global conflict would end in annihilation of the world. Wisdom prevailed. The United Nations was formed as a forum for airing national grievances. Offshoots were set up to promote global economic equality, development and common values. Like many a human stroke of genius, the plan hit the skids when it came to details relating to power and information made public. As the most influential member of the United Nations, the Unite States had the power to power to move the world through information as long as it exercised the wisdom of the common sense that Joe Biden brought back to America after Trump.

By 2021, the technology that drove the world for over 150 years with the industrial revolution turned into the digital revolution was at a crossroads. Climate change was undeniable as parts of the world burned and flooded by turns. In America, a new koan emerged to stimulate insight. What was the value of 2,000 Fb bffs when next-door neighbors couldn't be visited?

Those mysteries in the modern world called for global solutions and the irony of progress in the modern age was phenomenal. Technological improvements were aimed to reduce tedium and make life easier for all. Collaterally, they have increased stresses. Online bill pay, for example, has proven to be convenient but expectation of ease rendered any snag a major episode of frustration. The only solution to negotiating the snag was to exercise patience, a skill not learned on line.

Nations United by the US 2020 Election Debacle

Baseball, mom and apple pie, all warm fuzzy images of America, land of the free and home of the brave. Those symbols were nowhere to be found in the US election of the Covid year 2020, when many speculated that the world's great superpower was in decline.

Others saw America rebooting to a global reality after a long journey from the George Washington "cannot tell a lie" to Trump saying "stolen" when a legitimate election was held. Trump contested the result even though there was no basis. His claims were dismissed by all courts from local to the Supremes, and still a third of America believed the Trump lie about a fraudulent vote. The gullibility of those who believed the lie was perhaps telling about other vulnerabilities to address to prevent the feared decline.

The world was used to America as the leader in all things democratic, but the authoritative Pew Research Center has highlighted areas where America lagged behind other advanced economy peers. Voter participation was one. The 2020 election saw a record number of Americans voting at the rate of 77.5% of the voting age population. That number was up from the 55.5% who voted in 2016. But even with that record number, the voter turnout rate was below that of Denmark, for example, which had an 87% voter turnout in its last national election held in 2014, according to the Global Citizen activist group in a 2021 article on why the turnout rate was usually low in the United States,

Democracy loving America, it turned out, fell short on making it easy for citizens to vote. The 50 states had different systems and requirements. In 2002, an Act requiring a photo ID to vote was signed into law by George W. Bush, who was named president by a Supreme Court decision. As of 2021, 36 states required a photo ID to vote, which was not easily obtained by the elderly and many in rural and economically depressed areas with limited access to the government offices issuing the ID's.

Further, most states had complicated registration routines. Most democratic US peers had automatic voter registration whereby citizens were registered to vote in tandem with other certifying procedures. In the United States that would be based on Social Security number s.

States in America also had confusing laws regarding voting methods, including vote by mail, absentee and early voting. Some sent ballots automatically to eligible voters, in other states the ballots had to be requested by the voter. States differed on the voting status of groups such as prisoners and they had varying systems for counting the votes. Then on top of those hurdles, social influences regarding age, gender and socioeconomic circumstance factors could dampen the desire to vote. Finally, the Tuesday voting day was a deterrent for working citizens not in position to take unpaid time off from work to stand in long lines to vote. In the 2020 election, Trump made a tossed salad out of those state voting complexities.

According to the Global Citizen, Blacks who voted for Obama in 2014 did not show up for Hillary Clinton in 2016 because they lacked enthusiasm. Others failed to show because they felt their vote wouldn't make a difference. The combination handed Trump the presidency in 2016 and he later thanked Blacks for not casting a Hillary vote. That was a mistake they seemed intent to avoid in 2020.

The 11-hour wait lines for casting a vote created a sensation around the world, according to the BBC. Most of those lines were in predominantly Black and minority areas with few polling sites. Those lines became community sensations, with local eateries providing food and refreshments to those in line while voters themselves provided impromptu entertainment. In the 2021 ruckus created by Trump and allies in wake of his electoral loss, those amenities became the target of "voter security" measures instituted by Republican state legislatures intent on control of vote tallies even as the Trump mob threatened with bodily harm the state electoral professionals who had refused to taint the vote in Trump's favor.

In the Covid-weary global world of 2021 battered by fires and floods due to global climate change, the twice-impeached former US president was under investigation in multiple US states for a range of crimes ranging from tax evasion and election tampering to fomenting a coup. He was also floating the idea of another run for president in 2024 with Republicans at the ready to service his needs regardless of his decision. The mob that had staged the attempted coup to derail the democratic process was hailing itself as a band of patriotic heroes demanding protection of their Constitutional rights. Clearly democracy in America was derailed and in need of urgent, radical overhaul to properly function again.

The blueprint for such remedial intervention was amply mapped out by scholars and analysts. Political journalist Mehdi Hasan in 2018 noted seven areas where American democracy could be strengthened to make the government truly representative of its people. Elimination of the quaint Electoral College now skewed to the rural 1700's would give an equitable voice to the modern urban population. A new federal voting rights act could simplify the convoluted and fraud prone current state system.

Further, Hasan called for eliminating gerrymandering, the redistricting system that artificially delineated voting base areas for political advantage. Likewise, he said the filibuster had to go. It was a dated tool aimed at bipartisanship in an age when one party was obviously not interested in cooperative problem solving. The "dark money" allowed into politics by the 2010 Supreme Court needed to be reversed and term limits set on Supreme Court appointments instead of the lifetime appointments currently enjoyed. Finally, to make America a truly representative democracy, he said the vote the right to vote should be granted to the District of Columbia, Puerto Rico and the numerous territories that had a stake in the outcome of US elections.

The attempted coup in America created shockwaves around the world. Both allies and adversaries expressed dismay as live coverage carried images of the US Capitol being ransacked. "Canadians are deeply disturbed and saddened," said Canada's Justin Trudeau. "Disgraceful," said the UK's Boris Johnson. Venezuela condemned the acts of violence and brought attention to the US foreign policy of using aggression against legitimately elected democracies around the world. "The looking of democracy," said a Sweden's official. All called on Trump to accept the election result. They expressed faith in the American democratic institutions and in Joe Biden to steer America past the turmoil.

Plenty of the world's near-200 countries had their hands full with transitioning to a global world. Most were democracies emerging from autocratic rule. Coups were common in those countries fighting corruption as a major enemy. Other countries newly democratized as some in middle and eastern Europe were democracies in name with dictatorial leaders corrupting the democratic process to slide their countries back into veritable autocracies. But no stable democracy slid into an autocracy it had never known, a phenomenon made all the more appalling by the fact that one man was able to corrupt the democratic process in a feat the world had not seen since Germany nearly a century earlier.

In short, the attempted coup fomented by the sitting US President when he lost the 2020 US election brought America into alignment with the rest of the world's near 200 other countries. America was no longer exceptional, exempt by its Constitution from the troubles plaguing less advantaged countries. Coups were happening around the world, from Mali and Haiti to Guinea. The Army still held Myanmar. Cuban unrest against its communist regime was short-lived while China cracked down on Hong Kong democracy activists. Russia lay low, no doubt advising Belarus on how to handle pro-democracy activists working to topple a Russian backed dictator based on clear evidence of voter fraud. By contrast in America, a would-be dictator tried to bring down a democracy based on clear legal evidence of NO voter fraud.

The irony was inescapable among three of the world's most prominent powers. Russia and China were autocracies, in essence. Their dictator rulers held on to their positions by putting down opposition by any means possible. The opposition fought tooth and nail until the dictator was toppled. That day seemed far off in Russia and China but democratic America had been able fend off a hostile take-over by a dictator due to the strength of its foundation in democratic institutions.

According to the Democracy Index operated since 2006 by the UK-based Economist Group, America fell in 2015 from a ranking as a full democracy to the status of a flawed democracy. The drop was due to a measure of a population's faith in its institutions. Apparently, Trump saw America as a distressed property that he acquired in 2016. Unwilling to give it up when he bankrupted the country, he receded to background activity while duly elected Joe Biden repaired America's democracy.

Flawed or not by international standards, America's democracy had enabled it to fend off a hostile take-over by a marauding horde. The task after that was to strengthen the democratic institutions and the people's faith in them so that the persistent invader could not threaten again.